Lads and Ladettes in School

Lads and Ladettes in School:
Gender and a Fear of Failure

Carolyn Jackson

Open University Press

Open University Press
McGraw-Hill Education
McGraw-Hill House
Shoppenhangers Road
Maidenhead
Berkshire
England SL6 2QL

email: enquiries@openup.co.uk
world wide web: www.openup.co.uk

and Two Penn Plaza, New York, NY 10121–2289, USA

First published 2006

A catalogue record of this book is available from the British Library

ISBN-10: 0 335 21770 2 (pb)   0 335 21771 0 (hb)
ISBN-13: 978 0335 21770 0 (pb)   978 0335 21771 7 (hb)

Library of Congress Cataloging-in-Publication Data
CIP data applied for

Typeset by BookEns Ltd, Royston, Herts.
Printed and bound in Poland by OZ Graf. S.A.
www.polskabook.pl

To Penny

Contents

Acknowledgements   ix

Introduction   xi

1 'Don't revise, and be a bit bad, that's more popular':
  Social motives for 'laddishness'   1

2 'I don't want them to think I'm thick': Academic motives for
  'laddishness'   24
3 Combining insights to understand 'laddishness':
  Integrating theories about social and academic motives   36

4 'I don't like failure. I want to get good levels.'
  Testing times: Academic pressures and fears in school   47

5 'If you work hard in school you're a geek': Exploring the
  'uncool to work' discourse   74
6 Fibs and fabrications: Strategies to avoid looking 'stupid'
  or 'swotty'   85

7 Balancing acts: Who can balance the books and a social life,
  and how?   101

8 'If I knew how to tackle "laddishness" I'd bottle it, sell it,
  and make a fortune': Implications for teachers, schools and
  policy-makers   122

Conclusion   140

Notes   143

Appendices   149

References   159

Index   00

Acknowledgements

I would like to thank the Nuffield Foundation (SGS/00627/G) and the Economic and Social Research Council (ESRC) (RES-000-27-0041) for funding the two projects that provided the basis for this writing. In sections of the book I have drawn upon my earlier work that has been published in *Gender and Education* and the *British Educational Research Journal*; I am grateful to Taylor and Francis for permission to do this (www.tandf.co.uk).

I am indebted to the anonymous schools, teachers and pupils that gave their time and support so generously. I am also very grateful to: Gill O'Toole for undertaking the fifty Nuffield project interviews; Helen Bressington, Jo Dickinson and Laura Steeples for their help with questionnaire data inputting; Sheena Archibald for transcribing many of the ESRC project interviews, and Alice Jesmont who transcribed countless interviews from both projects at a speed that never ceased to amaze me.

I am very grateful to colleagues who provided helpful comments on chapters at various stages: Linda Marshall, Heather Mendick, Emma Renold, Nigel Sherriff and Jo Warin. I am particularly grateful to Penny Tinkler who, without grumbling, read all of my chapters more than once, as well as the whole manuscript in the final stages, and offered immensely valuable insights, ideas and comments. Furthermore, Penny did this while finishing her own book, *Smoke Signals: Women, Smoking and Visual Culture*.

Two friends – Jan Lees and Paula Shakespeare – deserve very special thanks for their support, patience and excellent cooking! My parents – Brenda and John Jackson – have been a constant source of support, encouragement and, at times, chocolate! Words are not enough to convey my thanks, but they're a start.

Finally, I return to thank (again) Penny Tinkler, to whom the book is dedicated, and whose support and encouragement has been boundless.

Introduction

> We have to crack the lad culture that stops too many young boys doing well at school ... The culture tells boys that it is fine to play around and not work hard. But this harms their chances of doing well, getting their exams and fulfilling their potential.
>
> (David Miliband, cited by Clare 2003: 5)

> 'Ladette' culture blamed for rise in young girls being locked up. The number of delinquent girls being held in secure units is rising sharply, according to government figures that will prompt renewed concern about the impact of 'ladette' culture in Britain's schools ... 'Girls are now behaving as badly as boys ... girls are hanging out more with boys and feeling they have to beat them at their own game'.
>
> (Henry 2003, online)

Concerns about 'laddish' cultures are pervasive in current education discourses.[1] Politicians, teachers, parents and researchers are now well acquainted with 'laddishness', and the terms 'lad' and 'laddish' are firmly established and regularly used components of an education correspondent's lexicon. The attractiveness of the concept 'laddishness' lies in its potential, according to popular discourse, to explain boys' 'underachievement'. For example, according to education correspondent Liz Heron (2002: 2):

> The girls' lead over boys at GCSE [General Certificate of Secondary Education examinations taken at 16+] has been put down to the growth of a 'laddish anti-learning culture' among teenage boys ... Educationalists pinpointed a possible cause several years ago in an attitude among teenage boys that it is uncool to be bookish, a swot, or good in class, coining the term 'laddish anti-learning culture'.

Numerous commentators have made links between 'laddishness' and 'underperformance' (see opening quote). Stephen Byers, during his period as Schools Standards Minister of England in 1998, stated that boys' 'laddish anti-school attitudes were impeding their progress at school' (cited in Francis 1999: 357). David Blunkett, Secretary of State for Education at the time, echoed this sentiment: 'We face a genuine problem of underachievement among boys, particularly those from working class families. This underachievement is linked to a laddish culture which in many areas has grown out of deprivation, and a lack of both self-confidence and opportunity' (DfEE 2000).

There are two key problems with these depictions. First, most representations of 'underachieving' boys in media, government and popular discourse are highly problematic. They all too often ignore important questions and issues, such as which boys are 'underachieving'? How is 'underachievement' defined – in relation to what or whom, and why? Which girls are also 'underachieving'? In most media and popular discourses nuanced, informed debates about achievement are replaced by 'simplistic, often alarmist descriptions' (Epstein *et al.* 1998: 3) about boys' 'underachievement'. There has then, rightly in my view, been severe criticism levelled at these unsophisticated, one-dimensional portraits (see, for example, Epstein *et al.* 1998; Delamont 1999). Second, such crude portrayals tend to present boys' 'underachievement' and 'laddishness' as synonymous; they are not. Not all 'laddish' boys are 'underachievers' and not all 'underachievers' are 'laddish'.[2]

Notwithstanding these important criticisms, there are reasons to be concerned about 'laddishness'. Evidence that 'laddish' anti-learning and/or anti-school approaches may be impeding boys' progress in school has emerged from the work of many educational researchers, both in the UK and overseas (for example, Younger and Warrington 1996, 2005; Parry 1997; Francis 1999, 2000; Martino 1999; Warrington *et al.* 2000; Jackson 2003; Archer *et al.* 2005). Indeed, McLellan (2002: 9) argues that 'Laddish masculinity may be the biggest challenge facing some schools that are attempting to raise boys' achievement'.

This book explores 'laddish' behaviours among 13–14-year-old boys *and girls*. The main aim is to understand the pattern of behaviours and attitudes that are labelled as 'laddish', in particular the 'uncool to work' aspect. In working towards this aim, I have drawn largely on theories and research from two disciplines, namely sociology and social psychology. I have also generated a substantial data set; the book explores data from 203 pupil interviews (from eight schools), 30 teacher interviews (from six schools), and questionnaire data from approximately 800 pupils (from six schools).

It is important to explore 'laddishness' among boys because although research suggests that 'laddish' cultures foster anti-learning attitudes, it is not clear *why* some boys so readily adopt 'laddish' behaviours (Connolly 2004). Without understanding boys' motives for adopting 'laddish' behaviours, it is not possible to challenge them successfully. Indeed, there is a real danger that current attempts by some schools to combat 'laddish' behaviour and tackle 'underachievement' actually serve to exacerbate the very behaviours that they are trying to discourage (Jackson 1999, 2002a).

The inclusion of girls in this study is both novel and important. Girls have been largely sidelined in the educational research, policy and practice agendas in recent years. The dominance of the standards discourse over the last decade, combined with performance data which shows that overall girls do better than boys at GCSE examinations, has meant that in general girls have been assumed to be fine. Dominant 'girl power' discourses represent girls and women as 'having it all' and 'doing it all' because of new-found confidence, ambition and opportunities (Hughes 2002a; Harris 2004; Renold and Allan 2004; Aapola *et al.* 2005). However, there is plenty of evidence to the contrary (Warrington and Younger 2000; Osler and Vincent 2003; Evans *et al.* 2004; Lloyd 2005). For example, Warrington and Younger's (2000) research suggests that: girls still feel alienated in traditionally 'male' subjects, career aspirations are still highly gendered; many boys' dominant and 'laddish' behaviours can have negative effects on girls' learning; and some teachers have lower expectations of girls. Although Warrington and Younger (also Francis 2000) have expressed concerns about the ways in which the 'laddish' behaviours of some boys might impact negatively upon the experiences and performances of girls, there has been no exploration of whether girls themselves are adopting 'laddish' behaviours. This is despite anecdotal evidence from teachers and parents that they are, and reports in the media – such as that cited at the start of this chapter – that highlight concerns about unruly schoolgirl 'ladettes'.

Discourses on the 'ladette' emerged alongside, and merged with, new girl power discourses. The 'ladette' represents a particular type of femininity that is portrayed almost without exception by the media as dangerous and problematic (see Jackson and Tinkler forthcoming). In this book I explore whether there is evidence that some schoolgirls are adopting 'laddish' attitudes and behaviours (becoming 'ladettes'), and if they are, in what ways 'laddishness' among girls is similar to, and different from, 'laddishness' among boys. A crucial question as far as educational experiences and attainment is concerned is: if 'laddish' attitudes are evident among girls, do they incorporate the notion that 'it's not cool to work' in the same way that they do for many boys? In other words, does being a 'ladette' involve overtly rejecting hard work? Are 'ladette' femininities likely to impede some girls' progress in schools in the same way that 'laddish' masculinities are seen to do for boys?

Theoretical frameworks: combining social psychological and sociological approaches to understand 'laddishness'

There is now a large and growing literature on masculinities and femininities in education (for example, Hey 1997; Martino and Meyenn 2001; Reay 2001a; Renold 2001, 2005a; Skelton 2001a, 2001b; Walkerdine *et al*. 2001; Frosh *et al*. 2002; Archer 2003; Haywood and Mac an Ghaill 2003; Martino and Pallotta-Chiarolli 2003). This literature has advanced our understandings of the complex ways in which girls and boys construct and negotiate their identities within schools, and it seeks to understand and interpret these constructions in relation to wider social structures. The vast majority of the work is written from sociological perspectives, and largely ignores theories and research from social psychology. This social-psychological blind-spot means that work on masculinities and femininities in education has largely ignored individual motives.

Individual motives are crucial to understanding why individuals act as they do. By contrast to the sociological literature, attempting to understand individual pupils' motives for their behaviours at school is central to the work of educational social psychologists. Only when we understand why a pupil does or does not engage in an achievement-related behaviour at school can we begin to understand how we might encourage or change her/his behaviour. As such, the study of pupil **goals** has been of particular importance as 'it is the *meaning* or *purpose* for engaging in academic behaviour, as construed by the students, that affects their motivation' (Kaplan *et al*. 2002a: 22).

However, while the work on goal theory is incredibly valuable, it has largely ignored the sociological literature on masculinities and femininities. It has failed to engage in an in-depth manner with the ways in which girls and boys negotiate and construct their identities as learners within schools in relation to their social, as well as academic, goals. Furthermore, literature on goal theory has tended to focus almost exclusively upon the microcosm of the classroom or school, and pays insufficient attention to broader social contexts and power issues. As Anderman and Midgley (2002: 2) admit, 'educational psychology as a field has been particularly negligent in terms of addressing socioeconomic issues'. In addition, it has also been negligent in terms of exploring 'race' and ethnicity issues.

This book draws together these two bodies of work: the (mainly) sociological theories and research on masculinities and femininities, and social psychological research and theories on academic motives and goals. It uses theories and research from both of these areas to further our understanding of the pattern of behaviours and attitudes that are labelled as 'laddish'.

Research methods

The data used in this book were generated during two research projects. The first was a pilot project funded by the Nuffield Foundation. The second, larger project and the one that is drawn upon more extensively in this book was an Economic and Social Research Council (ESRC) funded project. Both projects had similar aims in that they attempted to explore motives for 'laddish' behaviours in schools. In general, the methodological approaches were similar in both projects: they included questionnaires and interviews, and the interviews were broadly similar. However, there were also important differences, most notably, the ESRC project involved interviews with girls, boys and teachers whereas the Nuffield project involved interviews with boys only. The larger scale of the ESRC project meant that single-sex schools were included in the sample as well as co-educational schools, and the intakes of the schools were more varied than was possible in the Nuffield project. Information about both projects is provided below.

The Nuffield project

Two secondary schools – School A and School B – were involved in this project, which took place in the spring of 2002. The schools were both within the same town/city in the northwest of England, but had markedly different intakes. Both schools were mixed-sex comprehensive schools. School A was oversubscribed and had approximately 1400 pupils on roll. The proportion of pupils eligible for free school meals was below the national average; the school was predominantly white with a small number of pupils from black-African, black-Caribbean, Indian and Chinese backgrounds. The percentage of pupils gaining 5+ A*–C grades at GCSE (the GCSE benchmark) was well above the national average (compared with all schools and also similar schools). School B was considerably smaller than School A, with approximately 600 pupils on roll. The percentage of pupils eligible for free school meals was above the national average and the pupils' socio-economic circumstances were described by OFSTED reporters as below average. The percentage of pupils who spoke English as an additional language was higher than in most schools. The percentage of pupils gaining 5+ A*–C grades at GCSE was well below the national average compared to all schools, and below average compared to similar schools.

All Year 9 pupils (13–14 years old) completed a questionnaire that explored aspects of self-handicapping behaviours in school (self-handicapping is discussed in Chapters 2 and 6), general approaches to school, and background information. After completing the questionnaires, 25 boys from each school were interviewed. The boys were selected for interview on the basis of their responses to the questionnaire: a variety of response-types was sought. In both schools teachers commented that the interviewees included a mix of pupils in terms of attainment levels, behaviours, 'laddishness' and popularity. The interview sample contained a fairly even mix of boys from middle-class (mainly at School A) and working-class (mainly at School B) backgrounds. Owing to the composition of the schools' Year 9 cohorts, the majority of the interviewees were white UK/Irish, although two interviewees identified as Indian and one as Chinese. The interviews, which were undertaken with the consent of the boys and their parents, took place during the day in school and lasted approximately 30 minutes. They were undertaken by Gill O'Toole, a white British woman in her 40s who was a PhD student at that time. The (semi-structured) interviews covered six main areas, namely, performance at school and performance indicators, impending SATs (Standard Assessment Tasks – national tests for all 7-, 11- and 14-year-old pupils in England), reactions to failure, attributions for failure, pressure to achieve and pressure to work/not to work, and 'laddishness'. The interviews were audio-taped and then transcribed. The transcripts were analysed with the aid of the computer package Nud*ist Vivo, in which responses were coded relating to one or more of 17 key themes (for example, perceptions of effort-grade relationships, attributions for failure, pressure to achieve, characteristics of a 'lad').

The ESRC project

Six secondary schools were involved in this project: four co-educational, one girls' and one boys'. All schools were located in the north of England. The schools were geographically widespread except for the single-sex schools which were based in neighbouring regions of the same town/city. The schools were selected carefully to ensure a mix of pupils in terms of social class, 'race' and ethnicity, and a mix in terms of overall examination results, and gender of intake (single-sex and co-educational). Summary information about each school is provided in Table 0.1.

Pupil data

All pupils involved in the research were in Year 9 at the time of the study in the academic year 2003/04. Questionnaires were administered to Year 9 pupils in each school. There were three questionnaires in total. Two of the questionnaires explored students' academic goals in school, self-handicapping behaviours, and their perceptions of their learning environments in English and Maths respectively. Data from these questionnaires have been analysed alongside the interview data to assess the validity of these particular self-report scales, and to explore the implications for psychologists who use them; this aspect of the research is beyond the scope of this book and so data from these two questionnaires are not used here. A third questionnaire explored pupils' views about 'laddishness' and popularity. The 779 responses

Table 0.1 ESRC project sample school information (at date of most recent OFSTED inspection before the project, except for A*–C grade data).

School	Type	Approximate number of pupils on roll (Years 7–11)	Proportion of minority ethnic pupils	Pupils eligible for free school meals	GCSE results compared with all schools	GCSE results compared with similar schools	5+ A*–C grades in 2003
Elmwood	11–18 mixed-sex comprehensive	800	23%	19%	Well above average	Well above average	54%
Firtrees	11–18 mixed-sex comprehensive	1100	1%	21%	Well below average	Well below average	28%
Beechwood	11–16 mixed-sex comprehensive	650	31%	51%	Well below average	Average	16%
Oakfield	11–18 mixed-sex comprehensive	870	86%	42%	Well above average	Well above average	38%
Hollydale Girls'	11–16 girls' comprehensive	760	17%	9%	Well above average	Well above average	70%
Ashgrove Boys'	11–18 boys' comprehensive	620	5%	3%	Well above average	Well above average	83%

to this questionnaire (392 girls and 387 boys) are used at various points in this book (see Appendix 1 for the questions included in the questionnaire).

Interviews were conducted with 153 pupils; 75 girls and 78 boys (brief profiles of the interviewees quoted in this book are provided in Appendix 2). In five of the schools (Ashgrove was the exception) pupils were selected for interview on the basis of gender (I aimed for a 50:50 girl:boy split, except in the single-sex schools) and their responses to one of the questionnaires: they were selected to ensure a mix of response types.[3] In all schools teachers commented that the interviewees included a mix of pupils in terms of attainment levels, behaviours, 'laddishness' and popularity. In Ashgrove (the boys' school), because of practical constraints, the pupils were selected by one of the teachers. In this case I requested that the sample should be varied in terms of attainment levels, behaviours, 'laddishness' and popularity; the interviews revealed that the sample was varied in these regards. Although I planned to interview 25 pupils in each school, in two schools I interviewed 27 and 26 because pupils who had been absent on the day of their scheduled interviews (and so had been replaced with another interviewee) were keen to be interviewed and so were included as additional participants. The interviews were undertaken with the consent of the pupils and their parents. They took place over the spring and summer of 2004, during the school day, in school and lasted approximately 30 minutes. At the start of the interviews I introduced myself and the project, telling them that I was interested in pupils' attitudes towards school and school work. I assured them that their answers would be treated confidentially, that there were no right or wrong answers, that it was fine not to answer any questions that they did not want to answer, to ask for clarification if necessary, and I asked if it was OK to tape the interview. All pupils agreed to be taped except for one boy, who agreed to me taking written notes instead.

The interviews were semi-structured and covered a number of topics, including attitudes and approaches to schoolwork; SATs; pressures in school; 'lads' and 'ladettes'; friends and popularity (see Appendix 3). I con-ducted all the interviews – a white British woman in my mid-30s. After each interview I made notes on the process, my perceptions of the interviewee, and reflections on my interviewing style. The audio-tapes were transcribed in full. The transcripts were analysed with the aid of the computer package Nud*ist Vivo, in which responses were coded relating to one or more key themes, which were then subdivided. Examples of key themes included aca-demic pressure; academic self-presentation; SATs; 'lads'; 'ladettes'. All key themes were then subdivided, for example 'ladettes' was subdivided into: ability, aggression, loudness, language, drinking, dress and so on.

Each school also provided SATs results for the entire Year 9 cohort; these were available after all interviews had been completed.

Teacher data

An average of five teacher interviews were conducted in each school: 30 in total (17 women and 13 men). The teacher with whom I liaised about the research frequently recommended teachers to interview after discussions with me about the types of issues I would cover. The teacher sample was diverse in terms of: subject specialisms; number of years in teaching; sen-iority in school; time at that particular school. The interviews took place in school and ranged between 30 and 60 minutes in length. Teachers were pro-vided with a list of indicative questions in advance of the interview (see Appendix 4); predictably, teachers varied in terms of how much thought they had given to the questions before we met. Teacher interviews were audio-taped, with the exception of one which started as a quick chat but developed into an interview. In this case I made notes and wrote them up immediately after the interview. The audio-taped interviews were tran-scribed in full. The transcripts were analysed with the aid of the computer package Nud*ist Vivo, in which responses were coded relating to one or more key themes in a similar way to the pupil data, although the categories were not identical for the teacher and pupil data.

All school, pupil and teacher names used in this book are pseudonyms.

Book overview

In this book I argue that 'laddish' behaviours among boys and girls can result from both social and academic concerns. Chapters 1 to 3 introduce key concepts employed in the book and map out the theoretical framework. Chapter 1 introduces 'lads' and 'ladettes' and explores the relationships between 'laddishness' and popularity in schools. The first part of the chapter focuses on 'lads': it considers what it means to be a 'lad' and then outlines the ways in which the concept of hegemonic masculinity has been employed to explain 'laddishness'. The second part of the chapter focuses on 'laddish' girls or 'ladettes': it introduces and critically explores what it means to be a schoolgirl 'ladette', and unpacks the relationship between 'ladette' and 'popular' femininities. Overall, drawing largely on sociological literature, this chapter highlights the ways in which pupils' social status goals – desires to be 'cool' and 'popular', and/or the flip side of that: to avoid being uncool and unpopular – contribute to our understandings of 'laddish' behaviours in school. Central to 'laddishness' is the dominant 'uncool to work' pupil discourse, which means that to be cool and popular students must generally avoid overt academic work.

Whereas Chapter 1 focuses on how *social* motives can help us to understand the pattern of behaviours and attitudes labelled as 'laddish', Chapter 2 considers how *academic* motives (academic-related reasons for engaging or not engaging with school work) can help to develop this understanding. Two achievement motivation theories are introduced – achievement goal theory and self-worth theory. Drawing on these psychological theories, I suggest that many 'laddish' behaviours act as defensive strategies that are prompted by a fear of academic failure; 'laddish' ways of behaving can protect individuals from the damaging implications of academic failure (that is, that they are 'stupid') by blaming other factors (for example, that they did not do any work). 'Laddish' ways of behaving can also make academic success appear effortless.

Chapter 3 draws together and evaluates the theories discussed in Chapters 1 and 2. I suggest that focusing upon social *or* academic goals is insufficient; we need to consider both types of goals if we are to understand 'laddish' behaviours. I argue that many pupils find 'laddish' behaviours attractive for both academic and social reasons, and that for some pupils 'laddish' behaviours are underpinned both by fears of academic failure and fears of social failure.

Having established at a theoretical level the importance of working across disciplines to address both the social and academic motives that underpin 'laddish' behaviours, Chapters 4 to 7 offer detailed empirical elaboration of these two aspects of 'laddishness'. Chapter 4 introduces the 'academic credentials' discourse and examines the pressures on pupils to succeed and/or not to fail academically at school. It explores pupils' perceptions of pressures from teachers, parents and peers. Pressures and fears emerged most explicitly and were reported most vividly in relation to exams and tests, so SATs are examined as a particular 'pressure point'. It is clear that many students feel under substantial pressure to perform academically, and that many fear failure. These pressures and fears are contextualized and discussed in relation to the dominant education discourse on standards, testing and credentials.

Chapter 5 explores the 'uncool to work' pupil discourse, which is at the heart of 'laddishness'. This chapter explores students' views about the strength and nature of the discourse, and their responses to it. It also tackles the questions: is the 'uncool to work' discourse dominant for girls and boys and for pupils across social class, 'race' and ethnic groups? How do pupils respond to the discourse given the strength of the counter 'academic credentials' discourse? Do any pupils benefit from the uncool to work discourse?

Chapter 6 explores the ways in which some pupils respond to their fears of academic 'failure' (discussed in Chapter 4) by adopting self-worth protection strategies that deflect attention away from a lack of ability onto another, less damaging explanation for potential or actual 'poor' academic attainment. It is not only 'low achievers' who fear 'failure', as 'failure' is highly subjective and relative. For example, some pupils might consider their performance to be 'poor' if they are not positioned among the top five people in their set. While many of the defensive strategies discussed in this chapter are beneficial in terms of protecting academic self-worth, they are also beneficial in terms of constructing appropriately 'cool', popular forms of masculinities and femininities. As such, most of the strategies discussed in this chapter serve a dual purpose for pupils. First, they enable them to act in ways currently consistent with popular forms of masculinity and femininity in their schools. Second, they provide an excuse for academic 'failure' and augment success.

Chapter 7 explores the ways in which pupils attempt to balance the demands of the two competing, dominant education discourses: the 'uncool to work' pupil discourse and the 'credentials' discourse. I discuss some of the strategies that pupils employ to balance their social demands with the academic demands of school. I argue that some pupils are better resourced than others to be able to balance these demands successfully and that time is central to the equation.

Chapter 8 brings together some of the key theories and empirical findings discussed in the book and explores the implications for practice. I tackle the question: what can teachers, schools or policy-makers do to tackle 'laddishness'? While there are no straightforward ways of eradicating some of the problematic aspects of 'laddish' behaviours, I discuss various ways in which they might be reduced.

1 'Don't revise, and be a bit bad, that's more popular': Social motives for 'laddishness'

'Laddish' boys: boys who want to gang together and gain the approval of their mates and will do daft things to gain the approval of their mates. And for whom learning is boring and it's not fashionable, and it's more fashionable to go out and have fun and flirt with girls, and as soon as you possibly can, drink.

(Ms Cornish, Elmwood)

'Laddish' girls: I think it's something to be challenged. We've always had girls that have been disruptive but that's always related to personal issues, internal personal issues. I think what we're beginning to see now are girls that are seeing that [i.e. 'laddishness'] as a way to behave and therefore changing their behaviour in order to do that ... It's almost peer pressure: this is the way I get in with the group. And therefore the reasons for the loud and disruptive behaviour are different [to those in the past] and that has to be challenged, the same way as it does with boys.

(Ms Rimmington, Oakfield)

My main aim in this book is to explore and develop understandings of the patterns of behaviours and attitudes that are labelled as 'laddish'. With that aim in mind, this chapter explores *social* motives for 'laddishness' (the next chapter focuses on *academic* motives).[1] Social motives for 'laddish' behaviours among boys and girls are emphasized by the two teachers in the opening quotes. Ms Cornish argues that 'laddish' boys 'do daft things to gain the approval of their mates'. Ms Rimmington suggests that girls behave 'laddishly' because of peer pressure and to 'get in with the group'. In both cases, the suggestion is that pupils behave in particular ways – in this case in 'laddish' ways – in order to be 'cool' and popular, or at least to avoid being 'uncool' and unpopular.

Social relationships constitute a crucial component of school life; it is difficult to overestimate their importance both in terms of experience and enjoyment of school, and in terms of academic outcomes. It is unsurprising, therefore, that a great deal of research has focused on the ways in which girls' and boys' behaviours are shaped by dominant discourses on 'popularity' in school, discourses which are gendered, as well as mediated by class, 'race', ethnicity and age. In this chapter I explore the theory that pupils behave 'laddishly' in order to be popular, or to avoid being unpopular; in other words, that 'laddish' behaviours are shaped largely by social concerns and goals. Broadly speaking, social goals are an individual's self-construed meanings or purposes for engaging (or not engaging) in interactions with others. While researchers have explored a number of different social goals, for example social responsibility or social intimacy (Patrick *et al.* 2002), I focus on social status goals because they are concerned with 'popularity'. Social status goals refer to a student's desire for social visibility and prestige within the larger peer group (Patrick *et al.* 2002).

In recognizing and focusing on the importance of popularity in schools I am not suggesting that 'being popular' is a goal of all boys and girls. Pupils have different social needs, and for some having a close or 'best' friend may be more important than being 'popular' (Kupersmidt *et al.* 1996). That said, there is little doubt that pupil discourses about popularity affect all pupils; this was clear from both the pupil and teacher interviews. Very few pupils were unable to recognize 'popularity', and there are dominant discourses within schools about what being popular involves. But while there are dominant discourses on popularity, pupils engage with these in different ways (Frosh *et al.* 2002). For example, some aim to be popular, some attempt to avoid being unpopular, and others might attempt to resist the discourse. However, those who actively resist the discourse are frequently subject to various forms of bullying and so tend to be a minority (Frosh *et al.* 2002).

Overall, the chapter explores the relationships between 'popularity' and boys' and girls' 'laddish' behaviours. Discourses on 'popularity' are gendered, so the chapter looks separately at 'lads' and 'ladettes'. The first part of the chapter looks at 'lads'. I consider what it means to be a 'lad' and then outline the ways in which the concept of hegemonic masculinity has been employed to explain 'laddishness'. While 'laddish' boys have been the subject of much research in recent years, 'laddish' girls have been virtually ignored. The second part of the chapter focuses on 'laddish' girls, or 'ladettes'. It introduces and critically explores what it means to be a schoolgirl 'ladette', and unpacks the relationship between 'ladette' and 'popular' femininities.

'Lads'

What does it mean to be a 'lad'?

In the interviews I asked boys, girls and teachers what it means to be a 'lad' and whether 'being one of the lads' was a phrase used in their schools. Overall, there was a large degree of consistency among pupils about what 'lads' are like; 'lads' display a particular kind of masculinity. Nevertheless, there were some pupils (a small minority) who suggested that 'lad' is simply synonymous with 'boy'. For example, Paul (Firtrees) regarded the two terms as straightforwardly interchangeable.

> *Do boys in school ever talk about being 'one of the lads'?*
> No.
> *So a lad, the notion of a lad, wouldn't conjure up anything with you other than a boy? Or would being a lad be different to being a boy?*
> Not really, it's just, someone says 'you're a lad' you just think oh I'm a boy.

Dean (Ashgrove) also saw 'lad' to mean 'boy', and thought that it was a matter of dialect as to which term people chose to use. However, it is worthy of note that he refers to a 'lad' as a 'normal' boy, although he does not go on to explain what he means by 'normal', nor what would constitute 'abnormal'.

> *Do boys talk about being 'one of the lads' in terms of being a bit laddish?*
> That's just like a lad, it's just like being a boy.
> *It's the same as being a boy?*
> It depends what kind of slang you speak ... it's really the same word. Like 'the lads' is like the same as 'the boys', but it depends how you speak really.
> *So a lad isn't a particular kind of boy?*
> No. It's just like a normal boy.

However, the conflation of 'lad' simply with being male was a minority view; most associated 'lads' with a particular sort of masculinity.

That there is some confusion and ambiguity about the term 'lad' is unsurprising. In general parlance it is often used interchangeably with boy or man. However, it undoubtedly has associations with a particular form of masculinity. But these associations are fluid, not fixed; they vary across time and space. For example, among social scientists, the term 'lad' was, and perhaps still is, most famously associated with the work of Paul Willis (1977), in which it was used to refer to a group of white, working-class, anti-school boys. Francis (1999) argues that this association began to shift in the

1990s when the term 'lad' was appropriated by, and popularized for, middle-class males, and as such gained renewed prominence in popular and media culture. There is evidence to suggest that the behaviours associated with 'lads' now span social class and ethnic groups (Francis 1999; Martino 1999; Archer 2003; Jackson 2003; Power *et al.* 2003; Archer *et al.* 2005). However, while this may be the case, the increasingly widespread adoption of 'laddish' attitudes does not eradicate their working-class associations. As Griffin (2000: 179) argues: 'the new resonance of the term "lad" simultaneously retains its derogatory anti-working-class connotations and obscures them whilst celebrating and extending the acceptability of a particular form of boorish heterosexual masculinity. Although the latter has never been confined to working-class men, such practices are frequently associated with that group.' But for many middle-class boys and men, the working-class associations of being a 'lad' may be what make it attractive. Particular 'laddish' attitudes and behaviours may be dispositions of the working class that Skeggs (2004: 22) argues are 'being re-converted into temporary cultural dispositions (such as "cool") that can be tried on and used as a resource for the formation and propertising of the "new" middle-class self'. 'Laddishness' may be an example of what Featherstone refers to as the restrained hedonism of the middle class, as they attempt to become less restrained without forgoing any of the cultural privileges that their social positioning brings (cited in Skeggs 2004: 23).

Some pupils in this research seemed to recognize that the term 'lad' has associations with particular types of masculinity, but were unable to conceptualize and/or articulate the differences in the interview. Rob (Elmwood) provides a good example.

> *Do people talk in school about boys being 'one of the lads', you know 'he's one of the lads'?*
> No.
> *What does it mean for a boy to be a lad?*
> Nowt really.
> *Do you think being a lad means a particular type of thing?*
> No.
> *… Do you think you're a lad?*
> Yes.
> *Why?*
> 'Cause I look like one.
> *What do you mean?*
> I look like one.
> *So you look like a boy or you look like a lad?*
> I look like a lad.
> *So what does it mean to be a lad?*
> Nowt.

> *Do you think any boy is a lad or does being a lad mean something a bit different?*
> A bit different.
> *In what way?*
> All sorts.
> *Go on, tell me a bit more.*
> All sorts really.

For pupils like Rob, the characteristics of a lad seemed intangible; they could recognize 'lads' but were unable to explain why. 'Lad' is an elusive concept. Writing about femininity, Holland (2004: 9) argues that 'we "just know" what femininity means, what it is and how it is done – except, when asked to explain it, it becomes much more difficult'. This may well be because femininity, as an aspect of gender, is, as Butler (2004: 1) argues: 'a kind of doing, an incessant activity performed, in part, without one's knowing and without one's willing'. Some boys seem to have a similar difficulty in talking about 'laddishness' as a form of masculinity. In the quote below, for example, Martin (Elmwood) tries hard to explain what 'lads' do and what it means to be a 'lad', but it is clear that he has difficulty articulating this, and makes this explicit through his comment: 'it's hard to explain'.

> *I want to go on and talk a bit about lads and laddishness and that. Do people talk at school about being one of the lads?*
> Er, yeah. You've got all the, like, people who do, it's normally the people who like, do sport and stuff like that. And like, popular people like that. People who like, I don't know, people go around in like, big groups ...
> *Right. So what does it mean to be a lad?*
> Er, they'd be like, good at sport, and got a lot of friends and stuff like that. It's like, just, er, I don't know, really. It's hard to explain. It's just like, you, I don't know, you're all into sport and stuff like, you're all into the same things like.

Some boys explained that there were different groups of 'lads' and different ways to perform 'laddishness', for example:

> It all depends on the sort of crowd that you're with ... I know ages ago when you had like the Mods and Rockers, now it's like the Townies and Moshers. Moshers are like the people like hoddies – baggy trousers, skateboard and I'm into all of that, and Townies are like the people who just hang around and like, [they are] label-people basically and [they] do all the smoking and everything. They're the people that sort of like go round taking the mick out

of people purposely who are not a lad, so it all depends on what crowd you're in …

(Adrian, School A)

In some groups particular signifiers of 'laddishness' were more important than in others. For example, 'acting hard' seemed to be a very important marker of 'laddish' masculinity at Oakfield (where 55 per cent of boys were Pakistani and 26 per cent were Bangladeshi). While 'acting hard' was also an important signifier in the other sample schools, in general it was given slightly less emphasis in these schools than was the case at Oakfield. Conversely, while being good at sport (especially football) seemed to be a particularly important aspect of 'laddishness' at Ashgrove, Firtrees, Beechwood and Elmwood, it was emphasized far less at Oakfield. This was also reflected in the questionnaire data, which showed that although there were no statistically significant differences between schools, responses from boys at Oakfield revealed that overall they placed less importance on playing sports than their counterparts at other schools.[2] Francis and Archer (2005a) explore in detail the ways in which constructions of 'laddishness' are mediated to some extent by 'race' discourses, with some (although not all) of their sample of British Chinese pupils suggesting that there are differences between the ways in which British Chinese boys and boys from other ethnic groups construct and perform 'laddishness'. However, Francis and Archer suggest that there were key features in the definitions of 'lads' that crossed groups, in particular the identification of academic work as uncool: 'The positioning of academic achievement as non-masculine and/or swottish, and the prioritisation of "having a laugh" over school-work, were key themes for the British Chinese pupils, as with the pupils from the ethnically diverse sample' (pp. 501–2).

A similar picture emerged from my research; there seemed to be 'core features' of 'laddishness'. These were: popularity and going out or 'hanging around' with mates; playing sport (mainly football); wearing the 'right sorts' of clothes; messing around and being funny; and, particularly importantly, not being seen to put much effort into school work. Tahir (Elmwood) describes many of the 'core' aspects of 'laddishness' in the discussion below.

Do pupils talk in school about being one of the lads?
Yes, sometimes.
What does it mean to be a lad?
Messing at school. Dunno.
… If you had to think – now, let me think about a typical lad – whatever that means, what would you see that typical lad being like?
Sat at the back, in the corner, asleep when teacher's talking.
Sat back asleep in a corner?

Yes, when teacher's talking.
Ok. What else? What about in break time?
Playing football, hanging around with mates, going out and about
after school.
...
*Is there anything they wouldn't do because it wouldn't be seen to be cool
enough?*
Oh, act like a swot.
*Ok, so can someone, going from what you said about not acting like a
swot, can someone who works hard ever be a lad?*
I don't get the question.
If you work hard at school, can you be a lad?
Oh, no. 'Cos you'd get called.
If you work hard?
Yeh, swot or geek or whatever.

Tahir, like most boys, constructed 'laddish' masculinity in opposition to
being a 'swot'. Lewis (Elmwood) talked about 'laddishness' involving being
part of a group or 'gang' (being popular), playing football, being funny, and
being fashionable.

What do you think it means to be a lad?
Just like part of a gang, playing football and stuff.
So what would a lad do?
I don't know, play football and tell jokes and stuff.
… What about clothes and things, is it important the way you dress?
Sort of yes.
What do you mean?
It's like you want to look good.
So particular sorts of clothes and designs?
Yes.

Overall, despite some difficulties associated with defining the term
'lad', and notwithstanding the varying degrees of emphasis on specific signifiers of 'laddishness' between schools (and sometimes within schools),
there was a considerable degree of consensus among pupils about what
'core' features of 'laddishness' are for boys. Girls also spoke about the same
set of 'core' features of boys' 'laddishness'.

Penny (Elmwood)
*What do you think it means to be a lad, if I asked you to describe to me
what a typical lad might be like, what would you say?*
Erm, someone that like just hangs about and that.
What else?

Acts like cool in front of his mates and that.
So what would that be doing?
Showing off and stuff like that.
How?
Like making jokes and stuff like that.
What about at break times?
Like chasing after people and playing football and stuff like that.
In class, what would they do in lessons?
Messing about.

Some girls were very critical of 'laddish' boys, which is unsurprising given that these boys frequently disrupted lessons and learning (Warrington and Younger 2000; Younger and Warrington 2005). Examples are provided here from Hannah and Zoe.

Hannah (Firtrees)
Do boys talk about being one of the lads?
Some people use it but usually they're the horrible lads that are just stupid.
So lad would mean, what?
Like in their little group, because they have little groups.
So what would a lad be like?
Usually the people who disrupt the lesson and throw pens at people.

Zoe (Elmwood)
So what does it mean to be a lad?
I think it's, to be a lad, I think most people just refer to lads as being typical, just a typical lad who plays football all the time really. And whose got no brain cells really, but basically that's what 'to be a lad' is to most people I think.
And what else? Would there be anything else about them?
Erm, pathetic sense of humour really, but I don't really think there's anything else, that's about it.

Although individually some girls (and boys) were very critical of 'laddish' boys, dominant pupil discourses equated being 'laddish' with being popular. 'Laddish', 'cool' boys were labelled as popular by both boys and girls, particularly by 'cool' or popular girls. Furthermore, the most popular lads were those who were effortlessly 'laddish' (see also Francis 1999); they appear as 'naturally' funny, athletic, good-looking, fashionable and so on (see also Chapters 6 and 7). By contrast, those who have to try hard in these domains have less social status as they are regarded as inauthentic (see also Frosh *et al.* 2002 and Sherriff 2005 for similar findings regarding 'hardness', and Swain 2004 in relation to humour). For example, Martin (Elmwood) told me that some people try too hard to fit in, whereas others 'naturally have friends'.

> Like, people are always like, trying to fit in and stuff like that, and they don't want to be like, seen to be doing something that they think they're going to be getting like, criticized for and stuff like that. But some people like, they're not really bothered and they still like, manage to stay popular. Other people are like, scared of becoming unpopular if they do stuff like that and they like, pretend, stuff like that.
> *So you can tell people who, it's almost coming back to the effort thing again* [discussed earlier in the interview], *isn't it, there are some people who are just effortlessly cool, and popular ...*
> Yeah.
> *And some people ...*
> Like, really try to.
> *And how can you spot them?*
> They like, the louder ones are normally the most popular, and they have the most friends. But the other people like, they come in and they like, join you, and they're always trying to do stuff to like, make people laugh and stuff like that.
> *Right, so do they, are they the ones that try too hard all the time?*
> Yeah, some people like, naturally have friends, but they [others] are always trying to make friends like.

Martin conveys the ways in which fears of social failure motivate many pupils to try to 'fit in'; he points out that people are 'scared of becoming unpopular'. Such fears are unsurprising because, as Francis (2005: 10) points out: '"being popular" and "fitting in" are understood as vitally important, particularly given the heavy consequences of failure, which can result in marginalisation or bullying'. The ways in which fears of social failure shape, and are shaped by, constructions of masculinities and femininities underpin much of the sociologically informed work on gender identity constructions in schools, although it is not always explicitly articulated in terms of 'fear of failure'. Within this framework, boys' 'laddish' behaviours are explained principally in terms of conformity to dominant or hegemonic forms of masculinity. In other words, 'laddish' masculinity is a hegemonic form and so many boys strive towards it. This striving is underpinned by a desire to attain a 'laddish' hegemonic form of masculinity and/or a fear of being regarded as insufficiently 'laddish'. The next section briefly outlines this theory.

Employing the concept of hegemonic masculinity to explain 'laddishness'

As Renold (2005a: 66) points out: 'since the late 1980s "hegemonic mas-culinity" has become one of the key analytic concepts through which masculinities in school-based research have been theorised'. Connell's work (1995; also Carrigan *et al.* 1985) has been particularly influential in intro-ducing and developing the concept of 'hegemonic masculinity', which although challenged on a number of fronts, is still regarded by many as a useful concept and is described by Connell (2005: xviii) as 'still essential'. Hegemonic masculinity refers to the form of masculinity that is culturally exalted at any one time (Connell 2005); it is a high-status, dominant form of masculinity. Hegemonic masculinities are 'contextual constructs in that a particular form of masculinity acquires hegemonic status only in certain situations' (Mills 2001: 21). Furthermore, it is an idealized form of mas-culinity which very few boys or men can ever attain. Nevertheless, it is a standard against which boys and men measure their manliness, and influ-ences their understandings of how they need to act in order to be 'accept-ably' male (Frosh *et al.* 2002).

The desire to be 'acceptably' male and the fear of being 'unacceptably' male represent two sides of the same coin, as Mills (2001: 48–9) argues: 'The desire for manly success, and consequently societal respect, is also comple-mented by a fear of being one of those subordinated boys/men who provide a means by which other boys can assert their manliness.' Many boys fear being regarded as 'unacceptably' or 'insufficiently' masculine, the consequences of which frequently include a mixture of verbal abuse, being ostracized and physical violence. Because masculinity is a relational con-struct – which exists only in a contrasting relationship to femininity – being 'unacceptably' or 'insufficiently' masculine is equated with being 'too fem-inine'. So hegemonic masculinity is constructed in *opposition* to femininity, and also to other 'subordinate' forms of masculinity, such as gay male masculinity (which tends to be aligned with femininity).

Although hegemonic masculinity varies across time and space, it is currently generally associated in the UK with heterosexuality, strength and toughness, power, competitiveness, and subordination of gay men (Frosh *et al.* 2002). Like Frosh *et al.* (2002: 76), I found that my interviews with boys 'provided support for the existence of "hegemonic" masculinity as a pow-erful idea that regulates boys' behaviour'. Also, like Frosh *et al.* (and Francis 1999, 2000), I found a very large degree of overlap between hegemonic mas-culinity, popularity and 'laddishness' among boys. In other words, popular boys were 'laddish' boys and they acted in ways closely associated with hegemonic masculinity.

As we have seen, integral to popular 'laddish' masculinity is the posi-tioning of school work as uncool. Many sociologists of education draw exclusively upon the concept of hegemonic masculinity to explain this positioning. In a nutshell, this explanation is as follows. Evidence suggests (Epstein 1998; Frosh *et al.* 2002) that academic work is perceived by many young people as 'feminine'. As outlined earlier, hegemonic masculinity is constructed in opposition to femininity, and so boys must *avoid* any activities associated with femininity. Therefore, if schoolboys want to avoid the verbal and physical abuse attached to being labelled as 'feminine', they must *avoid* academic work, or at least they must *appear* to avoid academic work. If boys want to undertake academic work, but they want to do so without harassment, they must work covertly.

In Chapter 3, I argue that explanations that draw *only* upon the concept of hegemonic masculinities to explain 'laddish' behaviours in schools are inadequate. Hegemonic masculinity cannot explain fully the behaviours of boys, nor can it explain why many girls also regard academic work as uncool. My research reveals that the 'uncool to work' discourse is as relevant to, and influential for, schoolgirls as it is to their 'laddish' male counterparts. Girls who behave 'laddishly' have been branded 'ladettes' by the UK press. I now explore what it means to be a schoolgirl 'ladette' and consider whether 'ladette' femininity is a 'popular' version of femininity.

'Ladettes'

'Ladette': a young woman who behaves in a boisterously assertive or crude manner and engages in heavy drinking sessions.
(*The Concise Oxford Dictionary* 2004)

Defining 'ladettes' is even more difficult than defining 'lads'. The term 'ladette' is a mid-1990s creation of the UK media. Definitions of 'ladettes' vary, although they consistently position the 'lad' as an implicit point of reference. This positioning is evident from the term 'ladette', which, as Day *et al.* (2004) point out, is the product of a male-as-norm model; it is derived from a 'male' established term ('lad') and is adjusted with a diminutive suffix ('ette') to make a 'female version'. In general, 'ladettes' are presented as crude, loud, bold, (hetero)sexually assertive, hedonistic and into alcohol and smoking. For example, a five-part 'reality' television series entitled 'Ladette to Lady' broadcast in 2005 was described as setting out to 'turn a bunch of loudmouthed, heavydrinking ladettes into ladies. It takes ten bawling, brawling, boisterous young women and grooms them for five weeks at a finishing school to discover if they can gain true class' (Hardy 2005: 20). While there is constellation of behaviours and characteristics commonly associated with 'ladettes' in the UK press, young women do not need to display all, or even most, of them to attract the 'ladette' label; performance of only one or two is often enough (Jackson and Tinkler forthcoming).

Initially the term 'ladette' was applied almost exclusively to post-school-age young women. However, more recently it has been extended to include schoolgirls: 'the "ladette" culture has filtered down from women in their mid-20s to girls who are still at school' (Meikle 2004). Schoolgirl 'ladettes', like their older counterparts, are portrayed by the media as both trouble and in trouble (see Jackson 2006). For example, Laura Clark (2004) wrote under the headline 'The ladettes aged 15' that: 'Teenage Girls have always been thought to be a more mature and sensible influence on their troublemaking male classmates. But nowadays the roles have been dramatically reversed ... While 15-year-old boys are content to play on their computers, more girls are drinking, smoking and taking drugs.'

There are many reasons to critically explore and deconstruct popular discourses on 'ladettes' (see Jackson and Tinkler forthcoming). The term 'ladette' is not used unproblematically in this book, as indicated by the use of inverted commas. It is important to bear in mind throughout that the concept of the 'ladette', like the 'lad', is the product of a particular time and a particular set of discourses, many of which, from feminist perspectives, are contestable and highly problematic. By applying the term 'laddish' to girls' and boys' behaviours, I am not intending to essentialize them, far from it. Rather, I want to engage critically with the 'laddishness' discourse, and so I have chosen to use the terms 'lad', 'ladette' and 'laddish' while interrogating, problematizing and deconstructing them.

With these cautions and caveats in mind, in the next section I explore whether there is evidence of 'ladette' cultures in secondary schools, and if so, what this means, particularly for girls' academic identities (see Jackson 2006 for a more detailed discussion). I then move on to question whether and why some girls' behaviours in schools, which are labelled in popular discourse as 'ladette' behaviours, are a cause for concern for girls themselves and/or for those concerned with girls' educational experiences and outcomes.

Schoolgirl 'ladettes'

In the interviews pupils and teachers spoke about girls in school who exhibited the types of behaviours attributed to the 'ladette'. These girls were portrayed by pupils as loud, disruptive, rude to teachers, frequently swearing, sometimes 'hard', and mildly aggressive to other pupils. Girls portrayed them as similar in behaviour to the archetypal 'lad'.[3]

> They're quite disruptive, they just barge into classes, even if you're walking in the corridor and you get in their way they'd just push you away ... they think they're quite hard ... They talk back to the teacher, if the teacher says something they'd actually turn round, if a teacher turned their back they'd stick two fingers up maybe ...

Often I see them not in lessons. They're usually walking around the school doing nothing and often they're smoking outside ... They go outside of school and maybe just get drunk, smoke and just hang around outside by themselves and they stay out 'til late ... if you're standing in the way they just come out swearing at you saying anything ... We've seen them fighting a lot, punching each other and pushing, just mainly swearing and spitting on each other.

(Chloe, Hollydale)

While the 'ladette' is presented as a new phenomenon, unruly and disruptive behaviours among girls are not new.[4] Sue Lees (1993: 167), for example, cites a girl talking about schoolgirls in the 1980s whom Lees labels 'pro-school, anti-work' girls:

They just like mucking around. They don't want to work ... They're show-offs. They just muck around the streets causing trouble. They muck around with your books and start drawing all over you with chalk. They start throwing around your books and there's nothing you can do about it. They exaggerate. They say, 'I went out last night.' If they had to get in by ten, they say it was twelve. If you say anything they hit you.

While there are similarities between the girls in Lees' study (and other studies conducted in the 1980s) and those in mine, there are also numerous, important differences. For example, Lees reports that a key reason for girls' 'anti-work' attitudes was that they regarded education as having only limited value because they expected to secure part-time employment after leaving school and to fit paid work in around family responsibilities. This was not a view voiced by girls in my research, almost all of whom stressed the importance of educational qualifications for building a 'successful' career, and expected to continue in full-time education or get a full-time job. Claims such as 'girls have always misbehaved', while true on one level, mask complexity and change (see the quote by Ms Rimmington at the start of this chapter). For example, I put the view 'but girls have always misbehaved' to Ms Walters at Hollydale girls' school when she was talking about girls being disruptive today.

Some people would presumably say 'well these sorts of behaviours have been going on for years, you've always had disruptive girls, you've always had girls that have truanted and things and is anything really changing?' But it sounds from what you're saying that you think things really are different?

I think they are yes. I mean, I certainly think in the years gone by there were fewer and they certainly were a lot more devious shall we say, some of the things that they used to do. I mean if I told my daughter about them she'd be horrified because they were really clever. You know, if you were going to disrupt a lesson, who would think of bringing in a load of rotten fish and putting it in a desk? Now I wouldn't credit most of this lot as capable of those sorts of thoughts; what they would do is immediately resort to the physical, you know, by shouting out, by being objectionable, by being awkward, by facing up to teachers, by being disruptive, by getting out of their seats, maybe being quite physical, those sorts of things. So although we're getting a lot more of that it's really not as clever …

It's much more overt than it was?

Yes, very much more so. And 20 odd years ago if you wanted to disrupt a lesson you could do it quite, well very, easily. Now that incident I told you about was actually when the school was a grammar school, so it was over 20 years ago and that was actually a case when a group of Year 8 (second year) girls deliberately decided to disrupt a lesson. And it was a hot summer's day and the fish came in, in a bag, and it sat in the desk and it stank. So you can imagine what havoc it wreaked, and yet actually the girls themselves did nothing because they were clever enough to not do anything.

This delightful fish tale evokes memories of scenes from 'St Trinians' films, and in Ms Walters' account there clearly are signs of her viewing the past through 'rose-tinted spectacles'. But she was not alone in reporting changes in the ways that misbehaviours are manifest, nor about the increasing amounts of disruptive behaviour overall. OFSTED, for example, in 2005 reported that 'the proportion of secondary schools in which behaviour overall has been judged good or better has declined since 1996/97 from over three quarters [76 per cent] to over two thirds [68 per cent in 2003/04]'. Numerous teachers reported recent increases in 'ladette' behaviours (see Jackson 2006).

> … I had some girls who would be 'laddish' when I first started teaching [about 6 years ago] but they wouldn't be as rude as the girls who are 'laddish' now. So perhaps the 'laddishness' has always been there but perhaps it's the way it's expressed now and it's the lack of inhibitions and it's the fact that they're prepared to be rude and they're prepared to shout and answer back and stand up in your face.
>
> (Ms Cornish, Elmwood)

Can girls be 'laddish'?
Yes, there's getting more of them, more of them now. I used to think that girls did things to impress boys or to draw attention to themselves with boys and now I think it's almost like being as hard as boys ... I think more and more now you're getting girls who are louder than boys and who are [using the] same sort of disruption tactics ... but definitely more than it used to be.

(Ms Attwood, Firtrees)

So while it is important not to assume that contemporary girls' experiences and behaviours are unique to this particular time, it is equally important to recognize that the ways girlhood is lived and experienced today is considerably different to the ways it was lived and experienced in the 1970s and 1980s. It is beyond the scope of this book to map out and discuss these changes, but there is an increasing number of studies that do provide such discussions (for example, Harris 2004; Aapola *et al.* 2005).

Of particular interest as far as this book is concerned is the relationship between 'ladette' identities and academic identities. The 'ladette' identity generally seemed to be constructed in opposition to 'good girl' (passive, diligent plodders) and 'swotty' femininities.

I think most of us are like that [loud and disruptive in lessons]. We like talk back to the teacher and stuff ... like if a teacher shouted at one of the swots they'd just sit there and say 'I'm really sorry Miss, I'm really sorry'. But if they shouted at us we'd be like 'yeh whatever, don't talk to me, I'm going, see you later' and just walk out the door and just give them loads of backchat and stuff.

(Paula, Hollydale)

They just sit there and they shout out all the time and then they just mess around and then they start picking on someone just because they're doing their work or because of the way they look or something.

(Julia, Firtrees)

Outside of school, an important aspect of a 'ladette's' leisure time was 'hanging out' with girls and boys. To be popular among peers, girls (like boys) had to invest considerable amounts of time going out with friends (see Chapter 7). Furthermore, drinking was seen to enhance a girl's reputation in school for being 'cool', and again, 'coolness' was set in opposition to being a 'swot'. For example, Paula was a middle-class girl who got scores of 6 across the board in her SATs.[5] She was a self-identified 'ladette'[6] and was also identified as such by one of her teachers; she talked about how important it is to socialize and drink outside school to avoid being seen as a 'swot'.

> The swots just sit at home and do their homework. We go out and we just go to the park and stuff, and people drive past and they think 'oh they're up to no good' but you're not, you just sit there. You look like you're up to no good because you're like in a gang of fifty but you're not, you're just talking.
> *So is that a mixed [gender] group?*
> Yes.
> *So is drinking quite a big thing to do then among some groups?*
> … Most parents are like 'you can drink but don't drink a lot' and so they'll [school girls] say 'right I'm sleeping at my mate's house'. And then they'll be drinking all night and all day and they'll come home with big headaches and they'll go 'oh no I was fighting and I banged my head' and stuff like that, and 'that's why I've got a headache'. But if you don't drink then you're swotty. I don't like drinking that much. I don't do it all the time, persistently, but if someone says 'here you are, do you want some of this?' then I'll go 'go on then' just so I don't look like a swot.
> *So when you got grounded [mentioned earlier in the interview], did you say you were out all night partying?*
> All night drinking.
> *No wonder you got in trouble then [she'd told me earlier that her Mum does not allow her to drink]. So is there quite a bit of pressure to go out and drink?*
> Yes. It's like most of the girls in my year they've got like older sisters who go out clubbing and that, and they all know the bouncers and so they can get us into like night clubs and stuff. So we all go like clubbing in town and I'll say to my Mum 'right I'm sleeping at Sandy's house' and we'll go clubbing with her sister and stuff like that. But my Mum don't know anything.
> *So you've been doing that for a while or have you just started?*
> Since Year 7. In fact the bouncers know we're not eighteen but they let us in anyway because Sandy's sister will flirt with them and she gets her cleavage out and everything and they go 'alright let them in, don't tell anybody' and they know we're not eighteen. But if we came to school and went 'oh we went clubbing on Saturday' everyone would be like 'oh my god, wicked' and stuff like that. But if we went 'oh I stayed in and did my homework on Saturday' they'd be like 'oh my god you swot'. So it's good to be seen drinking, like walking round the street with a bottle in your hand. Even if you're not drinking, you just tip a bit on the floor so it looks like you've

had some and you walk down the street with a bottle in your hand and everyone would just think 'oh she's dead good'.

Paula was explicit about the importance of 'show' and image in the construction of 'cool' identities: she admitted that she is not especially fond of alcohol, but that it is really important to be *seen* drinking. As such, she drank, or sometimes pretended to drink, to create a 'dead good' image and to avoid being seen as a 'swot'. Paula constructed her 'ladette' identity in opposition to the 'swot' identity, and she was not unusual in this regard; most girls feared, and attempted to avoid, being labelled a swot. Swot identities were antithetical not only to 'ladette' identities, but to cool, popular femininities more generally. Indeed, there was a considerable amount of overlap between 'ladette' identities and 'popular' femininities.

Is 'ladette' femininity a 'popular' femininity?

Popularity and friendships are crucial aspects of girls' school lives. There is a considerable body of research from a range of disciplines documenting the importance of peer friendships for schoolgirls (for example, Hey 1997; Osler and Vincent 2003; McLaughlin 2005) and also the negative consequences of being unpopular or rejected (for example, Erdley 1996; Kupersmidt et al. 1996). Similar to the ways in which boys must adhere to dominant models of masculinity in school if they want to be popular, or at least avoid being unpopular, so too must girls conform to normative models of femininity. Steph (Hollydale) summed this up passionately and succinctly: 'you can't really live without friends because you need them to support you, so you do sometimes have to try and fit in with everyone else'.

So what does 'fitting in' involve? What are 'popular' girls like? Are 'ladettes' popular girls in the same way that 'lads' are popular boys? Across the schools in this research there were a number of 'core aspects' of popular femininity. Unsurprisingly, most of these aspects revolved around physical appearance, fashion and sexuality, all within a heterosexual framework (see also Renold 2005a). Popular girls were usually regarded as pretty (which involved being thin); fashionable in terms of wearing trendy clothes, make-up and having the latest mobile phones; and sociable in that they 'hung out' with friends inside and outside school, and were 'interested in' the popular boys. In addition, and perhaps more surprisingly,[7] a recurring theme as a marker of popularity among girls was that popular girls, like their male counterparts, had to avoid overt hard work and have an air of indifference about academic work. Other features that commonly arose in descriptions of popular girls were being loud, and for some, a relatively regular feature of socializing involved smoking and drinking. The quotes below give a flavour of girls' types of responses about what makes girls popular.

Jenny (Firtrees)
Most of the popular girls you see walking in groups together and they've all got the same hairstyle and their hair is perfectly straight. Like [they've got] the same coats and they're all dead skinny and there's all these little chubby girls walking behind them going 'oh I want to be like that'.

Sarah (Firtrees)
So what makes them [group of girls] popular?
I don't know, it's like the clothes they wear and the way they never do any work. And like as I say, smoking and drinking on Friday nights and everything, and like shouting at teachers and not doing as they [teachers] say; their own free will thing.

Wendy (Beechwood)
What makes a girl popular in school, are there particular things that you have to do to be seen to be cool or good or popular or whatever?
Just like annoy the teacher and everything.

Clare (Firtrees)
So what makes a girl popular in school?
Not caring about her work really, doesn't care about going to school and stuff like that.

Dana (Beechwood)
So, so what makes a girl popular in school? Are there things that make some girls more popular than others?
I don't know. I'm just loud, have a laugh with me mates, that's it.

Gail (Elmwood)
I wouldn't say they're popular because they're hard workers, I'd say it's maybe more of the opposite: some people might say that because they're not [hardworkers], I don't know. I wouldn't say that some of the girls from the allegedly popular group are the cleverest people in the class, but I think it [their popularity] is maybe to do with like what they wear and their appearance and stuff like that.

Nassima (Oakfield)
What sorts of things make girls popular in school, do you think?
Girls? Er, I'm not sure. Well now, it's whose got the best shoes I think, the best pointy shoes. And the best hairdos, best coats, bags, shoes, everything, makeup, best looks, whose with the best guy or who can pull the most.

Sally (Firtrees)
What about girls, what makes a girl popular in school?
Wearing loads of makeup and wearing the right kind of clothes and talking and [being] loud.

Clara (Hollydale)
So they'd be seen as particularly popular – this group – then?
Yes it's like the main group in the school. There's other groups, but they're like the main popular group and most people want to be seen with them and stuff.
Why is that do you think?
Because they go out with the popular boys and get drunk and stuff and not many other groups [do], they [other groups] go out with lads and stuff but they don't get drunk because they can't get it. Whereas they [popular girls] can, they know older people. They just dress like in all the latest stuff and they like all the latest like phones and stuff. So everyone wants to be seen with them.

Teachers generally echoed the girls' comments. For example, Ms Wood at Hollydale girls' school commented on how a girl's popularity is based heavily upon her appearance and sexual attractiveness:

Are there particular things that girls have to be seen to do to be cool, thinking again about Year 9?
Yes in school it's the shortest skirt, the trendiest shoes, makeup starts to feature quite heavily in Year 9, the straightest hair, very heavily based around appearance … and it's quite interesting because as teachers we can never understand why they felt that they had to be like that because there are no boys here. And the Head of Lower School … she's just asked Year 9 when she's had them in detentions and things, and they said that it was a case of being known within the year as being the sexiest girls. So among her peers that's their aim or whatever, their goal. So they still go in for the makeup and hair and skirt, tan is another one, fake tan.

Overall, popularity for girls was closely aligned with models of normative femininity. This is unsurprising as much research has demonstrated the ways in which girls' behaviours are policed, and those girls who deviate from these normative versions (which are premised on heterosexuality) are Othered (for example, Hey 1997; Epstein and Johnson 1998; Paechter 1998; Kehily 2001; Renold 2005a). There was also a large degree of overlap between popular femininity and 'ladette' behaviours. As mentioned earlier, while the 'ladette' label is readily applied by the UK press, it is impossible to identify clear boundaries about who can, and who cannot, be regarded as a 'ladette'. Instead, one might envisage a continuum of 'ladette' behaviours (so too with 'lad' behaviours for boys). How many 'ladette' behaviours a girl or woman would need to perform before she was considered to be a 'ladette' is highly subjective, although it can be as few as one for a woman to be labelled a 'ladette' by the press (see Jackson and Tinkler forthcoming). The overlap between 'ladette' femininity and popular femininity might be visualized in terms of overlapping continuums, with many of the behaviours on the 'ladette continuum' being shared with the 'popular girl' continuum. However, those at the 'extreme' end of the 'ladette' continuum may not feature on the popular femininity one. So, for example, being regarded as too 'hard' may well be incompatible with popular femininity. A finding that is of fundamental importance to this book is that avoiding overt hard work featured large on both 'ladette' and 'popular girl' continuums.

Are 'ladette' behaviours among schoolgirls a cause for concern?

Given that the association between boys' 'laddish' behaviours and uncool-to-work attitudes has been the cause of a great deal of concern, it is pertinent to consider whether there are similar concerns about this association for 'ladettes'. In other words, are teachers concerned about the potentially negative academic consequences of 'ladette' behaviours for some girls? If boys' 'laddish' attitudes are commonly linked in popular and some academic discourses to their 'underachievement', are teachers concerned that 'ladette' behaviours might result in some girls 'underachieving'?

'Ladette'-type behaviours – both inside and outside of school – were regarded as a cause for concern by teachers. Concerns about out-of-school behaviours related to girls' drinking, sexual promiscuity, fighting and general safety. In-school concerns related largely to their reported disruptive behaviours, rudeness and lack of respect for teachers. It is not surprising that teachers express concerns about some of the behaviours of girls, particularly when they regard these behaviours as putting girls 'at risk'. Furthermore, it is understandable that teachers are unhappy about some girls' behaviours in class when they disrupt learning and make their jobs as teachers more difficult. The fact that teachers find time to reflect on, and worry about, the welfare of girls in a system that is generally dominated by concerns about standards and academic performance could also be regarded as positive. However, it is important to interrogate critically these concerns and the discourses that promote and sustain them. Popular discourses on the 'ladette' position her as dangerous and problematic. These discourses are underpinned largely by essentialist assumptions about differences between men and women. Penny Tinkler and I (Jackson and Tinkler forthcoming) have argued that the 'ladette' is presented as particularly dangerous in popular discourse because of her perceived capacity for gender disorder and her disruption of dominant discourses on gender differences.

Indeed, we suggest that a moral panic about 'ladettes' has been driven and fuelled by fears about women becoming like, or apeing, men. In popular discourse 'ladettes' are portrayed as power-hungry 'wannabe lads', and are almost always presented as lacking relative to the male, authentic version. Furthermore, her lack of authenticity frequently marks the 'ladette' as worse than the 'real version', against whom she is unfavourably compared and judged.

This deficit model was evident in schools, where, when compared to the 'ladette', even the usually troublesome 'lad' fared favourably. 'Lads' were presented as being ahead in terms of 'laddishness': boys are more 'laddish' because 'laddish boys have got a head start on these girls' (Ms Attwood, Firtrees). However, despite the view that lads are more 'laddish' than 'ladettes', a number of the teachers suggested that 'laddish' girls were more difficult to deal with than 'laddish' boys (see also Younger *et al.* 1999) and/or 'laddish' boys were more charming than their female counterparts.

> The 'laddies' that we have, our 'laddish' lads, were high profile. I think if you ask most teachers I think they would be able to rattle off ten names – of the loveable rogue. Now, the girls don't fall into that, they don't have that same endearing quality that the boys do. The girls that we've got that, if you like, are the nearest parallel, are disruptive, which is irksome because they disrupt the learning. Whereas the 'laddies' didn't. They might have, em, not disrupted the learning, they might have made it wobble a bit, but they never wrecked it ... Girls are different. So I think we have got girls who don't conform to the stereotype of girls which is that, you know, the person who sits still and wants to do well and please the teacher. But they ['ladettes'] don't have that same, those same characteristics as the 'laddish' boys.
>
> (Ms Byatt, Firtrees)

> Some of the girls can be really quite vicious. Now you very rarely see that unpleasant side in lads. You do, there's odd ones who flip, you do see it, but not as much as the girls.
>
> (Ms Brian, Beechwood)

The ways in which *behaviours* are viewed differently by teachers depending upon whether they are performed by girls or boys demonstrate the predominance of gender double standards. Some of the ways in which boys disrupt lessons are seen as 'harmless fun' and the boys are regarded as 'loveable rogues'; they are regarded as 'boys being boys' (see also Younger and Warrington 2005).[8] Similar behaviours by girls are usually regarded very differently; girls simply are not allowed to be loveable rogues (see also Francis 2000; Osler and Vincent 2003). Reay (2001a: 161) makes a similar point in relation to the 'spice girls' in her research. These Year 3 girls were labelled by teachers in the staffroom as 'real bitches', 'a bad influence' and 'little cows' for displaying behaviours that countered traditional forms of femininity.

These same gender double standards are also evident in terms of the *concerns* voiced about 'laddish' girls and boys. For boys, concerns about 'laddish' behaviours in school centred largely on raising their academic achievements and reducing disruption in class. For girls, the focus was less explicitly on raising achievement perhaps because, according to dominant education discourses, girls are 'successful'.[9] Instead, concerns about girls seemed to relate much more to the ways in which they are seen to transgress normative models of femininity (see Jackson and Tinkler forthcoming; Jackson 2006). For example, Ms Walters (Hollygrove) suggested that she had noticed an increasing number of girls fighting over the last few years, adding later:

> you'll not always find it's men brawling, you'll find a lot of the time it's women, which is I think a sad reflection of society. I mean any form of physical violence like that is very demeaning at the best of occasions, and maybe I shouldn't say this and maybe it is a sexist comment, but I think it's even worse sometimes when you look at women. Because ... I think women are far more capable of negotiating things verbally than actually resorting to thumping each other; it's not the way to solve an argument.

For decades feminists have documented and attempted to counter gender double standards in terms of teachers' expectations about, and treatment of, boys and girls (for example, Spender and Sarah 1980; Deem 1984; Delamont 1984; Mahony 1985; Weiner 1985; Lees 1986, 1993; Arnot and Weiner 1987; Spender 1989). In the twenty-first century, contrary to 'women have made it, have it all and do it all' discourses (Hughes 2002a), gender double standards continue unabated (see, for example, Francis 2000, 2005; Warrington and Younger 2000; Osler and Vincent 2003; Davies 2005). So while popular discourses on 'underachieving' boys construct 'lads' as in danger of academic failure, 'ladettes' are constructed as in danger of 'gender failure' for performing behaviours that transgress normative models of femininity.

Discussion

This chapter has introduced 'lads' and 'ladettes'. I argued that there is a large degree of overlap between being a 'lad' or a 'ladette' and being popular. Central to popularity for both boys and girls is an overt rejection of school work, as in all schools visibly working hard was regarded as incompatible with popular ways of 'doing' boy or girl. As will be demonstrated and discussed more fully in later chapters, the complexities and difficulties often involved in constructing 'acceptable' academic and social identities are as salient for girls as they are for boys. Thus, we need to reconsider the view that 'learning and academic achievement is not so socially stigmatised for girls as it is for many boys ... and hence they are less deterred from application by social considerations' (Francis and Skelton 2005: 129). Time and time again girls across the schools in this research told me that it is not 'cool' for girls to be seen to work hard on school work (see also Whitelaw *et al.* 2000; Evans *et al.* 2004; Swain 2005). Although concerns about the implications of such attitudes are central to discourses on 'laddishness' and boys' 'underachievement' (Younger and Warrington 1996; Francis 1999, 2000; Martino 1999; Warrington *et al.* 2000, 2003; Jackson 2002a, 2003; Younger *et al.* 2002), they have not been raised in relation to girls.

That the 'uncool to work' pupil discourse is as dominant for girls as it is for boys raises questions about how we attempt to explain it. In recent research, explanations have been sought only to account for boys' oppositional approaches to working overtly at school, and reasons proffered have related to social status. As discussed, these explanations have drawn upon theories of hegemonic masculinity, in which school work has been positioned as 'feminine' and therefore in opposition to hegemonic, popular versions of schoolboy masculinity. This theory cannot account for why many girls also regard overt hard work as problematic. It would be possible to argue that 'popular girls' and 'ladettes', like 'lads', reject overt hard work in order to be popular, or to avoid being unpopular. However, concerns about popularity cannot explain fully the ways in which girls and boys hide their academic effort – this is discussed further in Chapter 3. While social goals, more specifically, concerns about social status, are undoubtedly crucial to understanding how and why girls and boys position themselves in relation to academic work, they cannot provide all the pieces to the puzzle. I argue that we need also to consider academic goals. The next chapter introduces academic goals. Chapter 3 then argues why we need to consider both social and academic goals in order to enhance our understanding of 'laddish' behaviours in schools.

2 'I don't want them to think I'm thick': Academic motives for 'laddishness'

> If you've tried your best and you've got a low mark then it's sort of like 'oh you can't do it and you're stupid'. But if you didn't try and you got a low mark it's like 'oh I couldn't be bothered doing it so I only tried a little bit'.
>
> (Lee, School B)

> There are few things more frustrating to teachers than being confronted with a student who actively and purposefully avoids learning opportunities. Increasingly, we are finding evidence that engaging in these frustrating avoidance behaviours may actually be encouraged by the motivational climate of the learning context.
>
> (Urdan *et al.* 2002: 56)

'Laddish' behaviours and attitudes in schools are regarded as detrimental to student learning because, as we saw in Chapter 1, they frequently involve overt rejection of school work, messing around in class, and generally prioritizing social over academic endeavours. The 'million-dollar question' for many teachers is how to tackle 'laddish' attitudes and behaviours and how to get 'laddish' boys and girls to engage with academic work; this question is fundamentally about motivation. Questions about motivation are central to attempts to understand pupils' behaviours in schools. Teachers, parents, researchers and policy-makers all regularly engage with questions about what motivates particular types of behaviours. For example, why do some pupils mess around in class and disrupt the lesson rather than work? Why do some students work really hard on a task whereas others do not even attempt it? Why do some students leave their work until the last possible moment? These questions, along with many others, present conundrums for educators on a regular basis. I argue that in order to answer these questions we must engage with pupils' motives. This is a view shared by Warrington and Younger (2005: 4) who (referring to boys) argue that: 'Given the focus on credentials in today's economy, a fundamental starting

point in any discussion of the factors which affect boys' academic performances at school must be to try to understand the rationale and motives
which underpin the behaviour and (lack of) engagement of some boys.'

Questions about how to motivate students to work in school are not
new; researchers and teachers have struggled with such questions for a long
time. But shifting social, educational and political climates render it necessary to recast some of the old questions, and to consider them in relation
to the climate and conditions of the time. Furthermore, continuing developments and advances in our knowledge and understanding of behaviours
and motives provide ever-developing foundations upon which to build
further our research and theories.

The last chapter focused upon how social status motives can help us to
understand the pattern of behaviours and attitudes labelled as 'laddish';
this chapter begins to consider how academic motives can help to develop
this understanding. With this aim in mind, I introduce two motivation
theories: achievement goal theory and self-worth theory.

Achievement goal theory

Research on achievement goal theory has boomed over the last decade
(Freeman 2004) and it now represents one of the major theories, if not *the*
major theory, in the field of achievement motivation (Midgley *et al.* 2001;
Covington 2002; Maehr and Arbor 2002; Urdan 2004a). It is widely
acknowledged to be of central importance in enabling us to understand the
factors that influence the amount and quality of pupil learning in school.
Achievement goal theory is regarded as a qualitative theory of motivation,
as 'rather than focussing on the level of motivation (i.e., high effort, low
interest), the focus is on the goals or purposes that are perceived for
achievement behaviour' (Middleton and Midgley 1997: 710). Achievement
goal theory emphasizes the importance of how individuals think about
themselves, and attempts to understand an individual's self-constructed
meanings for pursuing a particular course of action, and to explore the individual factors and contextual factors that shape these subjective constructions. In other words, it is underpinned by the assumption that a pupil's
motivation at school is affected by her/his self-constructed meanings or
purposes for engaging (or not engaging) in an academic task. This purpose
is termed the 'achievement goal'. Midgley *et al.* (2001: 77) define the
achievement goal as: 'the purposes for behaviour that are perceived or
pursued in a competence-relevant setting'. So when we ask what a pupil's
achievement goal is, we are asking *why* s/he engages in an achievement-
related behaviour (Kaplan *et al.* 2002a; Kaplan 2004).

Achievement goal theory has emphasized two main types of
goals, namely learning goals (also known as mastery or task goals) and

performance goals (also known as ego or ability goals). Learning goals are the darlings of motivation researchers as studies consistently show them to have positive effects on learning (Covington 2000; Midgley *et al.* 2001; Kaplan *et al.* 2002a; Freeman 2004; Kaplan 2004; Wolters 2004). Learning goals relate to a focus on self-improvement, learning new skills, and increasing understanding, and appreciation, of what is being learned. In other words, learning goals are about *developing* competence. In contrast, performance goals relate to a concern with social comparisons and with a *demonstration* of competence in relation to others; they involve 'outperforming others as a means to aggrandize one's ability status at the expense of peers' (Covington 2000: 174). While there is a general consensus among researchers that learning goals are beneficial for learning, there is no consensus about the effects of performance goals.

The mixed and sometimes contradictory research findings about performance goals prompted researchers to look more closely at them, and the result has been a division into performance-*approach*, and performance-*avoid*, goals (Elliot and Harackiewicz, 1996). Performance-*approach* goals refer to a pupil's concern to demonstrate high ability (for example, I want to be top of the class), while performance-*avoid* goals relate to a concern to avoid demonstrating low ability (for example, I don't want to be bottom of the class) (Kaplan *et al.* 2002b). Some performance-approach-oriented students[1] are successful academically, as they often invest considerable time and effort devising study strategies and ways to be successful. By contrast, performance-avoid-oriented students, who are eager to avoid appearing stupid, frequently adopt strategies that involve reduced effort on academic tasks and so are often unsuccessful in academic terms. For example, a student concerned to avoid looking stupid might decide not to do a piece of homework rather than run the risk of doing it and getting it wrong (this sentiment is expressed by Lee in the opening quote of the chapter). There is a general consensus that performance-avoid goals are 'maladaptive' in educational terms (Linnenbrink 2004). According to Kaplan *et al.* (2002a) performance-avoid-oriented students are likely to (a) feel anxious; (b) have a low sense of academic efficacy;[2] (c) avoid seeking help; (d) engage in academic self-handicapping;[3] and (e) have lower grades. While performance-approach goals are not consistently associated with the range of negative feelings, behaviours and outcomes that performance-avoid goals are, performance-approach goals may be associated with test anxiety and with self-handicapping. Importantly, both performance-approach and performance-avoid goals are associated with a fear of failure (Urdan *et al.* 2002); this is discussed in more detail later in this chapter.[4]

While much of the research in this sphere has concentrated on the goals constructed by individuals, researchers have also been interested in the ways in which learning contexts (such as classrooms) shape these goals (Kaplan 2004). So, while personal goals are those that individuals construct and pursue in specific learning situations, these are related to, and influenced by, the goals emphasized or encouraged in the learning context (Kaplan *et al.* 2002a; Linnenbrink 2004). The goals emphasized within a learning context have been referred to as 'goal structures'. Kaplan *et al.* (2002a: 24) conceptualize goal structures in terms of 'the various classroom- and school-level policies and practices that make mastery [learning] or performance goals salient, as well as the explicit goal-related messages teachers communicate to their students'. So, for example, some teachers might emphasize the importance of learning and personal improvement, reward students for effort rather than getting right answers, discourage competition and relative-ability social comparisons, and place little emphasis on tests and grades. Such a classroom climate might convey a learning goal structure. By contrast, other teachers might encourage competition for top of the class, place high value on, and reward, good grades, emphasize differences between students and encourage relative-ability social comparisons by publicly announcing test results. Such a classroom climate is likely to convey a performance goal structure. Examples from my own research illustrate the ways in which performance goal structures are constructed in classrooms. For example, pupil interviewees revealed that a lot of teachers encourage relative-ability social comparisons by reading out test results to the class and/or signal ability hierarchies by other means. This will be discussed more fully in Chapter 4, but here I include one particularly explicit example of the way in which a teacher signalled relative pupil performance levels in her class. Lawrence at Ashgrove explained that in his top set maths class pupils are seated according to relative ability: 'clever ones' at the back of the class, 'not as clever' ones at the front.

> *So is there a lot of pressure to do well in the top sets?*
> There's not too much from the teachers but there's quite a bit from the other pupils. There's a bit of rivalry in the classroom … 'cause part of the system is if you're not as clever then you sit at the front in the middle, which is better because it's easier to hear. Then the clever ones sit towards the back …
> *So it's quite an explicit way of ranking people in the class then?*
> Well, in my first lesson in maths I was sat right at the front after a bit, which I wasn't too worried about because it was the first time I'd been in set one. But it helped me because the very next test I was sat quite a bit further back and it wasn't, well it wasn't because of the extra pressure, it was more because I was at the front and I could see everything she was doing and I couldn't miss a word and you don't loose your attention as easily when you're sat towards the front. And I think that was the main aim of it rather than just to embarrass us.

The teacher's method of seating pupils according to ability is striking for its emphasis on performance goals; it is difficult to imagine a more overt and visual way of ranking a class according to individual (grade) performance. Lawrence initially suggests that pressure to perform well in this class comes mainly from the pupils rather than the teacher. However, pupil-pupil relative-ability comparisons are clearly facilitated and encouraged by the way in which the teacher organizes her classroom. Lawrence attempts to find positive aspects of this method of spatial organization: 'less clever' ones can see and hear the teacher and are less likely to get distracted. However, underlying his response is also a recognition that some students are explicitly positioned as bottom of the class, and that this can be embarrassing.

The portrayal of performance and learning goal structures discussed so far is too neat to reflect real classrooms and real life. There are two main factors that muddy the pool. First, as Kaplan *et al.* (2002a) point out, goal structures are primarily a subjective construction. Students may perceive, respond to and negotiate goal structures in different ways (see also Wolters 2004). Second, it is likely that while some classrooms err more towards performance or learning goal structures, most teachers are likely to create a climate whereby both performance and learning goals are emphasized at different times. Furthermore, while some teachers might aim towards creating a classroom climate that emphasizes learning goals, broader climates, frameworks, discourses and regulations may make this impossible to sustain. For example, the standards discourse that is currently dominant in England emphasizes results (performance), not effort. The regular SATs testing that occurs in England exerts pressures upon pupils to 'make the grade' and there are pressures on teachers to ensure that pupils do 'make the grade' (this will be discussed in more detail in Chapter 4). So classroom climates are not divorced from broader school and educational climates and discourses.

So far I have introduced both learning and performance goals, and have subdivided performance goals into performance-*approach* and performance-*avoid* ones. As a reminder, learning goals are about *developing* competence; performance goals are about *demonstrating* competence. Performance-*approach* goals refer to a pupil's concern to demonstrate high ability, whereas performance-*avoid* goals relate to a concern to avoid demonstrating low ability. Let's take a closer look at avoidance goals and behaviours.

In general: 'avoidance behaviours reflect motivation to move away from, or avoid, some perceived threat in the learning context' (Urdan *et al.* 2002: 56). According to motivation researchers, academic 'failure', or being regarded as an academic failure by others, is frequently the perceived threat. So fear of academic failure is central to understanding avoidance behaviours in schools. It is crucial that we understand avoidance motives in order to challenge them successfully. However, as Urdan *et al*. (2002) point out, most of the research on academic motivation to date has focused upon approach goals. In other words, it has concentrated on understanding how we can help students move *towards* engaging with academic work. In a way, this focus is understandable given that a key aim of the classroom teacher is to encourage pupils to engage in academic activities. However, as suggested above, in order to understand how to get pupils to engage in academic activities, it is vital to understand why some do not, and this is where avoidance motives come into play. Some motivation researchers and theorists have been interested in avoidance motives for a long time, but it is only recently that they have begun to attract more widespread attention.

Avoidance of academic work, or more precisely, *public* avoidance of academic work, is central to 'laddishness' (Mac an Ghaill 1994; Epstein 1998; Martino 1999; Jackson 2003; Archer *et al*. 2005). Time and time again teachers talk about 'laddish' students as ones who could do the work if they tried, but they do not try. This creates frustration among teachers and parents, as recognized in the quote at the beginning of this chapter: 'There are few things more frustrating to teachers than being confronted with a student who actively and purposefully avoids learning opportunities' (Urdan *et al*. 2002: 56). Achievement goal theorists' attempts to explain avoidance motives and behaviours have drawn upon many elements of self-worth theory, so it is it to self-worth theory that I now turn.

Self-worth theory

Self-worth theory is a theory of motivation that is underpinned by an assumption that the achievement goals adopted by students reflect 'a struggle to establish and maintain a sense of self-worth and belonging in a society that values competency and doing well' (Covington 2000: 181). Martin Covington (1992, 1998, 2000; Covington and Beery 1976), who developed the theory of self-worth motivation initially in relation to US society, argues that individuals are generally considered to be as worthy as their ability to achieve. In other words, there is a dominant performance discourse within which individuals are judged by their (measurable) achievements. The dominance of this discourse in English schools has now been well documented (see, for example, Gleeson and Husbands 2001). Of course, achievements are diverse; one might demonstrate high ability at playing the piano, at playing football or in one's capacity to wrestle with mathematical equations. However, academic prowess is the most highly valued and rewarded ability by secondary schools, and the values attached to different abilities are hierarchically ordered; for example, Skaalvik (1993) argues that theoretical subjects are regarded as more important than practical and aesthetic ones.[5] Reay and Wiliam's (1999: 345) discussion of

Hannah illustrates the ways in which pupils internalize this hierarchy of values and use grades as an indicator of their self-worth. Hannah was a Year 6 pupil who was afraid of doing badly in her SATs because poor performance would mean, in her words, that she would be 'a nothing'. Reay and Wiliam point out that Hannah: 'is an accomplished writer, a gifted dancer and artist and good at problem-solving yet none of those skills make her somebody in her own eyes. Instead she constructs herself as a failure, an academic non-person, by a metonymic shift in which she comes to see herself entirely in terms of the level to which her performance in the SATs is ascribed' (p. 346).

As in the case of Hannah, Covington argues that academic ability is valued so highly within the education system, and in Western societies generally, that academic ability is inextricably intertwined with feelings of self-worth.[6] In other words, 'self-worth is determined by an individual's own, and others', perceptions of one's ability, perceptions that are mainly tied to successful achievement' (Simons *et al.* 1999: 152). Successful achievement within schools is signalled primarily by grades; value is quantified (Reay and Wiliam 1999). Covington argues that for many students no single thing at school can boost feelings of self-worth like a good grade, nor devastate it so completely as a poor one – they are only as good as their grades.[7] But the competitive nature of the education system – which stems largely from its function of sorting and selecting (Brown *et al.* 1997) – means that not everyone can succeed academically, many must 'fail'. Arnot and Miles (2005) argue that the 'sorting and selecting' functions of schools have become more visible in the UK as a result of policies implemented by the New Labour government that are aligned with their agenda of performativity in schooling. The costs of failure in practical and emotional terms are high (see Chapter 4). Emotionally, a range of negative consequences is attached to feelings of failure, such as shame, anxiety and withdrawal (Thompson 1999). Covington argues that amidst this competitive climate a fear of academic failure is common, and as a result many pupils are motivated to avoid failure, or the implications of failure, and to protect their sense of self-worth rather than to achieve *per se* (see also Martin *et al.* 2003b).

Fear of academic failure in schools

There is now considerable evidence to support the notion that many students do fear academic failure and that their sense of self-worth, and aspects of their public image (sometimes referred to as social worth[8]), are bound to notions of academic competence. Most of the early research exploring fear of failure in schools was carried out in the USA, where, according to many writers (for example, Covington and Manheim Teel 1996; Covington 1998, 2000; Dweck 2000), schooling strongly emphasizes

the product over the process and thus encourages students to define themselves according to their test scores. Reay and Wiliam (1999) argue that
while the increasing disposition of students to define themselves according
to their test scores in the USA is more extreme than is the case in England,
the situation in England is moving closer to that of the USA. There is now
mounting evidence that many pupils in England feel pressurized at school
and fear academic failure (Reay and Wiliam 1999; Younger *et al.* 2002;
Jackson 2003). The pressures and fears have been exacerbated by the
increased emphasis upon assessment and standards in England, particularly
the introduction of national tests for all 7-, 11- and 14-year-old pupils (Reay
and Wiliam 1999; Warrington and Younger 1999; Gleeson and Husbands
2001; Walkerdine *et al.* 2001). Many of the pupils interviewed in my
research articulated very clearly their fears about failing academically and
about looking 'stupid' or 'thick' in front of their peers. This theme will be
explored further in Chapter 4, but at this stage a couple of illustrations will
suffice. Extracts from interviewees David and Alysia convey their desires
and strategies to avoid looking stupid.

> David (School A)
> *What do you tell your friends if you get a low mark? How do you explain
> it?*
> I probably wouldn't tell them, I'd probably say that I got a high
> mark.
> *Why would you do that?*
> Just to show off.
> *Why is that important?*
> 'Cause I wouldn't like them going round acting, knowing that I'm
> the dumbest one out of the whole lot of them.

> Alysia (Hollydale)
> *Do you compare marks with other people?*
> No.
> *Not at all?*
> No.
> *Why not?*
> Because if they've got like high grades and I've got like a low grade
> then they might think I'm thick or something. So I don't, it's not
> often I compare my grades with anybody else.

Both of these pupils were concerned about their image, about how they
appeared to their peers. They were concerned not to appear stupid in
school, and both employed strategies to avoid looking stupid. According to
the work of motivation theorists such as Dweck (2000) and Covington
(1998), defensive strategies may be provoked by situations that provide a

threat to one's sense of self-worth in school. As discussed, such situations are plentiful in schools where assessments and grading are abundant and social comparisons are rife. There are two obvious ways to protect one's self-worth. One is to avoid failure, which is not always possible in an education system in which not everyone can succeed. The second is to avoid the *implications* of failure. There are numerous strategies to circumvent the implications of failure and these have been termed defensive strategies.

Defensive strategies

Defensive strategies are generally false, but plausible, explanations generated by students to justify or excuse their behaviour, in this case (potential or actual) 'poor' academic performance (Covington 1998). There are numerous defensive strategies, which are also sometimes called avoidance behaviours or preferences (Urdan *et al.* 2002) and sometimes self-handicapping strategies. Many of these defensive strategies are interrelated, and in general they provide excuses that enable individuals to blame factors other than a lack of ability for academic 'failure'. Many of the behaviours that can serve as defensive strategies are the same behaviours that characterize 'laddishness' (Jackson 2002a). In this section I introduce the defensive strategies and avoidance motives that overlap most with 'laddish' behaviours. These are: (1) procrastination; (2) intentional withdrawal of effort and a rejection of academic work; (3) avoiding the appearance of working and promoting the appearance of effortless achievement; (4) disruptive behaviour. Chapter 6 explores how and why pupils in my research adopted these defensive strategies.

1 Procrastination

This 'technique' requires little introduction and explanation. Putting off work until the last minute provides an excuse for failure that deflects attention away from a potential lack of ability. Procrastination keeps open the possibility that success would have been possible if effort had been applied earlier: 'I could have done better if I'd had more time ...' The procrastinator is able to attribute failure to factors other than ability, and hence maintain self-worth. Further, self-worth may be enhanced if the procrastinator is successful, as success with little effort is regarded as a sign of 'true intellect'. As with many of these defensive strategies, there is a distinction between what students claim to do and what they actually do. Some may claim to leave work until the last minute, when in actual fact they have worked long and hard on a task. Covington (1998) calls these students 'closet achievers', but in the context of procrastination they might equally be called 'reported procrastinators'. Of those who actually do procrastinate ('actual' as opposed to 'reported' procrastinators), procrastination occurs along a continuum. Some individuals procrastinate but eventually do the work (although the work may be poor in quality), whereas others may procrastinate to the extent that the work is never undertaken. The latter scenario may then lead to the second of the strategies discussed here, namely an intentional withdrawal of effort and rejection of academic work.

2 Intentional withdrawal of effort and rejection of academic work

when 'wannabe' hegemonic boys do not 'win', they tend to adopt a 'can't win, won't win and don't want to play' stance.

(Warrington and Younger 2005: 5)

Intentional withdrawal of effort and rejection of academic work are inextricably linked as self-worth protection strategies. The notion that our self-esteem or self-worth is influenced by our pretensions dates back to the ideas of William James (1890: 310), who argued that 'our self-feeling in this world depends entirely on what we *back* ourselves to be and do'. If some students are able to convey the impression that academic success is not important and therefore that they are unwilling to take part in what Covington (1998; Covington and Manheim Teel 1996) calls the 'ability game', then these students are able to protect their self-worth:

I left two weeks' homework to yesterday.
Why's that?
Had *better things* to do. (Tahir, Elmwood, my emphasis)

What is difficult to know, is whether students who publicly denounce academic work really do believe that school work is worthless or whether such displays are primarily self-worth protection mechanisms because these individuals fear the consequences of academic failure. Galloway *et al.* (1998: 36) highlight the difficulty of making this distinction, arguing that 'some pupils may reject the goal of academic success in order to maintain their status in the peer group, not because they fear academic failure' (see Willis 1977; Marsh *et al.* 1978). These motives are not mutually exclusive; I argue throughout this book that rejecting academic work can serve a dual purpose. First, it enables students to act in ways currently consistent with popular forms of femininity or masculinity in their schools (to be popular among peers). Second, it provides an excuse for failure and augments success. This will be discussed in Chapter 6. Overall, the evidence that rejecting academic work acts as a self-worth protection mechanism is convincing. Covington and others concerned with self-worth protection (for example, Thompson 1999; Martin *et al.* 2003b) have built up a considerable body of evidence to support the theory that defensive strategies are often regarded as necessary to protect against the potential consequences of failure. Covington (1998: 88) argues that individuals may 'take a perverse pride in their unwillingness to achieve by downgrading the importance of work they refuse to do, or by attacking others who do try as hypocritical, foolish, or stupid'. However, Covington argues that this behaviour offers a deceptive cover for people to avoid any test of their abilities and thereby encourages a positive perception of their competence.

3 Avoiding the appearance of working and promoting the appearance of effortless achievement

From a self-worth protection perspective, 'effortless achievement' is the ideal. To achieve academically without hard work gives clear signals about an individual's ability. Avoiding overt hard work also provides a convenient excuse if success is not forthcoming – failure without effort does not necessarily indicate a lack of ability, but success without effort indicates true genius. It is perhaps not too surprising, then, that overt withdrawal of effort is appealing in many ways. As Galloway *et al.* (1998: 128) point out, effort 'is a "double-edged sword": the harder we try the more we feel let down if we do not succeed; and if we do not succeed in a task which other people find easy the effect is compounded'. A key difference between this strategy of self-worth protection and the last one (intentional withdrawal of effort and a rejection of academic work) is that the last one was concerned with *actual* withdrawal of effort, whereas this one is concerned with the *appearance* of withdrawal of effort. In fact, individuals who adopt an effortless achievement approach may well be Covington's (1998) 'closet achievers'. As mentioned earlier, closet achievers are those pupils who establish a pretence that they have done no work when actually they have spent a considerable amount of time studying. For closet achievers, then, the pretence of not working is principally a performance for others.

4 Disruptive behaviour

Disruptive behaviour provides another method of blurring the relationship between failure and lack of ability. Where pupils exhibit disruptive behaviours, failures may be attributed to being inattentive in class rather than to a lack of ability *per se*, and the behaviour may act to deflect attention away from poor academic performance and onto their behaviour instead (Skaalvik 1993; Gilbert and Gilbert 1998). While disruptive pupils clearly jeopardize their own chances of academic success, they also make learning more difficult for other members of the class. As such, one might argue that, to some extent, disruptive behaviour acts to sabotage the efforts of academically oriented peers – an 'if I can't win, nobody will' approach.

Overall, the potential benefits of disruptive behaviour for the perpetrator are fourfold. First, it can deflect attention away from poor academic performance by focusing attention on the behaviour. Second, poor performance can be attributed to not paying attention in class rather than to a lack of ability. Third, disruptive behaviour may sabotage the efforts and performances of classmates and so make grade social comparisons more favourable.

Fourth, disruptive behaviour in class can increase a pupil's status within her/his peer group, as being disruptive can increase popularity.

Summary

In this chapter I argued that in order to develop our understandings of 'laddish' behaviours we need to engage with questions about what motivates them. Two achievement motivation theories were introduced – achievement goal theory and self-worth theory – that in combination have the potential to offer important insights into debates about the causes of 'laddishness'. Many of the behaviours that are labelled 'laddish' are the same behaviours that have been identified by motivation researchers as defensive strategies. In other words, certain 'laddish' behaviours provide students with excuses for poor academic performance so that academic ability is not called into question. Some students recognized the potential of 'laddish' behaviours to provide these excuses, for example Shaun (School B) suggested that students use the argument that it is 'uncool to work' to hide their lack of ability:

> *Is it seen as cool to work hard?*
> No.
> *Why?*
> 'Cause like it's supposed to be like swotty or something like that, and people who don't work hard it's them that say it [that it's swotty] 'cause they're not as good as you so they make up excuses for them not being as good as you are.

The ways in which 'laddish' behaviours act as protection strategies are explored throughout the book. However, while the motivation theories discussed in this chapter are valuable, they also have a number of limitations which are discussed in the next chapter.

3 Combining insights to understand 'laddishness': Integrating theories about social and academic motives

> As the questions and problems of human behavior are inherently complex and multifaceted, there is a need to draw on a diversity of traditional disciplines to understand the phenomena of interest, especially in the area of human cognition and motivation ... motivational science should draw from multiple disciplinary perspectives in terms of theories, constructs, and methods to address questions regarding the role of student motivation.
>
> (Pintrich 2003: 668)

> The moment is surely ripe for the sociology of education and its related fields to enter into a more sustained dialogue with psychosocial ideas.
>
> (Redman 2005: 537)

Chapters 1 and 2 identified and discussed key factors shaping students' attitudes to school work; Chapter 1 focused on social goals and Chapter 2 on academic goals. Chapter 1 explored the ways in which pupils' social status motives can shape approaches to learning, and in particular how social status motives (desires to be popular or avoid being unpopular) and gender identities interact in this process. I explored the concept of the 'lad' and 'laddishness' and argued that most attempts by social scientists to explain 'laddish' behaviours in school – particularly the 'uncool to work' element – have drawn almost exclusively upon theories of hegemonic masculinity. I then shifted the focus onto 'ladettes', and explored the interplay between 'popular' schoolgirl femininities and 'ladette' identities, and examined the ways in which 'ladettes' are regarded as a cause for concern.

Chapter 2 introduced achievement goal theory and the related theory of self-worth protection. According to these theories pupils' approaches to academic work are shaped by individual goals. These goals are shaped and negotiated by students in the context of classroom goal structures (goals emphasized or encouraged in the classroom), school goal structures, and then societal educational frameworks, structures and discourses.

Goal theory and self-worth theory highlight the often contradictory educational discourses that pupils must negotiate. On the one hand, pupils are told that effort is important in school, that effort and hard work are valued and rewarded. On the other hand, the standards discourse is currently a dominant educational discourse in the UK and this emphasizes and extols the value of academic attainment. Students and teachers are expected to meet, and are rewarded for meeting (or ideally exceeding), specified targets in regular tests. The emphasis is on performance and on demonstrating ability. In an educational climate in which demonstrating academic ability is paramount, effort becomes a double-edged sword; after all, failure after effort implies a lack of ability, which in a performance climate can have detrimental effects on an individual's self-worth. As a result, some students are more concerned with protecting their self-worth than achieving *per se*, and there is a variety of defensive strategies for doing this.

This chapter explores the strengths and limits of the theories outlined in Chapters 1 and 2 for understanding 'laddishness', with a particular emphasis on the 'not cool to work' aspect. I then discuss how attempts to understand 'laddishness' might be enriched by bringing together the theories outlined in Chapters 1 and 2. This provides the theoretical framework for the book. I start by discussing key strengths and limits of achievement goal theory and self-worth theory for understanding 'laddishness'.

Strengths and limits of achievement goal and self-worth theories for understanding 'laddishness'

The combined insights of goal theory and self-worth theory have the potential to offer a great deal for developing understanding of 'laddish' attitudes and behaviours. Goal theorists – drawing on aspects of self-worth theory – are now increasingly concerned to explore and to understand how and why pupils attempt to *avoid* certain academic tasks and challenges (Middleton and Midgley 1997). This renewed interest in avoidance motives prompts questions about student behaviours that echo those asked by teachers, parents, politicians and researchers about 'laddish' behaviours. These include questions such as why do certain pupils avoid learning opportunities? Why do they hide work and effort? Why are some pupils disruptive? Why is work left until the last minute? Why do some students construct barriers to learning? And crucially, how can we break down these barriers and encourage students to engage with academic activities?

However, while research that draws upon goal theory and self-worth theory is useful for furthering our understanding of 'laddish' behaviours, there are aspects of this research, and the theories that underpin it, that are potential weaknesses and require further development. I flag two key areas here.

The first criticism relates to goal theory rather than to self-worth theory. Goal theorists look for answers to the types of questions outlined in the opening paragraph of this section by exploring pupils' *individual* motives for learning or avoiding learning. They are rightly concerned with the ways in which individual approaches to learning are shaped by different teachers, subjects and so on. However, goal theorists tend to focus almost exclusively on the individual and her/his immediate learning context, and neglect broader social structures and discourses. As such, intervention strategies tend to target the 'maladaptive' pupil (or sometimes teachers), using techniques such as attribution retraining whereby individuals are encouraged to change their personal explanations for failure from a lack of ability to a lack of effort (Covington 1998; Dweck 2000).

In light of the above, goal theorists and motivation theorists more generally (although self-worth theorists are a notable exception) are open to the criticism that they tend to lay too much blame for poor performance on the individual pupil, teacher and/or school (Kenway *et al.* 1990). Such a 'blame the individual' approach is readily appropriated by current neoliberal dominant discourses which position the individual as responsible for their 'failures', and absolve social structures and inequalities of blame. Neoliberalism is discussed more fully in the next chapter, but it is defined by Phoenix (2004: 228) as 'an economic system and philosophy based on laissez-faire free market values and freedom of globalized corporations. It enshrines values of competition, entrepreneurialism, market participation, privatization, lack of state intervention, individual responsibility (e.g., employability), surveillance, assessment, and managerialism.' Phoenix argues that education is central to neoliberal philosophy because education constitutes an important site for the operation and naturalization of all four key features of neoliberalism – change, choice, chances, competition. Neoliberal discourse locates the responsibility for academic standards, and for raising academic standards, squarely on the shoulders of individual pupils, teachers and schools, and has been severely criticized by some commentators. For example, Brown *et al.* (1997: 21–2) argue that according to this New Right discourse:

> raising educational standards for all is simply a question of school management and quality teaching. In other words, school success or failure is determined by the management of the school and the quality of the teachers. In effect, schools could compensate for society, so long, of course, as the appropriate leadership was in place to head the management team ... This then enabled questions about family and child poverty and their impact on educational performance to be regarded as irrelevant. Indeed, the New Right have been quick to criticize any one who raised the link between pupil intake and school performance as evading

responsibility. Well-managed schools coupled with pupil self-moti-
vation, it is assumed, will make inroads into the eradication of
poverty as individuals better themselves through education.

I agree with this critique. However, in recognizing its legitimacy I am
not suggesting that understanding individual motives are unimportant; I
argue throughout this book that they are very important. But to understand
these individual motives we need to look both at the local context within
which the individual operates and also at the bigger picture. We need to
consider both structure and agency. We need constantly to shift our focus
back and forth between the micro and macro levels, to use the macro to
help us to understand the micro, and to use the micro to help us to challenge the macro. There is much scope for theories of motivation to engage
in this shifting focus, and although some motivation theorists do this, in
general the focus is on the micro context. Self-worth theory is, though, an
important exception. Covington does engage with both micro and macro
levels, which is in part why the theory (in conjunction with goal theory)
seems to have much to offer. Indeed, self-worth theory is premised on competition being problematic, and has at its core a damning critique of competitive individualism. Covington (1998: 129–30) argues: 'Competition is
more than a dubious way to arouse children to learn. Competition is also
an ethos, a world view that determines the rules by which people relate to
each other – in this case, rules that set person against person and discourage cooperation.' Covington's critique of education systems that are built
on competition mirrors critiques of neoliberalism. For example, Susan
George (cited in Phoenix 2004: 229) in her critique of the way that neoliberalism blames the weak and poorly educated for failing in social competition argues that: 'The central value of … neo-liberalism itself is the notion
of competition – competition between nations, regions, firms and of course
between individuals.' Self-worth theory has much to offer in terms of
understanding individual motivation within the context of broader societal neoliberal discourses. However, self-worth theory pays almost no attention to social motives, which leads to my next point.

A second criticism of the motivation literature is that, although there
are some notable exceptions (e.g. Juvonen 1996; Juvonen and Wentzel
1996; Wentzel and Wigfield 1998; Patrick *et al.* 2002; Anderman and
Freeman 2004; Kaplan 2004; Ryan *et al.* 2004), social motives have received
very little attention. While this is a criticism of the motivation literature in
general, it is perhaps especially applicable to goal and self-worth theories.
Self-worth theory assumes that a school pupil's self-worth is shaped substantially by her/his ability to achieve academically. While this is a valid
argument, and is supported by research evidence, other research suggests
that social 'achievements' are also very important, yet largely ignored. Goal
theory has also neglected social goals, as Kaplan (2004: 101) points out,

there is 'a relative scarcity in theoretical conceptualizations and empirical investigations that attempt to bridge academic and social processes among students in school'. Covington (2002: 286) also identifies this gap, and argues that it needs attention:

> Though we are relatively well informed about the role of academic goals in motivating the achievement of individuals, our under-standing of how social goals enter into the process lags behind ... prosocial goals clearly interact with academic goals to influence achievement jointly, and it is at this juncture that we need to con-centrate our inquiries.

As discussed in Chapter 1, there is a substantial amount of research, undertaken predominantly by sociologists, on the complex interrelation-ships between social and academic identities. Motivation theorists have largely failed to engage with this literature and the theories generated within it. This is, in my view, a limitation of much of the motivation liter-ature, and one that is increasingly recognized, and voiced, by motivation theorists themselves (Covington 2002; Pintrich 2003; Anderman and Freeman 2004; Kaplan 2004; Ryan *et al*. 2004). Kaplan (2004: 98) points out that 'A broader outlook on valued processes in school that includes social processes seems imperative in light of the role of socio-cultural processes in learning.' However, the theories discussed in Chapter 1 have their own limitations, which will now be considered.

Strengths and limits of current approaches to understanding 'laddishness' that draw on theories of hegemonic masculinities

As discussed in Chapter 1, most attempts by social scientists to explain 'laddish' behaviours in school – particularly the 'uncool to work' approach – have drawn almost exclusively upon theories of hegemonic masculinity, because being 'one of the lads' frequently involves displaying characteris-tics associated with hegemonic masculinity (Francis 1999; Frosh *et al*. 2002). Drawing on this theory, researchers suggest that at school '"hege-monic" masculinity is pervasively constructed as antithetical to being seen to work hard academically' (Frosh *et al*. 2002: 197–8). Epstein (1997) explains this construction by locating hegemonic masculinities within a structure of gender/sexual power relations. She argues that it is within these gender/sexual power relations that boys define their identities against the Other; femininity falls squarely within the category Other (Kenway and Fitzclarence 1997) and so boys must *avoid* any activities associated with femininity. Evidence suggests (Epstein 1998; Frosh *et al*. 2002) that academic work is perceived by many young people as 'feminine' and there-fore, if boys want to avoid the verbal and physical abuse attached to being labelled as 'feminine', they must *avoid* academic work, or at least they must *appear* to avoid academic work. If boys want to undertake academic work, but they want to do so without harassment, they must work covertly.

This explanation for some boys' reluctance to engage overtly with school work has many supporters, including myself (Jackson 2002a, 2003). But while I see merit in the argument presented above, in my view it does not, *on its own*, explain fully boys' relationships to academic work. This theory positions a fear of *social* failure (being labelled as 'feminine' and so bullied) as key to understanding boys' approaches to academic work, but I would add that a fear of *academic* failure is *also* of central importance. At this point I will illustrate my argument by means of an example. In the chapters that follow I develop and evidence this argument much more fully.

If boys who hide work and effort do so *only* because they are concerned not to appear feminine, it would follow that they would do this pretty con-sistently within any given subject area.[1] However, contrary to this expecta-tion, a number of boys (and girls) told me that they would hide their work and effort especially, or only, if they got a low mark for a piece of work. For example, when we were discussing hiding work and effort, Craig (Beechwood) told me that: 'If I got a high mark I probably would tell them [friends] that I tried hard anyway, but if I got a low mark I wouldn't.' Similarly, Martin (Elmwood) said 'I'd tell people if I got a good mark and I have revised, then I'll say. But if I get a bad mark, I'll say that I haven't revised.' The responses of Craig, Martin and the boys in the examples below suggest less that they are concerned about appearing 'feminine' for working, and more that they are concerned not to appear 'stupid' for working and failing.[2] It is worth noting that these boys have different pro-files in terms of popularity. For example, while Rob suggested that he got called 'a little swot' and 'boring' quite regularly in school, Alistair told me that he was in the popular group of boys: 'like I'm best mates with proba-bly one of the most popular people cause I play rugby with him and stuff'.

Alistair (Ashgrove)
So would you ever pretend that you'd not worked hard at something when you had?
No. If I've worked hard at something and if it turns out good then I'll be proud of it and I'll say. I'm not really bothered what some people think of me and if they don't like it then that's their choice. Because if I work hard at something and I do good and if they ask me 'how did you do that?' I'll tell them and if they don't like it then that's tough.
What if you don't do very well?

If I don't do very well?
Would you then pretend that you'd not worked much for it?
If I did work for it and I did bad?
Yes.
I don't know. If someone asked me 'did you try at it?' I'd say 'yes' but you wouldn't just say 'I did my best'. And if it was a test and I revised for like three or four hours I wouldn't be saying that, I'd just go 'yes, well there's always the next time, I'll do well in the next test' or something like that.

Dean (Ashgrove)
Some [boys] would probably secretly [work] and ... say they're not coming out cause they've been grounded. And when people ask them at school [whether they have worked] they'll say 'no'. They'll just like lie to them.
So would you do that?
Not really because I'm not really bothered what they think.
What if you got a low mark in something, would you then be more inclined?
It depends how low it was, if it was like 20 per cent I would [lie about having worked] ... if it was like a really, really low mark I probably would, but not if it was just a normal mark I wouldn't.
... So you were saying if it was very low you'd be inclined to say you'd not revised?
Yes and lie. But if it was like high or OK I'd just say I'd revised.

Rob (Elmwood)
Would you ever pretend that you'd not worked hard at something when you had really?
No I would just tell the truth whether I have or I hadn't.
... What about your friends, what do you tell them?
Nowt really, I just say that I'd been revising.
And if you got a bad result would you then pretend you'd not revised?
Yes.
Yes? What would you do?
Just say I didn't really revise.

Some girls also suggested that they hid their work and effort, and did so particularly if they got a low mark, but were less likely to do so if they got a good mark. An example is provided below, which then leads on to my second point.

Zoe (Elmwood)
OK. And would you ever pretend that you'd not worked hard at something when you had?
I don't pretend that I don't work hard, but I do pretend that maybe I haven't worked as hard as I actually have.
Right. Can you give me an example?
Erm, projects and things, erm, everyone else has just done a few pages and I tend to do quite a lot ... so you just tend to cover it up as best you can.
... And if you got a good mark for something would you, would you do that as well, or would you ...?
Erm, if I got a good mark, I'd probably, depending on how good the mark was, if it was really good and I've never got one of them marks before, then I'd probably boast about it, and have a brag about it ... and then they'd probably be like 'well that's probably because you did all these pages' and that, 'it's because you did all that'. But I don't really try and cover it up if I've got a good mark for it.
OK. Would you try to cover it up if you got a low mark?
If I got a low mark, I think it depends how low the mark is. If it was a B or something I probably wouldn't be bothered, possibly C depending on the subjects. But if it was a C minus or like, I don't know, like 17 out of 30 or something, there's a possibility that I wouldn't really be telling a lot of people.

My research revealed that many girls regard overt academic work and being cool/popular as incompatible and so hide their work and effort; this provides a second reason for looking beyond theories of hegemonic masculinities to explain boys' relationships to academic work. While the underlying motives of boys and girls for these types of behaviours are not necessarily the same, there are striking similarities both in the methods used by boys and girls in negotiating school work and 'cool work' and their explanations for their behaviours. These will be explored fully in later chapters. However, this finding among girls does raise questions about why overt engagement with school work and being 'popular' are regarded as incompatible for many girls. It is clearly inadequate to straightforwardly apply to girls explanations regarding hegemonic masculinities that have been put forward for boys' 'not cool to work' approaches; suggesting that girls avoid hard work because they do not want to appear 'feminine' is at best over-simplified. So for girls – and I would argue for boys too – we need to look for more complex explanations.

Combining theories: Summary of the theoretical framework adopted in this book

> The social, cultural and psychological are so strongly entwined with each other that a disciplinary teasing apart does violence to the actual mechanisms.
>
> (Walkerdine *et al.* 2001: 15)

The limitations of the individual theories and approaches outlined previously are reduced considerably by bringing the two sets of theories and research together. Research on masculinities and femininities that has been undertaken largely by sociologists has much to offer social psychological research on motives and goals, and vice versa. By bringing together the work of sociologists and social psychologists, we can circumvent the problems associated with 'the inability of sociologists to recognise the complexities of the person and the unwillingness of psychologists to recognise the dimension of social power' (Haywood and Mac an Ghaill 2003: 13). Bringing together work from different disciplines allows us to construct a fuller picture than can be crafted from any discipline in isolation. In this case, I attempt to bring together achievement goal theories, self-worth theory and theories about masculinities (especially hegemonic masculinity) and femininities to explore why some boys and girls behave in ways that have been defined as 'laddish'. Understanding motives for 'laddishness' has important implications for teachers (discussed in Chapter 8).

Although I believe that there are many benefits to be gained to working across disciplines and with different theories, there are also dangers involved in such an approach. I am aware that psychologists may feel that there is not enough psychology, and that sociologists may feel there is too much psychology! However, I hope that whatever their disciplinary allegiances, readers will engage with the ideas presented here, and find some value in them. I now conclude this chapter by summarizing the key arguments and theoretical framework adopted in this book.

As flagged earlier in this chapter (and discussed more fully in Chapter 4), neoliberalism is a dominant discourse in contemporary UK society. It is within this broader social context and set of discourses that we need to locate and consider education discourses, which are currently dominated by concerns about standards. The standards discourse, like neoliberal discourses more broadly, prompts schools and teachers to reward attainment and academic success. While lip service is paid to the value of effort, it is performance that counts. As such, current educational discourses encourage performance cultures, climates and goals in schools. Some teachers and pupils can and do attempt to resist these performance discourses, but countering such dominant discourses is very difficult to do, and the performance and neoliberal discourses are incredibly powerful.

Evidence suggests that performance climates encourage self-worth protection strategies among some students. This is because when faced with pressure to attain results in a climate in which so much value is attached to academic success, many pupils fear failing. Fear of academic failure prompts some individuals to employ defensive strategies to protect their self-worth from the damaging implications of failure. I argue that many of the behaviours labelled as 'laddish' can act to protect an individual's self-worth from the implications of academic failure. In other words, 'laddish' behaviours can operate as self-worth protection strategies for some individuals. Chapters 4 to 7 discuss this in more detail, and provide evidence to support the claims made here.

However, I am not suggesting that individuals display 'laddish' behaviours *only* to protect their self-worth from the implications of academic failure. Drawing upon theories on masculinities and femininities, I argue that individuals perform such behaviours also to protect themselves from social failure. In relation to boys, 'laddish' behaviours in school are aligned closely with hegemonic masculinity. As we have seen, hegemonic masculinity is constructed in opposition to femininity. There is evidence to suggest that academic work is constructed as feminine, so boys must avoid overt hard work in school. However, as I have argued earlier in this chapter, while social motives are clearly very important to boys, there is evidence to suggest that these are not the only motives for hiding work and effort. So to understand the complex ways in which boys negotiate school work and 'cool work', we must consider academic *and* social goals.

Girls too show evidence of self-worth protection strategies. As we will see in Chapter 6, many girls hide work and effort both to be cool and to avoid the implications of academic failure. The finding that school work is socially problematic for girls counters earlier findings that it is a problem for boys to work hard at school, but that it is OK for girls. It is not entirely clear why this pattern of findings has emerged now. Explanations may relate to changing models of femininity, which were flagged in Chapter 1. For example, while for boys displaying behaviours associated with any type of femininity is problematic, displaying *particular types* of femininity may be increasingly problematic for girls in some school contexts. Traditional discourses of femininity present girls as hard-working, diligent plodders in school. Girls' success is portrayed as being by virtue of effort rather than genius (in contrast to discourses about boys). These 'good girl' discourses remain, but they merge with newer discourses around girls and femininities. Some girls may be rejecting the traditional 'good girl' model of femininity, which now seems rather old-fashioned compared to 'newer' versions of femininity, that hold more appeal. For example, 'girl power' discourses present girls no longer as plodders, but as having it all, doing it all, and having new-found confidence, ambition and opportunities. Aapola *et al.* (2005: 8) argue that the girl power discourse presents girls as feisty, sassy, attractive and assertive. 'Girl power' girls (including 'ladettes') may, there-fore, be eschewing the old-fashioned, hard-working, good girl image, and instead embracing a party animal, rebel, effortless achievement image more akin to their male counterparts.

Overall, I'm suggesting that some pupils find 'laddish' behaviours attractive both for academic and social status reasons. For some pupils, 'laddish' behaviours are underpinned both by fear of academic failure and fear of social failure. Fears of academic failure are taken up in the next chapter, which explores the pressures on pupils to succeed and/or not to fail in school.

4 'I don't like failure. I want to get good levels.' Testing times: Academic pressures and fears in school

> With ... Year 7 [and] Year 8, at the end of every topic – which generally lasts about six weeks – they have a test. This is all the new government Key Stage 3 strategy. Year 9 is the same, and then there's the Key Stage 3 test which is so important, it's pushed onto them ... They move into Year 10 and immediately they're onto modular exams, so they've two modular exams every twelve weeks, and it's just continuous. And if they're not accessing what's going on in the room, it's just putting more and more pressure on them, so their attendance falls, 'cos why do they want to come to fail? Who wants to keep going to the same classroom, knowing you're failing every time? ... And they won't. The attendance in exams isn't what it should be for the same reason. You know 'what's the point of doing an exam when I know I'm going to fail?'
>
> (Ms Brian, Beechwood)

Social scientists, in particular sociologists, have built up an extensive body of research and writing about changes that are occurring in UK contemporary society in a period that is commonly referred to as 'late modernity'. This period, many argue, is characterized by increased choice and risk and by intensifying individualist values. Neoliberalism is now a dominant discourse which 'promotes a social world where the individual is fully self-responsible' (Aapola *et al.* 2005: 36). So as self-inventing, self-determining, neoliberal subjects, we are expected to plan our lives and to make the 'right' choices. Accordingly, if we do not make the 'right' choices and/or if we do not succeed, we have only ourselves to blame. As Hughes (2002a: 33) argues, success in Western societies is defined 'through the ability of individuals to navigate the social system in an upwardly mobile way. This is achieved through education and paid employment, the two main institutional arenas where, though importantly not unambiguously, competitive individualism is celebrated.'

It is within this broader social context and set of discourses that we need to locate and consider education discourses, and the lived experiences

of pupils and teachers. The changes that have occurred in educational policies and practices over the last two decades or so reflect the concerns and
shifts in society more generally (Furlong and Cartmel 1997). It is beyond
the scope of this book to provide an in-depth discussion of the political and
educational changes and priorities of this period, such discussions are provided by other writers (for example, Brown *et al.* 1997; Arnot *et al.* 1999;
Gleeson and Husbands 2001; Walkerdine *et al.* 2001; David 2004; Arnot and
Miles 2005). However, I will flag some key features of the educational landscape, in particular those that promote fears of academic failure and 'laddishness' and so relate most closely to the concerns of this book.

The emphasis on competitive individualism in society is reflected in a
schooling system in England in which market competition is now an established feature. The marketization of education was cultivated by legislation
introduced in the 1980s and 1990s. This legislation was underpinned by the
assumption that increasing competition within and between schools would
raise standards because education 'consumers' would be offered a greater
choice of schools, and so those schools that could not raise their standards
would simply 'go out of business because they cannot attract "customers"'
(Brown *et al.* 1997: 21). So we have witnessed a period in which there has
been increasing pressure upon schools to raise standards, coupled with the
introduction of various mechanisms to monitor and publicize their performance. The most notable of these mechanisms are SATs at ages 7, 11, 14
and 16 years; regular inspections by Office for Standards in Education
(OFSTED) inspectors; publication of national league tables of schools; and
the public 'naming and shaming' of 'failing' schools. These extra pressures
on schools to raise standards are coupled with a growing emphasis on the
importance of academic and professional credentials in contemporary
society (Brown 1997). There is widespread recognition that young people
are 'increasingly forced to chase credentials' (Furlong and Cartmel 1997: 13)
in order to secure a chance of successful entry into the world of work; something that I refer to in this book as the 'credentials discourse'. Furthermore,
as Reay (2001b: 338) points out: 'Against the backdrop of powerful blaming
discourses a lack of credentials can all too easily mark out the individual as
a failure.'

This constellation of factors come together to create climates within
schools in which a fear of academic failure is commonplace. Both teachers
and pupils identify and articulate pressures to perform in schools, and to
perform in measurable ways, ways that can be documented and audited.
This pressure to perform is particularly pronounced around exams that are
used to publicly rank schools. Linking back to Chapter 2 where I introduced
learning versus performance goals, the educational culture within which
schools and pupils are placed is one of performance. Schools are ranked
publicly according to results, not according to effort.[1] So teachers who try
to create learning goal structures (classrooms that encourage learning goals)

in their schools have to attempt to create a 'learning goal' microcosm within the performance culture education system. But the boundaries to the microcosm cannot be maintained; the classroom is part of the broader educational climate and system and it cannot be kept separate; so teachers who endeavour to establish a learning goal climate are battling against a performance tide. As we saw in Chapter 2, performance climates encourage and foster defensive behaviours among many students who fear academic failure. Many of these behaviours are labelled as 'laddish'. Ironically then, defensive 'laddish' behaviours may be borne, in part, out of the very mechanisms and strategies that policy-makers have implemented to attempt to raise educational attainment levels in schools.

This chapter explores in detail, at the micro-level, the pressures on pupils to succeed and/or not to fail academically at school. I explore pupils' perceptions of pressures from teachers, parents and then peers. Predictably, pressures and fears emerged most explicitly and were reported most vividly in relation to exams and tests (see Ms Brian's quote that opened the chapter), and in many cases particularly in relation to SATs; so I'll focus on SATs as a particular 'pressure point'.

Pressures on pupils to succeed and not to fail

Fear of academic failure was a recurring theme throughout the interviews. These fears were articulated in a number of ways, sometimes directly and sometimes indirectly, but they were voiced by pupils across schools, social classes, 'race' and ethnic groups, and ability levels. Fears about failure and desires to succeed co-exist in an uneasy relationship; while they are conceptually distinct (see discussion in Chapter 2 about approach and avoid motives), in practice they can be difficult to disentangle. Pressures to succeed are frequently transmuted into pressures not to fail; in schools, the attractiveness of success is frequently conveyed by contrasting it with its Other: failure. Both parents and teachers seize readily upon the potential dangers of failure, and attempt to instil into children a fear of it, with a view to encouraging them to flee from failure and therefore, by default, enter the realms of success. Many students spoke of teachers and parents telling them that they need to work hard and succeed in school if they do not want to end up with a 'dead-end' job and a bleak future (see also Reay and Wiliam 1999). This message seemed to have been taken on board by almost all students: questionnaire data revealed that 72 per cent of pupils chose 'very true' and 18 per cent chose 'mostly true' in response to the statement 'doing well in school is important in order to get a good job in later life' (these represented points 5 and 4 respectively on a 5-point scale). In the interviews, most students' accounts conveyed both the pressures to succeed academically in school, and also pressures not to fail. I explore pressures from teachers first.

Pressure to perform from teachers

> There's never a break; it's continuous testing. They are put under pressure and they are put under pressure to achieve and perhaps our expectations of them are very high. That's perhaps one of the reasons why I like teaching here ... because to me this is a very good school and it has high expectations of the pupils who come through the door. And sometimes it is very difficult for girls to live up to that.
>
> (Miss Walters, Hollydale)

As discussed in Chapter 2, while perceptions of the goal structures emphasized in a classroom are subjective, and are shaped by a variety of factors, teachers are nevertheless very influential in the creation of classroom climates. There is growing evidence to suggest that some teaching practices emphasize performance goals (which promote fears of failure) rather than learning ones (Kaplan *et al.* 2002a; Linnenbrink 2004). A performance goal structure is likely to be encouraged by, for example, promoting competition for top of the class, 'good' grades being highly valued and rewarded, emphasizing grade differences between students and encouraging relative ability social comparisons. Perhaps one of the most explicit ways of encouraging relative ability social comparisons, and thereby reinforcing the importance of 'performance', is by teachers reading out class test results to the whole class. In all of the schools in this research there were instances of this practice, although it was more prevalent in some schools than in others. Furthermore, it was a practice identified by a number of pupils across the schools to be a significant pressure that added to the other general performance pressures that they experienced. Clare at Firtrees, for example, suggested that the public reporting of scores made tests much more stressful.

> It doesn't bother me doing tests, but it's just that she shouts them out – your score. If she just like gave them you then that would be alright. But your mind's like, when you're doing a test, that she's going to shout it out – the score that you've got – and then you just try and do your best to get a higher mark.
> *So why is it particularly important that she calls them out, is it about being so public, can you say a bit more about why it matters so much?*
> 'Cause if she shouts them out and you've got a low mark everyone looks at you and your friends are like 'are you alright, you've got a

low mark but you'll be better next time' and you're a bit embarrassed.

Richard at Elmwood also disliked the public announcement of results. He, like Clare, was concerned not to appear 'stupid' and feel embarrassed if he got a low mark, and suggested that people get laughed at for poor performances.

Some people have told me that teachers actually read out the results in some classes.
Yeah, I don't really like it 'cos if you get a rubbish score ... some people laugh at you sometimes.
So do they do that very often?
Yeah, they do it near enough all the time. Some teachers don't [read out the scores] 'cos they know some people get embarrassed and get upset when they read the answers out.
Why do you think teachers do that?
To see if you know, that if you do get embarrassed, you know you have to try harder so that you won't get embarrassed.
And does it work like that, do you think?
Yeah, sometimes.
So if you got a bad score would you think, I'll work harder then?
Yeah, so I don't get embarrassed.

Richard's analysis of why teachers announce test results to the class is insightful; it is likely that these teachers do believe that such practices will motivate pupils, that they will shame them into working harder so that they are not bottom of the class. However, what is missing from this lay model of motivation is how pressures to demonstrate success (or not to demonstrate failure) can encourage among some students a range of defensive patterns of behaviour that ultimately are more likely to reduce rather than improve attainment levels (these strategies were introduced in Chapter 2 and will be discussed further in Chapter 6). Furthermore, in a competitive, performance-oriented classroom climate in which achievement hierarchies are explicitly flagged, there are always going to be 'winners' and 'losers'. While some of the 'winners' may like the system, the 'losers' seldom do, as Lyn (Elmwood) signalled:

Another girl was telling me that one of the teachers she has reads out the [test] scores.
Yeah, I hate it when they do that. I hate it when they read them out in class.
Do they do that a lot?

Yeah, it's really embarrassing if you've got something bad; you can't lie about it then.
... So do you think anybody likes it?
No, no-one likes it unless you're really, really, really clever and just want everyone to know how well you've done, but not many people are really like that.

At Ashgrove, the boys told me that it was general practice to read out the results unless individual boys wanted to opt out, in which case they could get their scores privately during the lesson.

Damian
The teachers read them [marks] out in class; if you don't want it reading out then you say 'can I see you later' and they'll say 'yes'.
So what do people usually do, have them read out or not?
Yes, most people anyway. It depends if you're good in that subject. If I was good in a subject I'd say 'yes read it out'. But if I weren't so good I'd just say 'I'll come and see you in a bit to get it'.
So do they do that in all subjects?
Yes.
Is it like a school thing, a school policy?
Yes.
... Why are people worried about other people knowing about it [a low score], *do people get picked on or laughed at or...?*
No, I just think they don't want their mates to know that they're not so clever; they're not exactly bright so they just keep it to themselves I think.

Although boys could opt out of the public results system, it was assumed that any boy wanting to receive his score privately was expecting it to be low. As such, 'opting out' was frequently read as a sign of weakness amidst the competitive classroom climate, as an indication that he was lacking in confidence and unable to cope with the academic challenges and demands of competition that most other boys were perceived to be able to manage. Furthermore, given that popular, 'laddish' boys were expected to display a certain public nonchalance about academic work, overt anxiety about, and blatant attempts to hide, potential academic failure was not in keeping with a cool, laid-back, relaxed attitude. So opting out of the public results system struck a double blow to a boy's masculinity, because as Kerfoot (cited in Hughes 2002a: 92) argues: 'Ever concerned with their own and others' judgements of themselves as to their competence at being "on top" of situations, masculine subjects must at all times labour at being masculine and to conceal or downplay personal fear and weaknesses that stimulate a questioning of this competence.' Unsurprisingly then, only a minority of boys opted out of the public results system at Ashgrove.

Public announcement of marks was one very palpable way in which pupils felt under pressure from teachers to get good results. But pressure from teachers is frequently less tangible, more subtle, operating at different levels through general classroom and school climates and discourses. As indicated earlier, pupils in this research, like those in other studies (Phoenix 2004), were well aware of the importance of good exam results for optimizing their chances of a successful career; the performance and credentials discourses are powerful ones in schools. Teachers contribute to these discourses in a variety of different ways. There is space here for only a few examples, but there is further discussion of how teachers exert pressure in the later section on SATs. Many pupils spoke about teachers exerting pressure verbally. For example, Faya at Hollydale spoke of teachers telling her and her peers that they needed to get good marks in order to live up to the school's standards and to not let the school down: 'The teachers are like pressuring you "oh you need to get good marks". And at GCSE level as well, people say "you need to live up to the standards of last year's GCSEs, we did really well, we don't want to drop, blah, blah, blah, don't let us down kind of thing"'. Neelam (Hollydale) spoke of feeling under pressure from the school and teachers, but couched the pressure more in terms of fears about her own, rather than the school's, future.

> They just say that your exams are really important if you don't want to make a mess of your life and stuff like that all of the time. And it makes you want to do it [work] but sometimes you get too pressurized.
> *In what way?*
> They say to you ('cause I'm in a low set for maths) they say that you might have to be put on a foundation paper and you can only get a D and you'd have to re-sit it in college.

Interviewees commonly reported receiving warnings from teachers about needing to get good marks in order to do well in later life and/or not to 'mess up' their futures: 'they say "it's really important and you've *got* to get these marks or you won't get nowhere" and everything. And "you've *got* to do well and you've *got* to go to bed early the night before [an exam]"' (Clare, Firtrees). While some pupils resented the pressure, others felt it was necessary and at about the right level: 'they tell you to work hard but it's not right over-pressure, you just know you've got to try' (Paul, Firtrees). Students spoke about pressure from teachers becoming particularly intense leading up to SATs, in this case Year 9 SATs. This will be discussed later in this chapter as a separate section. I now want to consider the pressures exerted on pupils about school performance by their parent(s).

Pressure to perform from parent(s)

In addition to feeling pressured by teachers to do well academically, most pupils also spoke about the demands and expectations of their parents. The majority of students described their parents as supportive and encouraging rather than as overly pressurizing (see also Martin 2003), but signs that they felt under pressure were evident nevertheless. Quotes from Tom and Zahir illustrate this common view.

> Tom (Elmwood)
> *Is there any pressure on you to get good marks at school?*
> Sometimes, yes.
> *Who from?*
> Well, like parents. They say 'if you don't get good marks in school, you'll get bad grades and you won't end up with a good job'.
> *So do your parents put a lot of pressure on you?*
> No, they don't put a lot of pressure on me. They just always encourage us to get good grades and do as well as I can.

> Zahir (Ashgrove)
> My Mum and Dad put a bit of pressure on me and, not a lot of other people do.
> *So the school don't?*
> Well the school obviously do, but my Mum and Dad put the most on ... They just want me to do well and ask me to try my hardest and help me and stuff like that.
> *So do you find the pressure helpful or do you find it can get a bit much at times?*
> Helpful.
> *Are there any points where you find pressure to do well (from wherever) just gets a bit overwhelming or?*
> No. They don't put too much pressure on me, like completely over the top, they just put enough on.

Although teachers and parents often spoke in similar ways about why students need to work hard – usually to get a good job – most students spoke in more positive terms about pressures from their parents than from their teachers. This may be explained in part by students feeling that pressures from parents were underpinned exclusively by concerns about them, the pupils. By contrast, while many pupils suggested that pressure from teachers was also based on them caring about their students and wanting them to have successful careers, it was also sometimes seen to be underpinned by teachers' concerns about their own reputations and the status of the school (see also Fielding 1999). This issue is revisited later in the section on SATs.

Francis and Archer (2005b) point out that there are racist stereotypes of certain minority ethnic groups in Britain as 'oppressed by their home culture' and under undue pressure from their parents to achieve in schools. They argue that while there is evidence of middle-class white families exerting pressure upon their children to perform well in schools, this is generally not presented as a cause for concern in popular discourse, rather, it is minority ethnic groups that are presented as oppressive or pathological. This stereotype was mentioned by a few Asian pupils in my research, and they clearly resented it. For example, Nassima, a middle-class Pakistani girl from Oakfield who for numerous reasons felt under pressure to do well in school, was annoyed that teachers and other pupils would assume that she was overly pressured by her parents.

> Because I'm an Asian girl, like teachers, and I think pupils, think it's because she's Asian, she's going to get in trouble by her parents if she doesn't get good grades. And oh her mum's Asian, that's why … they're not going to understand it if she gets a low mark. And that's one thing that really gets to me, and I don't want people to think that, but yet I want to impress my parents.

While there were Asian pupils who reported high levels of pressure from their parents, there were white UK pupils who did too. Overall, reports of parental pressure seemed no more apparent among the Asian pupils than among the white UK sample. This finding is supported by the questionnaire data, in which there was no significant difference between Asian (mean (M) = 3.56, mode (Mde) = 5; median (Mdn) = 4) and white (M = 3.42, Mde = 4; Mdn = 4) pupils in response to the statement 'there is a lot of pressure in school to get good grades' (U = 44100.0, ns, r = −.051).

Although the vast majority of pupils suggested that they could cope with, and sometimes welcomed, pressure from their parents, a small minority reported feeling under immense pressure from home. Aisha, a working-class Pakistani girl from Oakfield, clearly felt over-pressured academically.

> It's at home, they're always saying 'you should get this level, you should get the highest in the class and everything'. I mean, even if you didn't get the highest level in class at least you know that you tried and everything, but it's like they weren't that bothered. They just wanted you to get the highest level and the highest mark. And that's what was going on at home. And then in school, the teachers they were just like 'oh we're expecting this from you, we're expecting that from you, and if we don't get it, that's bad' and everything … My mum and everyone they used to say that 'we expect you to get a really high level' … then at nights, and this was about one or two weeks before the SATs, then I was like studying every night. I

only used to get about two or three hours sleep and then I was just
thinking if these are only the SATs, then if, if it's like this in the
SATs, what's it going to be like in the GCSEs? And then, that's why
I just feel a bit over-pressured and everything ... I can cope with it,
but when it gets too much then I just, you know, 'cos I've got a
temper problem, and then I just, you know, I lose my temper and
then just start shouting and everything.
Right. At home, or...?
At home and in school. I sometimes react quite, I don't react quite
good with the teachers if they like, put too much pressure on me.
Or say like, you know, just keep on going on and on about the SATs
and work and everything, then I just change.

Like Aisha, Terry, a middle-class white British boy from School A,
reported feeling under tremendous pressure to be academically successful in
school. In his case, he felt under so much pressure from his parents that he
would hide test results and lie about his performances. The rather lengthy
extract that follows is only one section of Terry's extensive reporting about
his fears, pressures and strategies for coping.

*Can you tell me about the last time that you felt you failed an exam or
a piece of work or the last time you felt very disappointed by a mark?*
The last time was the last maths test we had just before Christmas.
We had a quick test and I was quite disappointed because even
though the highest mark was only around 70 per cent my mark
was only 53 per cent. So I was feeling a bit worried 'cause I didn't
really want to tell my parents and because of that I decided that I'd
tell them a lower highest mark. So I said it was only 60 per cent so
it sounded like I got a quite high mark. So they were quite pleased
with that but I didn't tell them that the highest mark really was 70
per cent.
Why did you do that?
Because I didn't want to disappoint them really 'cause ... all the
time I'm really worried about exams. Dad gives me this really long
lecture about how hard the girls [his sisters] worked and how bril-
liant they were at school and I don't really want to know that
'cause they just carry on talking about that all the time. So I try not
to tell them so it's then like I don't want to disappoint them all the
time 'cause if I get a lower mark than like the girls did I'll disappoint them.
How does that make you feel?
It makes me feel quite nervy really 'cause if I've done something to
upset my Mum and Dad like get a bad result, I don't know, I just
feel nervy and things like that because I think they might shout at

me for not doing that well. But it's never happened because my Dad he usually just listens and tells my Mum afterwards, but I still, I just feel quite nervy really in case I disappoint them. When I go home, and say I've got a test paper in my bag, I'll have the test paper and think what am I going to do? So I just hide it down my trousers and go upstairs and say I need the toilet and go upstairs and hide it under a pile of books. So I've got a couple there now.

... I'm thinking that if I tell them then they might get quite cross ... 'cause my parents, say if I have a bad grade they usually write to the school and say 'why has he got a bad grade and how can he improve on this?'

The importance of competition, judged by Terry's *relative* position in his class is delineated clearly in the first part of the extract. His test score of 53 per cent is presented as accepted by his parents only because he told them that the top mark was 60 per cent; he is convinced that had he told them the real top score (70 per cent) his parents would have been unhappy. The signals here are clear – it is his performance relative to his peers that is important, not his individual progress or enjoyment of learning. The same was evident in Aisha's account: 'They just wanted you to get the highest level and the highest mark.' Terry and Aisha's accounts of their school-related stresses are heart-rending. Fortunately, these types of accounts were unusual. However, they did represent an extreme version of what most pupils talked about in a more 'diluted' form; the pressures on pupils to perform in school can be intense.

Terry's account refers to within-family competitions: his performances are juxtaposed against those of his sisters. Sibling rivalries arose as an issue in numerous students' accounts when they were discussing family pressures; in most cases, this translated into competition to perform as well as, or better than, siblings.

Stu (Ashgrove)
Was there pressure to do well, did the school put pressure on you to do well [in the SATs]?
No, it's more my Mum and Dad saying you need to do well because your sister got this.
So when did your sister do her SATs?
Two years ago, she got 7,6,6, so if I get all 7's then I've beaten her; my other two sisters will have something to beat then.

Jake (School A)
Is there pressure on you to get good marks?
Yes 'cause I've got an older brother and he's constantly saying he's more clever and whatever and better at everything. So if I get lower

marks he'll be like 'oh I got a better mark at that than you, you're rubbish' or whatever. And so I've got to try and keep up with the competition of my brother.

Clara (Hollydale)
And were you worried about them [SATs] *in advance?*
Yes.
Why is that?
Because my sister got really, did well on hers and I didn't want to like get lower than her.
What did she get?
6,7,8, so I had to try and get the same or beat it ... she like sets marks and then I have to try and either get the same or beat it ...
So your reason for wanting to get the same or better, does that come from you or from your family or, where does that come from?
My Dad really and my Mum. If my sister sets the thing then they always expect me to like be the same or better. So I try and prove them right.

While sibling rivalries are not new, the introduction of standardized tests at the end of Key Stages has undoubtedly facilitated social comparisons among siblings. There are now numerous points at which family members can compare the achievements of different children, as measured by 'objective' and 'standardized' measures. The fact that Stu and Clara (and others) were able to recall without hesitation the SATs levels of their siblings is evidence of the ways in which within-family comparisons are highlighted and competition is fostered. Such is the importance of these comparisons and competitions that Clara was not only able to recall the individual SATs levels of her sister, but she also knew, without having to calculate it, the sum total of her levels: 'my sister got ... if you add up like the 6,7,8, you get like 21 or something'. Clara's account conveyed a high level of emotional investment in her SATs, so much so that re-reading her interview transcript prompted me immediately to check her SATs results to see if she managed to outperform her sister; unfortunately for Clara, she did less well.

On the basis of a study that explored the importance of social class for girls' experiences of schooling and growing up, Walkerdine *et al.* (2001) argue that parental pressures upon middle-class girls to succeed in school can be particularly intense. They argue that these pressures stem from a powerful fear of failure within middle-class families; a fear that educational failure will lead to their children falling off the middle-class conveyor belt, that they will become working class (see also Reay 2001b). For these parents, it is a fear of their children becoming *unlike* themselves (not middle-class) that pushes them to keep their children on a trajectory for 'success'. For working-class aspirational parents, however, Walkerdine *et al.*

argue the story is very different. Pressures upon their children to succeed at school and forge a successful (middle-class) career stem from aspirational working-class parents' desires for their children to be 'better' than they are themselves. So for these working-class parents, it is a fear of their children becoming *like* themselves that pushes them to keep their children on a trajectory towards 'success'. The latter is fraught with emotional difficulties, contradictions and complexities, both for parents and children, as a desire to escape from the lifestyle of the parents suggests that the lifestyle, and parents, are lacking. As Reay (2001b: 334) notes: 'In England, in the minority of cases when the equation of working class plus education equals academic success, education is not about the valorization of working classness but its erasure; education as escape.'

My research did not set out to explore parents' hopes and fears for their children. Yet there was evidence in some pupils' narratives of parents using different points of reference for encouraging success. So while the quotes from Stu, Jake and Clara (middle-class students) above articulate pressure to do better than their 'successful' siblings, others (working-class students) reported pressures to do better than their 'unsuccessful' parents or 'unsuccessful' siblings. For example, Jane (Firtrees) said of her parents: 'they want me to do well. They want me to get where I'm going 'cause they said that they wish they'd done well at school and done better and stuff. So I think they want me to do good.' In a similar vein, Graham (Elmwood) felt under pressure to be the one in his family that gets 'graded'.

> *Is there pressure on you to get good grades?*
> Yeah, 'cos in my family none of the boys, my big brother's not done his GCSEs and it looks like my nearest other brother won't be doing them because he like, misses school a lot. So my mum keeps telling me 'you're going to be the one that's going to get graded' so I'll get good grades.
> *Right. How does that make you feel?*
> Alright. Just puts pressure on me a bit.

Overall, while many students, both middle and working class, fear academic failure in schools, the specific sources and strengths of these fears, and the particular ways in which these fears are manifest, recognized and managed, are undoubtedly influenced by social class.

Family pressures represent another layer of pressures that interact with those from teachers and peers. It is pressures from peers to which I now turn.

Pressure to perform from pupils

Peers exert pressure on one another to perform academically in complex ways; a number of different and sometimes contradictory discourses are evident. Most interviewees suggested that peers do not pressure each other explicitly to perform well academically. This finding fits with other aspects of this and other research (Francis 2000; Frosh *et al.* 2002) that suggests that to be cool and popular, boys (and this research suggests girls too) must display a certain nonchalance about academic work. However, although pupils may be overtly nonchalant, almost without exception pupils expressed to me very clear concerns about not wanting to look 'stupid' academically in front of their peers (performance-avoid motives). There was a palpable fear of academic failure in the accounts of most pupils. While students' conceptions of 'failure' were highly subjective, they were almost always relative (see Walkerdine *et al.* 2001). So some students regarded not being top of the class as 'failure', while others had more modest criteria. However, it was very clear from the interviews that peers' perceptions about one's academic abilities were incredibly important, frequently more important than those of teachers or family. As Lyn (Elmwood) told me when talking about academic performances and pressures to get good grades: 'I don't think you ever mind what the teachers think as much as you mind what other people think.'

Peer rivalries and competitions were relatively common, particularly among boys: 'I think they [friends] want to do better than me, but they ain't gonna succeed, some of them' (Wayne, Beechwood). During the ESRC project interviews (the Nuffield ones included only boys), approximately twice as many boys as girls reported academic competition between peers. Some boys also talked more explicitly than their female counterparts about 'beating' other pupils, especially boys, in their classes (see the comments of James and Liam below). The greater importance attached by boys than girls to outperforming others was also reflected in the questionnaire data. Overall, boys (M = 3.25, Mde = 5; Mdn = 3) scored significantly higher than girls (M = 2.86; Mde = 2; Mdn = 3) in endorsing the statement 'I like to be "the best" at activities that are important to me' (U = 63560.5, p < .001, r = −.14). The girls who spoke about competition in the interviews conveyed a recognition that while they and others like to do better than their peers, and sometimes boast about good marks, overt competition is regarded as somewhat problematic. For example, Sarah used the phrase 'It's like people don't want to admit it, but ...', and Amy displayed ambivalent feelings about her secret competitiveness.

James (Elmwood)

And what about friends? Do they, is there pressure from friends to work hard and do well?

No, not really, just like a little competition every now and then.

Is there? In what way?

Well, say we're all doing a project on something, we might compete to try and get the best grade or see who does the most work or something like that.

Liam (Ashgrove)

Do you compare marks with other people?

Yes 'cause I'm in the top sets you like look at the other people who you think are the top in the year and see how well you've done in relation to them. Sometimes you beat them and sometimes you don't.

So is it quite competitive?

Yes, me and one lad are like top in all the lessons we're in and it's always who can get the better edge on it.

Sarah (Firtrees)

It's like people don't want to admit it, but I know some of my friends and even the popular people, like when the popular people do better than you they always make sure that you know about it. It's like in science if they do an experiment better than you and get better results then they'll boast about it to you.

Amy (Hollydale)

Do you compare your marks with other people?

Yes I do yes. It sort of puts you at a challenge with everyone, so it's like 'I'll do better than her' – secretly. But no, I don't know, we do compare yes.

… So are you a bit competitive with them?

Yes I suppose I am in a way, but it's sort of my little way, like inside me. I like to think, it sort of makes me feel more confident in my work when I sort of say to myself 'I'm better than', like 'I can do better than her'. I know it's like horrible to say that about my friends but it sort of makes me feel a bit more confident inside myself and makes me feel a bit more better.

Both boys and girls engaged with complex and frequently contradictory discourses about academic achievement, academic work, popularity, and constructions of masculinities and femininities. The influence of dominant discourses on the importance of school success and gaining academic credentials was a dominant theme in pupil narratives; almost without exception students regarded exam success as important for post-school life and so wanted to do well in school. Yet discourses around constructions of cool, popular versions of femininity and masculinity conflict with key aspects of the academic credentials discourse because constructions of 'cool popularity' involved a rejection of overt hard work at school (see also Phoenix 2004). However, there is an important distinction between effort and achievement; paradoxically while effort is 'uncool', so is appearing 'stupid' or 'thick'. As Frosh *et al.* (2002: 81) point out in relation to boys: 'popular masculinity does require an insouciant sharp-wittedness that runs counter to "stupidity", and this seems to be drawn out of the image of the hegemonic ideal as fast and cool, never to be a dupe'. These discursive tensions and the difficulties they create for many students are highlighted by Mr Lee (Beechwood), in this case in relation to three 'lads' whom he is recalling.

> It's not cool to be seen to be clever by your male peers, but it's also not cool to appear to be dumb in front of your mates. I mean, these three lads [spoken about previously in the interview] were ruthless with each other. If one of them gave an answer and it was wrong, then they just burst out laughing ... they didn't contribute, they stopped, 'cos they were, I felt they were just frightened of being made fools of by their friends, being ribbed by their friends ... I mean, if they gave the right answer their mates would be 'ooh!' you know, 'aren't you a smart arse?' you know. They couldn't win.

The tensions between these dominant discourses were also evident in pupils' narratives: many depicted the ways in which pupils attempted to manage their fears of both academic and social failure. But while many pupils talked openly in interviews about feeling under pressure from family and teachers, and about the academic rivalries and competitions in class, students, especially boys, seldom spoke to one another about these things.

> Anthony (Firtrees)
> *And what about friends? Do they put pressure on you?*
> No. Don't normally talk about it. Normally talk about, it's mainly footie that they talk about, so, don't talk about stuff like that.

Many girls also said that they preferred to talk to each other about non-work things. Jane (Firtrees) suggested that this was in part because adults talk to them about work, whereas friends converse about other things.

> We don't speak about revising and stuff, sometimes if you say you're coming round for a bit then yes we'll bring our revision books and help each other then but that's about it.

So is there pressure from friends to do well or does it not matter?
I don't think it matters. I think really people just want to do it themselves and don't really want people to help them, especially friends because you want them to be there for different things.
What like?
Problems with friends and boyfriends, you want someone else, and not an adult and telling you 'oh you shouldn't be worrying about boys, you should be worrying about your exams'. Your friends are someone you can talk to about those sorts of things.

There is evidence from previous research that girls are more likely than boys to support each other's learning (Osler and Vincent 2003). This pattern was also evident to some degree in this study. So while most girls reported not talking to their friends much about work, among some girls, particularly those at Hollydale, there was a sense of greater mutual support about work than was evident among the vast majority of boys.

Julie (Hollydale)
And friends, any pressure from them?
No, they'll help you; my friends always help me. I've got a couple of friends who are in higher sets in English and science and like if I say I'm stuck on my homework ... they say 'oh you do this'. But they don't tell you the answer directly, they just give you advice like a teacher would and they help you.

By contrast, with a few exceptions, boys suggested that they don't really help each other out. The next section looks at the SATs as a particular pressure point.

SATs as a particular pressure point

As far as I can see that's all we do in school, like prepare for tests, learn the stuff for tests.

(Mick, Ashgrove)

The SATs featured large in both of the research projects. The interviews took place either shortly before or after these exams. In the case of Oakfield and Ashgrove, some of the results were just starting to come through as the interviews progressed. The Year 9 SATs were a clear pressure point for the vast majority of students in this research; almost without exception, students felt under extra pressure because of them. For example, when asked about whether teachers put pressure on students to do well in school, Graham (Elmwood) said: 'Some do, some don't. Depending on what time of year it is; if it's coming up towards SATs then they put loads of pressure on.' Most students were nervous about the SATs, and their nerves were underpinned by fears of failure.

Test nerves and a fear of failure

> I don't pray a lot ... but before the SATs I just started to pray and I used to, you know, ask God to help me and stuff like that.
>
> (Shareen, Oakfield)

Overall, 68 per cent of interviewees reported being nervous about the SATs. Many of those students who were nervous explained their nerves in terms of fears about failing (see also Reay and Wiliam 1999). Explanations for nervousness tended to be along the following lines:

> Erm, scared that I might get [a] low level, 'cos [they're] really hard.
>
> (Jawad, Oakfield)

> Well, I don't like failure. I want to get good levels.
>
> (Salma, Oakfield)

> 'Cos I thought I might fail or summat, and [I] thought it was going to be really hard.
>
> (Rehana, Oakfield)

> 'Cos I think I'm going to get rubbish marks.
>
> (Graham, Elmwood)

> I'm in like, bottom set for lessons so if I don't do good, I might get, people might start calling me, calling me like thick and stuff. So I don't want people to start calling me stuff like that.
>
> (Richard, Elmwood)

> [I was] scared of going down to bottom sets.
>
> (Mark, Beechwood)

> In case I did bad or anything.
>
> (Tamina, Beechwood)

Although both girls and boys spoke of their nervousness in the interviews, a greater proportion of girls than boys (75 versus 61 per cent, respectively) reported being nervous about the SATs (Reay and Wiliam 1999 report a similar pattern in relation to Year 6 SATs). Furthermore, in general, girls were more likely than boys to offer vivid, colourful descriptions of how nervous they felt.

> Jenny (Firtrees)
> *Were you worried about them [SATs] beforehand?*
> Yes I was scared to death! I thought oh no I'm not going to be able to do them, I'll get stuck half way through and I won't be able to answer any of the questions.

> Steph (Hollydale)
> *Were you nervous about your SATs?*
> I was yes. Going in I was shaking because there was so much pressure almost like put on you before them. You almost like, you know people were willing you to do well and inside you were thinking I don't know if I can do it, but yes I was quite nervous.

> Sarah (Firtrees)
> When it was near the SATs I was really worrying and I was revising like all the time and I didn't really go out at night anymore because I was scared that I was going to not do well. And I know that my Mum would be disappointed in me and it's just, you get like pressure from all areas. Like even your friends because I feel that you always want to do one better than them, or like be the same as them, so there's pressure also coming from there.

The silence of boys relative to girls in discussing in detail nerves and fears is likely to be a reflection of dominant social constructions of masculinity whereby boys and men are expected to show no fear, and rather like Ian Fleming's James Bond, to cope coolly and calmly. Traditional gender discourses present girls as more emotionally fragile than boys, and so speaking in detail about nerves may still be regarded as more socially acceptable for girls than boys. However, this may be starting to change, as increasingly, neoliberal discourses position successful subjects, whether male or female, as those who can handle life's demands, those who can cope. This is discussed further in the final section of this chapter. The next section explores whether, and in what ways, pupils considered the SATs to be important.

Pupils' perceptions about the purposes and importance of SATs

> They [the school] said they was the important, most important tests that you've ever done.
>
> (Zuber, Oakfield)

The school attended, as well as gender, seemed influential in students' responses about their anxieties about the SATs. Broken down by school (in the ESRC project), the percentages of interviewees saying that they were nervous about their SATs were: Oakfield 85 per cent; Firtrees 76 per cent; Beechwood 72 per cent; Hollydale 68 per cent; Ashgrove 56 per cent; Elmwood 50 per cent. While the reasons for these differences are not entirely clear, patterns in the interview data suggest that they may be linked to students' perceptions about the purposes and importance of the tests, and these varied between schools, and sometimes, between individuals within schools. Interviewees generally regarded the 'unit of assessment' in the SATs to be the school, the teacher or the individual pupil. In the three schools where there were the highest proportions of pupils reporting being nervous about the SATs (Oakfield, Firtrees, Beechwood), most pupils regarded the 'unit of assessment' to be the pupil. These students reported that the SATs were important because they were used to determine Year 10 sets, and therefore, they had important implications for the GCSEs.

Sikander (Oakfield)
They said they were important to see what set we were going to be in for GCSE, 'cos if you don't get good results [in the SATs] you ain't going to get entered for the higher paper [in the GCSEs].

Jane (Firtrees)
*What did the school say about the SATs, did they say they were impor-
tant tests?*
Yes, non-stop talking about them, we got a bit fed up with them keep saying it.
What did they say, what sorts of things?
Your SATs are coming up, you need to start revising and if you don't want to revise then it's up to you and we can't force you to do anything.
What did they say about the tests, did they say they were important?
They just said they were important and they would sort you out for your sets in Year 10. And when you go on for your GCSEs, you'll be put in the right sets for your GCSEs either intermediate or foundation and stuff like that.

Amina (Beechwood)
They said whatever you get now depends on what sets you end up in Year 10 so you have to work hard for them because if you go in Set 3 you're not going to get a higher paper to do are you? So you won't get enough marks to get a GCSE high result.

By contrast, in Ashgrove and Elmwood many more students suggested that the SATs were to assess the teachers and/or to rank the school. Furthermore, in both of these schools the students suggested that sets for Years 10 and 11 were not based principally upon SATs results.

James (Elmwood)
Em, so are you nervous about your SATs?
No, not really, 'cos they're like, just something that grades the teachers and not the pupils really. It's more the GCSEs you want to be bothered about.
… So are the teachers quite up front about it? I mean, you say it grades the teachers rather than you. Is that something you got from the teachers or from elsewhere?
Oh, I've, the teachers have said it before, because they said, 'don't worry about your SATs, it's just how we're teaching you, they want to pick up on that'.

Gail (Elmwood)
Do they [teachers] give the impression that they're very important tests?
A lot of the teachers do yes, well the subject teachers that are taking the SATs tests they do.
And why is that, what are they used for?
Well I've heard that they're just used for the school's reputation basically, but I don't know whether that's true. I know in some schools it depends what like sets you're put in the year after but in our school that's not the case because we get the SATs results back after we've been put in the sets.

Pete (Ashgrove)
Did you work hard for your SATs?
I didn't do any work prior to them.
Why is that?
Well the teachers said they don't matter for any pupil purpose, they're just for the school so that the Government can check or something.
So did the school suggest that you shouldn't be worried about them or … ?
Yes they said we shouldn't bother about them at all because they don't matter in the slightest.
So did they suggest that you should work for them or not?
No, they said we should try our best in the hall but not before.

Dean (Ashgrove)
English said it was a load of rubbish and just do your best. And maths said they can't do much of it because they do different papers and then science didn't really say much about it.
So why did they say 'it's a load of rubbish'?
Because they thought the questions they gave us were just rubbish. Some were like too hard and some were just too easy. They were just a waste of time and money and the fact that they change it every year is just like a waste of time for the schools to be doing that when they could be doing something else.

At Hollydale, although teachers were reported to have stressed the importance of the tests and encouraged the girls to work hard for them, the importance of the tests for the individual girls was not always entirely clear to them. Some reported that the SATs were used, along with other performance indicators, to determine sets for upper school (Years 10 and 11), but others were less clear about this.

Lisa (Hollydale)
Did teachers suggest they were important?
Yes they do, they put a lot of pressure on you to say that they're really, really important the SATs. But then other people say that they're just for other reasons and they don't affect you so I wasn't sure what the SATs were really for.
So what do other people say about them, what sorts of other reasons?
They say they're just for like the Government, just for general schools, see how the school is doing and I wasn't really sure if they were for both or which one.
What did the teachers say?
They said that you had to try your best obviously, but then they do use them with other things to set you in the Upper School.

Paula (Hollydale)
So is there pressure do you think to get good marks?
Yes. The Head of all the school she says the same conversation over and over again. She goes like 'you're at the middle of the slope, you can either go down or go up and it's hard to go up and it's easy to go down. You've got to go up, you've got to go up or we're just going to give up on you.' And she says it to me every single time, she says it to me like twice a week and I'm like, right I'm bored of this conversation. And she puts so much pressure on you, and what it is, it's like, she is saying we want you to do well for you but the only reason she wants us to do well is so it looks good for the school's reputation. So it looks like oh they've got all the good

pupils, we'll send our little girl there and stuff like that, and that's what everyone thinks about it

Thus, the schools seemed to cluster into two groups: Elmwood and Ashgrove in one (SATs less important), Oakfield, Firtrees and Beechwood in the other (SATs more important), with Hollydale bridging the two. The comments from pupils at Elmwood, but particularly from Ashgrove, were strikingly different from those at Oakfield, Firtrees and Beechwood. Data from Ashgrove convey the distinct impression that the school can rely on its long-established reputation for excellent results and for being a 'good' school with grammar school traditions, and so its staff and students do not need to engage seriously with the 'Government SATs game'. This contrasted with the climate in Oakfield, Firtrees and Beechwood, where, while some of the teachers did not support the Government's requirement for SATs, they were positioned by 'market forces' such that they had to 'play the game'. While Ashgrove appeared to be the cool, popular, effortless achiever among this group of schools, some of the other schools appeared to be the anxious, hard-working, less popular relatives. The anxieties about results at Beechwood, particularly GCSE results, and the consequences of 'failure' are conveyed clearly by Ms Brian:

> If we don't get 20 per cent [A*–C grades at GCSE] the Government will close us. So that's, we've been told that by the head. And so obviously all the departments are now thinking, you know, come August we're all going to be a nervous wreck, but nobody will sleep the night before the results come out. And if your results aren't at 20 per cent how are you going to feel? You know, could you have done any more? ... And yet I think, you know, we've done every-thing we possibly can to get it. So this is the Government dangling this in front of us, saying, not looking at the children, not looking at the children that come in, because value added, we're well above ... No, this is the magic figure, 20 per cent. So, whether we get it or not I don't know ... So we've been working on that really hard to do it this time. So all the staff are under the pressure of failing and if your department doesn't do well, there's like what happens next?

In summary, there is some evidence from the interviews to suggest that the climate of the school, and the way in which the school regards and communicates the value and importance of the SATs to its pupils, may influence the students' levels of anxiety about them. Fewer students reported feeling nervous about the SATs in schools that could afford to take, and convey to their students, a more relaxed approach to SATs because of their reputations for being very good schools. In these schools, the SATs were not used to determine sets and their significance to the individual pupil was minimized. However, even in these schools, half or more of the students still reported SAT-specific anxieties. Furthermore, at Ashgrove, although the SATs were not used to determine sets for Year 10, the end of year school exams were, and as a result pupils were much more anxious about these tests. So at Ashgrove, the test anxieties were to a large extent transferred from the SATs to the school's in-house exams. Furthermore, some of the students complained about the extra pressure of having two sets of tests: the school's end of term ones and the SATs.

> Alistair (Ashgrove)
> The SATs I found quite easy but in the end of year [exams] I just, I don't know what happened in them. I know I was more relaxed in the SATs rather than the end of year because, I don't know why, because the teachers put sort of pressure on you saying that the SATs don't matter, these are just really saying what you should be getting, just showing to the Government. And then they're saying the ones that you really want to be concentrating on are our end of year ones ...
> *It's interesting, the school were saying that the end of year ones are much more important than the SATs?*
> Yes. They just say that we're not really going to use the SATs results, we're just going to use the end of year ones to grade you and to put you into next year's sets. I'd prefer them to do it on SATs 'cause there's more pressure again with having to do two lots of tests and I don't see why they don't just use our SATs ones rather than making us do two lots of tests.

So, overall, the vast majority of students reported feeling anxious about exams at the end of Year 9. In many cases these anxiety-producing exams were the SATs, but in some cases they were the school's end of year exams. Where there were SATs and end of year exams, some students reported feeling nervous about, and pressured by, both sets.

Discussion

This chapter explored the ways in which Year 9 pupils experience pressures to be academically successful in school. It is clear that many students feel under substantial pressure to perform academically, and that many fear failure. However, while fear of failure is common, it is rarely discussed among pupils; most students attempt to hide their academic fears and vulnerabilities from one another. The chapter explored these pressures, fears and vulnerabilities at the micro-level of the individual pupils and schools. But these micro-level processes also need locating within, and analysing and understanding in relation to, macro-level processes which were flagged in the chapter's introduction. The education system in England is now underpinned by policy that has market competition as its cornerstone (Brown *et al.* 1997). Competitive individualism, which is required by market societies, is at the core of contemporary schooling. Furthermore, as Hughes (2002a: 65) argues, 'Discourses of capitalist individualism, of course, fully subscribe to the notions of competition and survival of the fittest that are endemic in market societies.' Interviews with students in this research revealed their awareness of, and familiarity with, these notions. Ironically, while these notions of competition and survival of the fittest underpinned many of their pressures, fears and concerns, they also acted to make these same pressures, fears and concerns feel illegitimate. In other words, because survival and success require individuals to cope with what-ever is thrown at them, succumbing to pressure was regarded by some as not coping.[2] So despite evidence presented in this chapter that most stu-dents are placed under considerable pressures from numerous sources to perform well in school exams, students were aware that to be truly success-ful one has to be able to 'handle pressure', to cope with it. For example, Gail from Elmwood conveys self-disapproval at feeling pressured by the SATs because 'you're not supposed to get yourself worked up about them'.

> *Is there pressure on you to get good marks?*
> Sort of. Recently I've felt quite under pressure for these SATs tests, but I know that you're not supposed to get yourself worked up about them. So I'm trying not to let it get on top of me but I have felt like there's been pressure on me.
> *Who's that from?*
> I think the teachers and things mainly. But I think also a bit of it is me myself putting pressure on me and I've got to try and get out of the habit of doing that.

Gail conveys a sense of dissonance between what she thinks she *should* feel in relation to exams and what she suggests she *does* feel. Furthermore, she individualizes the source of the 'problem': she says that she puts pres-sure on herself which she should stop, and anyway, she should be able to cope with pressure. The contradictions and tensions inherent in students' dialogues about academic pressure and coping may reflect many students' attempts to conform to dominant discourses within which the successful subject is able to self-manage. Exams are a point at which an individual's capacity to cope is put to the test, where they have the opportunity to show their 'mettle', and to emerge as a winner or a loser. The ambivalence of students' accounts about their relationships to pressure and coping are evident in the lengthy section of interview below. Hazel (Hollydale) suggests at the start of the extract that she feels under so much pressure that she wants the world to swallow her up – a clear sign of not coping. However, by the end of the extract she positions herself as one who can handle pressure, indeed, who hardly feels it – she can cope.

Do you feel that there's pressure on you to get good marks?
Er, sometimes. The school keep on giving us homework, lots of homework, and then tell us to revise. And I sometimes feel like, oh, I just want the world to swallow me up kind of thing. But then I find a way round it and it's alright, but sometimes I feel like there's a lot of pressure.
In what way then? Is it pressure to do too much work, or just pressure to do well or both?
Er, at the start of the year they say 'oh it's your SATs coming up, you have to do well' kind of thing, 'you have to get good marks', and at first I thought oh it's pressure. Now I've got used to it and I understand why ... 'cos they've explained. But at the start of year it's like, they just kind of like, pressure us and everybody just felt the pressure on us. But now we understand why really.
Right. And when you said that 'sometimes you want the world to swallow you up', what do you mean by that?
Er, sometimes I feel like oh I can't do this or, really annoyed kind of thing. But then I thought hang on a minute, I'll just try my best really and I sit down and do it and then half an hour later I've done it, so, that wasn't so bad.
Mm, so sometimes the thought of it's worse than actually doing it?
Yeah.
OK. So what sorts of things do the school say? I mean, in terms of trying to get you to realize the importance of the exams?
Em, they say, they just keep on repeating it in the assemblies kind of thing. And the first few times you're like yes I've heard this before. Then after a couple of, like, when it gets to like, six times they've said it, like, you realize like, oh yeah, you know, it's like important kind of thing, so.
Mm, so do you find it helpful, or do you find it a bit too much?
I find it helpful because I realize why the SATs are important and I realize why I have to get good marks, so it's more important, but sometimes er, my friends say 'oh it's only to make the teachers look good'. But I just kind of like forget that and I just listen to what the teachers say. 'Cos my friends say it's only to make the teachers look good, they're sounding like 'oh there's no point in getting good marks, just try and make the teachers look bad', but it's just helping your future career really, so.
... Mm, and so you say the school put pressure on, in a sense, about, particularly about SATs, what about family, would you say?

Em, my family don't put any pressure on, and the school don't put that much pressure on. Sometimes my friends say 'oh they do put a lot of pressure on' and I'm like, 'well I haven't felt really any pressure', it's just at the beginning I thought 'SATs, SATs, SATs' but it's all right.

These ambivalent expressions may reflect the complex and frequently contradictory nature of the discourses that these students must negotiate. The discourse on the importance of academic credentials was clearly dominant for all pupils in this research, and many students felt under considerable pressure to succeed in school in order to earn the academic credentials that would enable them to '"purchase" income, status and employment' in the labour market (Brown *et al.* 1997: 13). The broader, competitive individualism discourse emphasizes that the survival of the fittest depends on being able to cope, to manage, to juggle life's demands. Within this discourse, succumbing to pressure is read as a sign of weakness, of not coping, of failure. So as we have seen, fears of failure extend beyond fears about simply making the grade academically, they also depend crucially on *how* one makes the grade. To be 'truly successful' one has to be academically and socially skilled, and these skills should come apparently effortlessly.

5 'If you work hard in school you're a geek': Exploring the 'uncool to work' discourse

> It's not cool to bring your equipment, and it's not cool to have a pen in your pocket, it's more cool to have a packet of fags or a bottle of something to drink.
>
> (Ms Austen, Beechwood)

The 'uncool to work' pupil discourse is a powerful one in many schools and is seen to be at the heart of 'laddishness'. To attain social status pupils need to be popular; many fear being unpopular because of the negative consequences that ensue. As we have seen already, to be popular girls and boys have to demonstrate a relaxed, laid-back approach to academic work because hard work is widely regarded as uncool. This chapter explores students' views about the strength and nature of the 'uncool to work' discourse, and their responses to it. It tackles the questions: is the uncool to work discourse a dominant one in the sample schools? Is the discourse dominant for girls and boys, and for pupils across social class, 'race' and ethnic groups? How do pupils respond to the discourse given the strength of the counter 'academic credentials' discourse? In other words, how do students manage their fears of academic and social status failure when academic failure stems from a lack of hard work but social status failure results from overt hard work? Finally, I consider whether any pupils benefit from the uncool to work discourse.

Is the uncool to work discourse a dominant one?

Without a doubt, the uncool to work discourse was dominant in the sample schools. In response to the question 'is it seen as cool to work hard in school?', the vast majority of students conveyed the clear message that it is not cool to be seen to work hard.

Sameena (Oakfield)
Is it seen as cool to work hard in school?
Em, oh not really. No, some people just call you swot.

Jan (Beechwood)
If you work hard in school you're a geek.

Fran (Beechwood)
No, [to] mess about is seen as cool.

Jade (Firtrees)
No, not really because the bad ones don't really work hard and then they get really popular. And then you get the good ones who work hard and they get like called spiffs and stuff because they work hard.

Simon (Ashgrove)
No. It's usually like, the people who don't work hard they get more street cred, and then the people who work hard they'll get called swots if they got a good mark.

Danny (Beechwood)
Well, people that don't work hard in school are all hard and all that, and when you work hard you're a swot.

Jim (Ashgrove)
No, you get called a geek or something.

While making clear that it is uncool to work, many students' narratives revealed the complex and nuanced 'rules' of the discourse. For example, Zoe, Becky and Martin all suggested that it is OK to do *some* work but uncool to do *too much*.

Zoe (Elmwood)
Is it seen as cool to work hard in school?
No, not really. It depends how hard you work to determine how wrong it is, how uncool it is.

Becky (Beechwood)
So you say it's not particularly cool to be seen to work hard, I mean do people hide the fact that they work then, or how do people manage?
Even the cool people and stuff like that, people who are popular, more popular than me and stuff like that, they usually do work, they don't mind doing some work. They work, they might do a few questions and then stop, but they do work. Enough to stop them getting in trouble anyway, half the time.

Martin (Elmwood)
You wouldn't really get called uncool if you do good at something. But if you like tried hard at everything and you just like, pushed everything else away and you just tried at your work, then you probably would [get called uncool] then.

Other students suggested that while it is generally uncool to work, some exceptions apply. For example, it is more acceptable to do some work if you are already popular.

Mark (Beechwood)
Is it seen to be cool to work hard in school?
Yeah.
Yeah? But you said [earlier] *that if you work too hard you get called a swot.*
Yeah, but if I'm cool and do my work then they go 'alright'.

Aisha (Oakfield)
Em, I don't know. It's like, you know, if you're really popular, especially the boys, if you're really popular and if you do work hard, then it's for you. But if you're not popular and you work hard, then they're going to start calling you a swot and everything.

Liam (Ashgrove)
If you were really clever and really good at sport would that be different?
Yes, because people would ignore the side of you which is swotty and think oh he's a good sportsman, he must be cool.

As we will see in Chapter 7, some students have enough 'popularity points' by virtue of, for example, their sporting prowess (boys) or their good looks (especially girls) that they can afford to do some academic work without becoming unpopular. As we saw in Chapter 2, the bases of popularity are gendered. Liam (quoted above), along with other pupils and teachers, suggested that sport was a key route to popularity for boys, and in addition, that being good at sport could be used to offset some of the negative consequences typically attached to overt academic work. This is discussed much more fully in Chapter 7, but Ms Cornish's comments provide a further illustration here.

So can lads be high academic achievers?
If they're good at sport they can, it's almost like they're forgiven for doing their work because of the sports and having a girlfriend …

Whereas the ones that aren't necessarily as good at sport can't cope with the label of being good at academic stuff.

(Ms Cornish, Elmwood)

Overall, while responses about whether it is cool to work in school varied slightly and frequently conveyed the complexity of the 'rules', there was a deep-seated acknowledgement underpinning almost all responses that the dominant pupil discourse in school was that it is not cool to be seen to work hard.

Is the discourse dominant for girls and boys and for pupils across social class, 'race' and ethnic groups?

The dominance of the uncool to work discourse was apparent from both the interview and questionnaire data. Furthermore, both sets of data revealed that it was evident and applicable to girls as much as it was to boys. In response to the statement on the questionnaire 'It's cool to be seen to work hard in school', there was no significant difference overall between the answers of girls (Mean (M) = 2.03, Mode (Mde) = 1; Median (Mdn) = 2) and boys (M = 2.12, Mde = 1; Mdn = 2) (U = 70505.0, ns, r = −.04). Table 5.1 shows the distribution of boys' and girls' responses, and reveals that on a 5-point scale – where 1 represents 'not at all true' and 5 represents 'very true' – 72 per cent of girls and 68 per cent of boys selected 1 (not at all true) or 2 (a little true).

Table 5.1 Distribution of girls' and boys' responses to the statement 'It's cool to be seen to work hard in school'.

	1 Not at all true	2 A little true	3 Somewhat true	4 Mostly true	5 Very true	Totals
Girls						
% of girls	44	28	16	7	6	101
Number	169	107	62	25	23	386
Boys						
% of boys	41	27	20	6	7	101
Number	155	102	76	22	27	382

While there were no significant differences of opinion overall between boys and girls about whether it is cool to be seen to work hard in school, there were significant differences between pupils according to school attended (H(5) = 17.52, p < .005). The pattern of responses across each of the six schools is shown in Table 5.2. As the table shows, Ashgrove had the greatest proportion of pupils disagree most strongly with the statement that 'It's cool to be seen to work hard in school', and Oakfield the smallest proportion. The percentages of pupils at each school who thought that it was 'not at all true' or 'a little true' that it's cool to work hard in school were: Oakfield 56; Beechwood 60; Elmwood 70; Firtrees 73; Hollydale 75; Ashgrove 77.

Table 5.2 Pupils' responses to the statement 'It's cool to be seen to work hard in school', broken down by school.

	1 Not at all true	2 A little true	3 Somewhat true	4 Mostly true	5 Very true	Totals
Oakfield						
% in school	22	34	24	11	9	100
Number	22	33	23	11	9	98
Beechwood						
% in school	36	24	20	6	15	101
Number	32	21	18	5	13	89
Elmwood						
% in school	42	28	15	6	9	100
Number	61	41	22	9	13	146
Hollydale						
% in school	44	31	18	6	2	101
Number	58	41	24	8	2	133
Firtrees						
% in school	47	26	18	5	5	101
Number	91	51	35	9	9	195
Ashgrove						
% in school	56	21	15	5	4	101
Number	60	22	16	5	4	107

In order to ascertain where there were statistically significant differences between schools, six Mann-Whitney tests were conducted.[1] Opinions about whether it is cool to work hard in school differed significantly between Oakfield and Elmwood (U = 5679.5, r = –.182), Oakfield and Hollydale (U = 4667.5, r = –.253), Oakfield and Ashgrove (U = 3362.5, r = −.325), and Ashgrove and Beechwood (U = 3584.5, r = −.227). However, differences were non-significant between Oakfield and Beechwood (U = 3990.5, r = −.076) and Ashgrove and Elmwood (U = 6631.5, r = −.138). In other words, one might cautiously regard the six schools as falling broadly into two groups, with Oakfield and Beechwood in one and Elmwood, Hollydale, Firtrees and Ashgrove in the other. Overall, smaller proportions of pupils in Oakfield and Beechwood disagreed strongly with the statement that 'it's cool to be seen to work hard in school' than in the other four schools. It is possible that some of these school differences may be explained in part by intake differences. Oakfield and Beechwood are the two schools where there are the greatest proportions of Asian pupils (84 per cent and 30 per cent of respondents respectively). Overall, white UK students (M = 1.94, Mde = 1; Mdn = 2) were more likely than their Asian counterparts (M = 2.58, Mde = 2; Mdn = 2) to disagree strongly with the 'it's cool to work' statement (U = 34411.0, p < .0001, r = −.214).

There are two main points to highlight from these questionnaire findings, findings that were also mirrored in the interview data. First, the notion that it's not cool to work in school is *not* just a 'boy thing'. Girls, just as much as boys, suggested that it is not seen to be cool for them to work hard in school. Indeed, this view was voiced loudly at Hollydale, the girls' school. Second, the perception that it is uncool to work in school is *not* specific to working-class pupils. Ashgrove had the highest proportion of middle-class children of all the schools in the sample; it also had the greatest proportion of pupils disagree strongly with the statement 'it's cool to work hard in school'. So the discourse that it is uncool to work hard in school is neither gender nor class specific. Neither is it specific to particular 'race' or ethnic groups, although there are some indications that white UK pupils are more likely than Asian pupils to identify the 'not cool to work' discourse as a dominant one in school.

So far in this chapter, I have established that the 'not cool to work' discourse is a dominant one in my sample schools. However, this tells us little about how pupils respond to this dominant discourse; so it is to students' responses that I now turn.

How do pupils respond to the discourse given the strength of the counter academic credentials discourse?

The uncool to work discourse is a dominant pupil discourse in schools. However, as we saw in the previous chapter, the academic credentials discourse is an equally dominant, yet contradictory, discourse. For most students the resulting tension between wanting to appear 'cool' and popular in school, and also wanting to do well academically and attain good exam results, was very difficult to manage. Most attempted to handle it by trying to balance academic and social demands: to be 'popular' in school (or at least not 'unpopular'), and to do well academically. In other words, these 'balancers' recognized and attempted to negotiate both the 'uncool to work' discourse and the 'academic credentials' discourse. This balancing act is very demanding for most students. Andrew Martin's (2003: 29) research with boys in Australia revealed that one of the five most frequently reported difficulties the boys experienced at school was 'juggling the competing demands in their life (for example, schoolwork, sport, work and friends)'. Nevertheless, it is a course that most of the students in my research attempted to navigate.

> Steph (Hollydale)
> *You said about the importance of fitting in and things and sometimes making out that you'd done less work that you had, so is it not seen as cool, or whatever the word is, to work hard?*
> No it's not. People are always like, they think it's cool to like just sit back and do nothing and be cheeky to the teachers ... I just try and work hard but then you try and fit in at the same time. But people who work hard, even though they come out with the grades, they don't have as many friends and they're not as popular within the year so it's not very good.

> Jade (Firtrees)
> *So could somebody who worked hard be popular?*
> Yes I think so, but I think they might smoke as well to be popular and drink. Because there's a girl in my maths class and she works quite hard, but I think she might smoke and drink at the same time, but she's popular.

> Martin (Elmwood)
> *Can someone at school who works hard be a lad?*
> Yeah. But, depends like, if you devote all your life to like, your work and stuff like that, then you're not, but like, you can be good in class but like, not like, talk about work in everything you do.
> *Right. So you'd just have to go out at night and things, you wouldn't stay in and do your work all the time?*
> Yeah.

Frosh *et al.* (2002) reported very similar findings from their study of 11–14-year-old boys. They argued that most of their sample of boys attempted to negotiate what Frosh *et al.* call a 'middle way'. In other words, they tried to do their school work in ways that prevented them being branded as swots. While few of the boys in Frosh *et al.*'s work who opted for the middle way were regarded as popular, most managed to avoid being unpopular. In Chapter 6, I explore the strategies that pupils adopt to balance academic and social demands. Not surprisingly, some are more adept at this than others; Chapter 7 discusses who can and who cannot manage to balance these demands successfully, and importantly, why.

None of the interviewees in this research adhered wholeheartedly to the notion that it is uncool to work and that academic work should be rejected completely. This finding was also broadly supported by the questionnaire data which revealed, for example, that only 3.6 per cent of girls and 5.33 per cent of boys chose 'very true' in response to the statement 'I'd rather mess around in class than work hard'. However, some interviewees suggested that they sometimes prioritized social over academic goals, where being socially adept, or 'popular', meant accepting aspects of the 'uncool to work' discourse.

Rehana (Oakfield)
In your classes for example, are there just a few girls relative to boys?
There's only about five or six girls in our classroom and the rest are boys. But us lot [girls] try hard but sometimes we can be a bit like them [boys], by messing about too.
Right.
And getting bad reports.
OK. So what makes you mess around?
It's just that when they start to say that 'oh you're swotting away', so then we just leave our work and we think oh we're not swotting away now – we've stopped. And so we just start to chat at the back of the classroom.
So why, why do you stop if they say you're swotting away?
'Cos like, it makes us lot feel bad and we don't want to be like that.

Ruth (Elmwood)
So in your group then, would it not, would it not be seen as cool to work then?
I think it's a case of, there is girls in my set that try to have a competition how bad they can be, but there is some that do try …
Right. But you say you have a competition to see how bad you can be. What do you do?
Well, like if a teacher tells you to move, you just sit there and ignore her, and like, your mates'll say 'don't move, don't move'. So you just sit there; the teacher will just grab your stuff and move it. And then they'll [the teacher] call for staff response or summat … and you'll be still sat there saying you don't want to move. And all your mates will be egging you on to stay where you are, and

they'll like, call for a staff response, or threaten to put you in a DT
[detention] or something. And you just sit there and laugh.
Right.
And it just seems to get you into more trouble, laughing.
So is that more important than working?
It's more fun. People think it's more fun, to wind teachers up.

Tahir (Elmwood)
*Is there anything they wouldn't do because it wouldn't be seen to be cool
enough?*
Oh, act like a swot.

By contrast, a minority of pupils attempted to reject the uncool to work
discourse and subscribed to the academic credentials one instead. Within
their own groups these pupils attempted to redefine school work as cool.
For example, Rosie (Elmwood) reported that: 'There's two different groups
at school … some girls and lads who don't work, they're in one group, and
some girls and boys who do work. So it's cool [to work hard] for one group
but not for the other.' This attempted redefinition was not, though,
accepted by the majority. For example, Paula (Hollydale) talked rather critically about the 'swots' in her discussion of the different groups in school:

It depends what group you're in cause there's a big group of Year 9
and they're all like sort of good but they're all like really slaggie.
And then there's another group which I'm in and they like, they
hang round with Year 10s and 11s and they just don't care about
anything. And then there's like the swot group and they're really
good and *they all look at each other as being good.* (my emphasis)

The price most of these pupils pay for prioritizing school work over
'cool work' is being labelled as unpopular and called names by their
'popular' peers. Some of these students seemed to comprise what I have
termed a 'swot but I don't care' group. Typically, such students – who were
a small minority – reported that they do get called swots but they do not
care; as Jim (below) told me, he would rather be called a swot and do well
at school than mess around and end up as a dustbin man.

Judy (Beechwood)
*You say people get called swots for working hard; do you get called a
swot?*
Sometimes but I just turn round to them and say 'well I'll get a
good job'.

Amy (Hollydale)
Is it seen to be good to work in school or are there any people that think it's not good to work?
There are a few and it's like 'oh you swot'. But if a swot means getting good grades and … ahead in college and doing well then I'll be a swot happily.

Jim (Ashgrove)
So do you get called swot?
Sometimes yes.
How does that make you feel then?
I'm not really bothered by it because I'd rather like work hard and then get a good job and get good money than not work hard and be a dustbin man or something when you're older.

Anthony (Firtrees)
I'm not bothered what people think. Like, some people'll say 'oh you're a spiff' or 'you're an idiot' or something like that because they're jealous. Because like, it's mainly the people that call them spiffs are the ones that can't do it, so they're jealous 'cos they [spiffs] can do it and they try. But the ones that like, are naughty and that, they don't try and they can't be bothered.

Notably, even students voicing 'swot but I don't care' views told me that external factors – usually jobs and/or money – motivated their hard work rather than intrinsic ones such as a joy of learning. This predictable but rather depressing finding was common across the whole interview sample where, without exception, students spoke about the value of school and school work in terms of getting results and credentials which could lead to money and good jobs.

Overall, while the 'uncool to work' discourse was clearly a dominant one in these schools, few girls or boys regarded it as unproblematic, largely because of the strength of the competing dominant discourse of credentialism. So while the uncool to work pupil discourse was accepted by a small minority, and challenged by a minority, the majority of pupils attempted to negotiate it.

Who benefits from the 'uncool to work' discourse?

It is worth considering whether and in what ways any pupils benefit from the uncool to work discourse, and which pupils are most disadvantaged by it. Pupils who could be seen to 'benefit' are those who need, or think they need, excuses for poor academic performances. For these pupils who fear academic failure and so invoke self-worth protection strategies, the overt rejection of academic work inherent in the 'uncool to work' discourse provides an excuse for failure and augments success (Jackson 2003). While the 'benefits' of many of the self-worth protection strategies are short term and frequently involve self-defeating behaviours, they can seem very appealing for the reasons discussed in Chapters 2 and 6.

Those who seem to be most disadvantaged as a result of the discourse are: (1) those who attempt to balance academic work and popularity but cannot manage to do both successfully; (2) those who take on board the discourse wholesale and reject academic work, or at least who prioritize 'popularity' at the expense of school work; (3) those who overtly resist the discourse – the 'swots' or 'geeks'. The ways in which these pupils are disadvantaged varies. Those in group one who are unable to balance academic work and popularity risk either limiting their educational qualifications or being picked on in school for being a 'swot', depending upon where they invest the bulk of their energies. Those in group two are likely to sacrifice academic success for 'popularity', thus limiting their career and further education options at age 16. Those in group three may suffer at school as a result of being bullied for being a 'swot' or 'geek'.

Summary

In this chapter, I argued that the 'uncool to work' discourse is a dominant one in schools. Furthermore, it is a dominant one for girls and boys, and middle-class as well as working-class students. It is also not confined to particular 'race' or ethnic groups, although there is some evidence that it is more influential among some groups than others. Although the discourse is clearly a dominant one, most pupils attempt to negotiate it rather than accept or reject it fully. Discourses about the importance of academic success and gaining credentials make it difficult for pupils to take on board uncritically the 'uncool to work' discourse. However, the 'uncool to work' discourse is difficult to reject because of the negative consequences attached to not being seen to be cool. Furthermore, the 'uncool to work' discourse may be particularly appealing to pupils who fear academic failure, as they can draw upon it to explain their academic 'failures' in ways that protect their self-worth.

6 Fibs and fabrications: Strategies to avoid looking 'stupid' or 'swotty'

The current educational climate in the UK is dominated by concerns about standards and testing. This was discussed in some depth in Chapter 4, where it was argued that a fear of academic failure is relatively common among secondary school pupils. This chapter explores the ways in which some pupils respond to their fears of academic failure by adopting self-worth protection strategies that deflect attention away from a lack of ability onto another, less damaging explanation for potential or actual 'poor' academic attainment.[1] Thus, the chapter draws upon the theories of self-worth protection outlined in Chapter 2. While self-worth protection strategies can be prompted by fears of academic failure (fears about looking 'stupid'), they can also be prompted by fears of social status failure (fears about being unpopular). Overall, I argue that defensive strategies that are seen to characterize 'laddishness' in schools can be appealing to many students – high and low achievers – because they can help them to: (a) avoid the implications of academic 'failure'; (b) augment success by making achievements appear effortless; and (c) protect against social status 'failure'. The emphasis in this chapter is on academic self-worth protection and augmentation, although the social status benefits of the strategies discussed are also highlighted.

Lies

> We all tell people when we've got good marks, and you don't really tell them when you've got bad marks.
>
> (Nigel, Ashgrove)

Probably the least sophisticated strategy used by pupils to deflect attention away from (actual) lack of ability was simply to lie about their marks; several pupils reported that they would hide low scores and tell their friends that they got a high mark.

Imran (Oakfield)
And what do you tell your friends if you get a low mark?
I don't tell them nothing; I lie to 'em.
Do you? What do you say?
I say I got a high mark?
Yeah? Why's that?
'Cos I don't want my mates to think bad of me, to think that I'm dumb or anything.
Right. So what if they find out though? Do they ever find out?
No, I haven't told them.

Sandy (Hollydale)
And what if you got a low mark, what do you tell your friends then?
I tend to say that I got quite a high mark ...
So if you got a low mark are you saying you'd tell your friends you'd got a good mark?
Yes, I don't know why though. I'd just feel really daft if everybody else got like a higher mark than me and then I'd think they're looking at me as if to say I'm thick.

However, lying about poor marks is not a fail-safe strategy for self-worth protection. In classrooms where social comparisons are rife and where marks are sometimes publicly announced, the strategy of pretending to have higher marks than have actually been awarded is unlikely to be successful on all occasions. As such, many students resorted to more complex strategies that were less easy to disprove.

Behavioural self-handicapping

As outlined in Chapter 2, there are numerous ways of providing excuses for failure that enable individuals to blame factors other than a lack of ability (see Jackson 2002a, 2003). In some cases individuals create impediments to successful performance, which can be active (for example, getting drunk the night before an exam), or inactive (for example, not revising for an exam). When individuals undertake behaviour (or lack of behaviour) before an exam to provide a reason for their (potential) failure, these strategies are known as 'self-handicapping strategies' (Urdan and Midgley 2001; Urdan 2004b). Although different researchers define self-handicapping in slightly different ways, Urdan and Midgley (2001) argue that self-handicapping is a proactive strategy that occurs before a performance and provides a basis for an attribution (how it is explained), it is not the attribution itself. A variety of activities have been identified as potential academic self-handicapping strategies, including procrastination, lack of effort, drug or alcohol use, lack of sleep, over-involvement with friends and over-commitment to a range of activities (Urdan and Midgley 2001). These activities are not in and of themselves necessarily self-handicapping strategies, but if these activities are undertaken deliberately before performance on an academic achievement activity in order to provide an excuse for poor performance, then they would constitute self-handicapping. For example, not sleeping the night before an exam because of noisy neighbours would not constitute self-handicapping, whereas deliberately going to bed late in order to use tiredness as an excuse would. There were several examples of students in this research who seemed to undertake behavioural self-handicapping. For example, Clare (Firtrees), who in Chapter 4 recounted how she gets very nervous about tests for which the teacher reads out the results to the class, also talked about revising very little for tests in which she expected to perform poorly. It is unlikely to be coincidental that the subject in which Clare's teacher publicly announces test results to the class is science, and here Clare talks about leaving revision of her chemical elements to the last minute.

> ... sometimes if I know that I'm alright then I'll study more but if I think like, say like if I'm learning elements or something, then I'll leave it until last thing because, I don't know, it's like playing on my mind overnight as well so.
> *I'm quite interested in this because I think that sometimes people do quite deliberately put obstacles in their way and then use it as a reason for not doing so well. But also in the process you trip yourself up a bit I guess. Is that something that you do?*
> Just sometimes but not often no.
> *So you were saying in the form of maybe not doing revision until the last minute?*
> Yes, but I do revise like hard but like if I know that I'm not going to do well in it I only revise a bit.
> *Does that then help you to think it through afterwards in terms of, almost like 'oh I could have done it if I'd tried harder'?*
> Yes, if I get a low score I think oh if I would have revised more then I would have got a higher score or something.

Methodologically, attempting to ascertain whether or not people self-handicap is not straightforward. Most research assessing self-handicapping has utilized self-report questionnaires. While self-report questionnaires were used in this research, their value is limited. As Martin *et al.* (2003a: 617) argue, self-handicapping is a strategy that 'may be manifested in a variety of ways for a variety of subtle or not so subtle reasons. It is not until individual respondents are interviewed that the richness of this information can be used to better understand the constructs and their relationships.' While I agree with this view, interviewing individuals about their motives for behaviours is not without its own problems, particularly when some of the behaviours are motivated by defensiveness. Even if individuals are willing to speak openly about their motives (which most of the pupils in this research *seemed* to be), they may not always be entirely aware of them; as Dweck (2000: 139) points out: 'they are things that we can *become* aware of, but at any given moment we may not realise that they're present and how they are affecting us'. Motives operate at varying levels of consciousness, frequently we do not reflect on why we behave in particular ways, especially if our actions are motivated by defensiveness. This came across in a number of the interviews; Lyn (Elmwood) provides a good example.

> *Do you think some people leave it* [work] *to the last minute, then if they don't do very well, they've got an excuse?*
> Mm, yeah.
> *Do you do that?*
> No, I don't know why I leave it to the last minute. It's stupid really. Or, have I mentioned that I put it off because I don't like doing it? Mm. Yeah, probably that. I do, sometimes if I get homework that's just straightforward and easy, like some sums in maths, I just do it like when I get home or something, or that night. But if I get like a big project – it should really be the other way round – but if I get a big project, I just put it off. My mum can tell what I'm doing, because I go and offer help, I say 'mum do you want some help?' and she says 'go and do your project'.
> *Yes, you do anything but what you're meant to do. Yes, I know what you mean there. So do you reckon some people, do you think some people might leave it to the last minute so they've got an excuse if they don't do well?*
> Mm, 'cos everyone wants an excuse if they don't do well don't they. 'Cos they don't want anyone to think that they've not done well just 'cos they're dumb or anything.
> *Do you get the impression that that's quite a concern to people?*
> Mm, yeah, probably. I don't really know. You see, these aren't usually the things that I think about a lot.
> *Yes. Well, that's interesting. That's one of the interesting things with this research I think, because some of the things that you do, you don't necessarily consciously think about.*
> Yeah, you do it without thinking. Mm.

While many interviewees had not necessarily considered their own, or other people's, motives for particular behaviours (or lack of behaviours) before the interviews, most thought carefully about them in the interview

itself. However, it was difficult attempting to access complex and sometimes sensitive motives without leading the interviewees; some readers may
feel that parts of the dialogue in this section are rather too interviewer-led.
But attempting to tease out motives was an important part of the process,
and proved valuable in that interviewees frequently engaged in complex
dialogues about motives, and clearly thought very carefully about their
responses. The lengthy extract below, for example, demonstrates the way in
which I attempted to unravel Talha's (Ashgrove) motives for hiding his
work, and to delve deeper to see whether or not he undertook behavioural
self-handicapping; there are some clear signs that he did.

*So would you ever pretend you'd not worked at something when you had
really?*
Yes when I've not got a good result I'll say 'I didn't revise that
much' and I knew I had.
Even though you had done?
Yes.
So why would you do that?
Because they'd say even though you revised you got not a very
good mark so I'd just say I didn't revise and so they'd not think like
he's done all that revision for nothing so what was the point of it?
*What do you think it would make you look like if they knew you'd done
loads of revision and got a low mark?*
Not very clever.
Right so you don't want them to think that.
Yes.
Do you think a lot of people do that?
Probably.
Are there any examples where you know other people have done it?
No.
*Are there any occasions where you'd actually put obstacles in your way
so you'd have a reason for not doing very well? Do you know what I
mean?*
Not really.
*Some people might deliberately not revise for something so that they
could have a reason for themselves if they didn't do very well.*
I wouldn't *really* do that.
You wouldn't really, *does that mean you might sometimes or...?*
I might sometimes, it depends what subject it is.
Explain to me a bit more. So you say you might not revise sometimes ...
'Cause if like, erm, I don't know.
*So is it about not revising or is it about doing other things? Again people
might not revise on purpose so that if they don't do well they can explain*

it, or leave work until the last minute so that if they don't do well they can say that's why, you know, quite deliberately do it.

I wouldn't, I don't know, I wouldn't really do that because what's the point. You might as well revise and get a good mark than not revise and get a bad mark.

So what sort of thing would you do, give me an example?

It's like, revise for a few weeks before the test and then revise the night before as well so like it's fresh in my mind.

So you would revise?

Probably, if I remembered and if I wasn't busy.

But you might be busy?

It depends.

Tell me a bit more.

If I've got like a cricket match the day before the test and then I'd come back late from the cricket match and then I wouldn't have any time for revising so I'd do some on the bus and just before the lesson.

So you'd put the cricket match before the revision would you?

I'd probably do some revision a few weeks before but I'd probably have forgotten most of that anyway.

So would that be a good reason if you didn't do very well, would you then see that as, because you'd been playing cricket rather than revising?

Yes.

So are there occasions where you might hope there was something the night before so you didn't have to revise?

Yes.

Tell me a bit more.

Yes if I've got like a German test and I don't really want to do it, I don't really want to revise for German, I just like say 'oh please let me go out, let me have a cricket match that day' so I couldn't revise 'cause I don't really like German.

And if you'd not got a cricket match would you maybe do something else instead or would you ...?

I might do.

What sort of things?

Like just go out or something or just like stay in and watch the tele instead of revising.

So afterwards then, if you say didn't do very well, would you think then well that's 'cause you didn't revise?

Yes.

And would you tell other people that?

Yes that I didn't revise so I didn't get a good mark.

Talha's account is interesting as he conveys his hopes and desires to have 'legitimate' reasons not to revise: 'I don't really want to revise for German, I just like say "oh please let me go out, let me have a cricket match that day" so I couldn't revise.' However, he suggests that if a 'legitimate' excuse is not available, he sometimes creates an excuse for potential poor test marks by watching television instead of revising. This suggests that there may be a hierarchy of excuses for not revising, some are more convincing and generally better than others, both to the individual self-handicappers themselves and to their intended audience. In this case, having a cricket match the night before an exam largely externalizes the reason for his non-revision; after all, Talha did not book the fixture, it is just the way it turned out. Also, many boys would declare publicly that a sports fixture was a very good reason not to revise; in the current 'cool masculinities' hierarchy, sport would always gain more kudos than revision. So here we catch glimpses of the ways in which academic self-protection strategies and social status motives interact. The interaction of these dual sets of motives may also come into play in relation to disruptive behaviours in class.

Disruptive classroom behaviours can also constitute a form of behavioural self-handicapping. Although not all disruptive behaviour is likely to be self-handicapping, there are hints that some of it may be. Disruptive behaviour provides another method of blurring the relationship between failure and a lack of ability (Swain 2004 makes a similar point about using humour in class). Where pupils exhibit disruptive behaviours, failures may be attributed to being inattentive in class rather than to a lack of ability *per se*, and the behaviour may act to deflect attention away from the poor academic performance and onto their behaviour instead (Skaalvik 1993). A teacher interviewed by Younger *et al.* (1999: 335) suggested that disruptive behaviour can sometimes relate to self-handicapping: 'There are two boys in my German set, and if they don't understand, they'd rather cause trouble than ask, because they're embarrassed about it. Or they just copy other people's work.' Teachers in my research voiced similar sentiments. For example, Mr Garner (Firtrees) said that:

> I seem to think that quite a lot of it [disruptive behaviour] is to put the fact that they're not very academic on the backburner kind of thing. If they can't do the work or they're struggling with the work, rather than ask for help they won't admit that they can't do it. They'll kick off or they'll do something stupid or they'll stab someone with a pencil or do something to try and get a bit of attention to them, but to distract the attention from the fact that they can't do the work.

Some students also thought that messing around was a self-handicapping strategy for pupils:

Liam (Ashgrove)
Is it seen as cool to work hard in school?
No, everyone is like 'oh why didn't you join in with us?' and I'm
like 'well I wasn't really too bothered I was trying to do this work
and finish it off', or something like that. And they're just like 'oh
you swot, you swot'.
So why is that do you think?
I don't know, if some people aren't very good at something they'll
just mess about to hide the fact that they're not very good and say
'I only got a low mark because I was messing about all the time'.
Do you think that's quite a deliberate strategy then on their part?
Yes a lot of the time.

Masoom (Oakfield)
*So do you think the boys who mess around a lot, or mess around all the
time, mess around because they can't do the work or because they don't
want to or ...?*
I think it's because they can't, they can't do their work, and get
scared if they get a low mark, that's why they mess about.
Right. You think that's why?
Mm.
Can you say a bit more about that?
Like if they mess about, people think they're cool, and if they not
mess around and get a low mark, people will take the mickey out
of them.
Right. So you say it's because they're scared of getting low marks?
Mm.

While disruptive pupils clearly jeopardize their own chances of academic success, they also make learning much more difficult for other
members of their classes. As such, one might argue that, to some extent, disruptive behaviour acts to sabotage the efforts of academically oriented
peers; an attitude that might be summed up as: if I can't win, nobody will!

As discussed in Chapter 2, there are both self-worth protection and
social status benefits for disruptive pupils in class. First, disruptive behaviour in class can increase a pupil's status within their peer group. Second, it
can deflect attention away from poor academic performance by focusing
attention on their behaviour. Third, poor performance can be attributed to
not paying attention in class rather than to a lack of ability. Fourth, disruptive behaviour may, in some cases, serve to sabotage the efforts and performances of classmates.

There were more examples of behavioural self-handicapping than I am
presenting here. However, although *behavioural* self-handicapping was

evident among the sample, it was certainly not as prevalent as *self-reported* self-handicapping. Self-reported self-handicapping will be discussed now.

Self-reported self-handicapping

As outlined earlier, most writers agree that self-handicapping involves *deliberate behaviour* before (or during) a test that can provide an excuse for poor performance. So there is a distinction between the self-handicap: the *behaviour* undertaken to provide an excuse for poor performance, and the attribution: how the poor performance is *explained*. It is possible, then, for people to make attributions for their poor performance without having undertaken any self-handicapping behaviour. For example, a pupil could suggest that s/he did poorly on an audio-recorded mental arithmetic test because s/he could not hear the tape, when in fact s/he could hear it perfectly well. However, when individuals are claiming handicaps strategically in order to attempt to influence other people's perceptions about the causes of their (potentially) poor performance, these attributions are very similar to handicapping (Urdan and Midgley 2001). Cox and Giuliano (1999) refer to public explanations for poor performance that do not involve low ability as self-reported self-handicaps. So they draw a distinction between behavioural self-handicapping and self-reported self-handicapping. Self-reported self-handicappers, unlike behavioural self-handicappers, have not undertaken deliberate behaviours to impair, and provide an excuse for, their performance. Instead, self-reported self-handicappers simply claim an impairment to provide an excuse for their performance. In one sense, the latter might be seen as a more sensible choice of self-handicapping, as it 'provides a plausible excuse for failure without actually spoiling one's chances of success' (Cox and Giuliano 1999: 422).

Avoiding the appearance of working and promoting the appearance of effortless achievement are self-reported self-handicapping strategies; they are not behavioural self-handicapping strategies (they would be if the students did actually avoid work). Avoiding the appearance of working and promoting the appearance of effortless achievement are self-worth protection strategies as they involve manipulating the perceptions of others about one's ability (self-presentational), and in some cases, may also involve an 'excuse' for the individuals themselves (self-delusional) – this will be discussed further later in the chapter.[2] The following section considers pretending not to work to provide an excuse for failure, the section after that focuses on pretending not to work to augment success.

It's no effort: Pretending not to work to provide an excuse for failure

It was clear from this research that many pupils, both boys and girls, were well versed in providing excuses for failure that enabled them to deflect public attention away from a lack of ability onto a lack of effort. Graham, Paula and Ruth, for example, all explain how they would tell friends that they had not revised or tried hard if they got a low mark for a test or some work.

Graham (Elmwood)
What would you tell your friends? What would you say to them about why you'd got a low mark?
I'd just say I hadn't tried, I weren't trying or something.
And would that be true?
No.
Then what would you say that for?
So they wouldn't think I'm like dumb and stuff.

Paula (Hollydale)
Would you ever pretend that you'd not worked hard at something when you had?
Yes. If I'd tried my best and then I got a low mark I'd be like 'I didn't try, I couldn't be bothered doing it', because [otherwise] everyone would think oh my god she got a low mark and she tried and everything. You'd get a bit of a reputation for being stupid.

Ruth (Elmwood)
Would you ever pretend that you'd not worked hard at something when you had?
Yeah. I do that a lot.
In what way?
... if someone says like 'have you revised?' I'll say 'no' when I've been revising all weekend.
So why do you do that?
I don't know. In case I get a poor mark; they'll think you revised and you still got a poor mark.

In these cases, the students are aware that 'failure' after effort implies low ability. So, following a 'failure' they suggest that they had not worked hard so that they can blame their 'failures' on lack of effort rather than lack of ability. The implication is that they could have done well if only they had tried. Urdan and Midgley (2001: 131) argue that self-protection strategies involve complex cognitive processing. They argue that individuals 'must be aware that (a) performance in an achievement situation can reveal information about ability; (b) more effort suggests less ability; and (c) it is possible to manipulate others' perceptions of one's ability by decreasing effort'. It is apparent that Graham, Paula and Ruth, along with the majority of pupils I interviewed, were well aware of these factors.

Another way in which boys and girls tended to hide their work and effort was by using the excuse of a lack of time, and therefore effort, as a reason for poor performance. Claiming to have left work until the last minute again allows the blame for the failure to be attributed to factors other than a lack of ability. Josh (School B) provides an example of this.

Would you ever blame a [poor] piece of homework on it being late?
If I didn't do good at it I'd tell my mates 'well I only did it the other day and I rushed it so'.
Why would you do that?
So if my homework was bad then I could just blame it on that instead of saying I'd spent loads of time on it.

It is worth at this point considering whether the 'excuses' are principally presentational (aimed at manipulating the perceptions of others) or whether they are actually believed by the pupils themselves (self-delusional). In a review of research on self-handicapping, Urdan and Midgley (2001) argue that while the research is not conclusive, self-handicapping, seems to be primarily a self-presentation strategy. In this research most students suggested that their (self-reported) self-handicapping strategies were presentational. However, a few pupils seemed to convince themselves by their strategies; this was apparent especially among those who attempted to present themselves as 'effortless achievers'.

It's no effort: Pretending not to work to augment success

... people get much more respect if they don't like revise or anything but they still do well.

Andrew (Ashgrove)

As discussed in previous chapters, overt hard work in school can pose dual problems for students. First, being seen to work hard academically is generally inconsistent with models of popular masculinity and femininity; achievement *per se* is not usually a problem, but working hard to achieve is problematic (see also Epstein 1998; Martino 1999; Frosh *et al.* 2002).

Lyn (Elmwood)
Is it seen as cool to work hard in school?
No. Not really.
Is that for boys and girls?

Mm.
So could it … [interrupted]
It's good when you get good marks, but when you're actually doing the work, it's not cool to like do the work.

Second, academic 'failure' after hard work signals a lack of ability, which in a society where ability is so highly valued, has detrimental consequences for an individual's self-worth. These factors create a conundrum for students, as most do not want to abandon academic work because of the importance attached to 'ability', which is signalled largely, and increasingly, via academic credentials. In this context 'effortless achievement' might be regarded as the ideal solution. It represents a way for pupils to negotiate the complex demands of their school lives.

Louise (Ashgrove)
If somebody wanted to be very cool, how would they be able to negotiate working?
They'd probably say that they didn't do it. And then get good marks. And that way they'd think they were really good.
What way?
I don't know. If they think, if they tell people that they don't do any work and then they get really high marks, then they probably think that they're like on top of people. And people would probably think that they want to be like them 'cos they don't have to do any work and they're still clever and things like that.
So is that the sort of ideal position?
Probably.

From a self-worth perspective, to achieve academically without hard work gives clear signals about an individual's ability. It also provides a convenient excuse if success is not forthcoming – failure without effort does not necessarily indicate a lack of ability, but success without effort indicates 'true genius'. Michele Cohen (1998) argues that the notion of 'effortless achievement' as a sign of true intellect is not new. She points out that in the nineteenth century the English elite male was supposedly distinguished by his 'natural' mental superiority. Such a view of ability means that hard work is in fact evidence of a *lack* of 'natural' mental superiority. Such notions were also evident among Mac an Ghaill's (1994) 'Real Englishmen', for whom a key element of their identities was a 'highly public display of a contradictory "effortless achievement" to each other and outsiders' (p. 67). Pupils who pretend to do no work when they actually have worked hard – 'closet learners' as Covington (1998) calls them – may be seen to be in a 'win, win, win' situation in relation to their peers. First, they may be able to present themselves as 'cool' and popular to their friends for not working.

Second, if they fail academically they can attribute their failure publicly to a lack of effort rather than to a lack of ability (although privately this may not be so straightforward). Third, if they do succeed as a result of their hard work, they may present it to their friends as effortless achievement which signals genius. Examples of students wishing to appear as 'effortless achievers' are provided by Lee and Jan, who both declared that they pretended to their peers not to have worked hard at something when they actually had. In both cases there is also the suggestion that it makes them feel better about themselves (self-delusion):

Lee (School B)
Would you ever say you'd not worked hard at something when you really had, so if you were doing revision for a test would you ever sort of say 'no I didn't really work hard for that, I didn't do much'?
Yes I would.
Why?
Like if I got a higher grade than them, I'd say no I didn't really revise cause that would make me sound brainier 'cause I already knew it and I didn't have to revise it.
OK so that's important is it?
In a way yes.
Why?
It sort of makes you like feel better about it.
What to yourself or others or ... [interrupted]?
Both. To yourself if you said that and you make yourself sort of believe it that you didn't [work] and you had [got a good grade] and if they think that you hadn't revised and you got a good grade then they have to work harder.
But you had worked hard but you'd say that you hadn't and that would make you look better would it?
Yes.

Jan (Beechwood)
With my mates I've got an image that I do well without really trying ...
So are there benefits from looking like you get really good marks without trying?
Yes 'cause I can do it [work] and not have anyone knowing, 'cause sometimes you get called a swot and everything if you do a lot of work; I don't like being called a swot 'cause that really annoys me ...
So if you do well without trying it stops you being called a swot but does it also then make you look more clever as well?

Yes.
Go on, tell me a bit more about that?
I don't know, it makes you look as if you've got bigger brains than what you actually have 'cause you don't bother trying but you get good grades as well ...
You said that works on two levels, on one level it works in terms of not being picked on and looking cool?
You don't really get picked on but say, they'll call you a swot because, my Mum would say because their jealous but I'm not that bothered, so what.
But you also said it makes you look good because it makes you look like ... you're more intelligent, that you're effortlessly intelligent. So is that really then a strategy that you present to other people but don't believe yourself or can you convince yourself that you've done less than you have really?
I don't know, I do it without even realizing now.
What do you mean?
I do it, I do the work but when I get scores I'm like 'I didn't do this' 'cause I don't remember doing it or anything.
So you almost convince yourself that ...
Yes, I haven't done anything.

Interestingly, effortless achievement as the 'ideal position' was not restricted to academic endeavours (see also Francis 2000; Frosh *et al.* 2002; Renold 2005a; Sherriff 2005). There were also examples of pupils striving to be regarded as effortless achievers socially and on the sports field. Martin (Elmwood), for example, talked about his desire to appear as an effortless sports star:

Would you ever pretend that you'd not worked hard at something when you have really?
Erm no, not really. If I were like, doing summat like sport, I would pretend that. I'd like pretend that I didn't work, if I'd done really good ... so they'd like, think that I'm better than I really am.
Right, so if you'd done well, you'd say you'd not worked hard, at sport, or at other things?
Yeah. Yeah.
Right, so why would you do that?
'Cos everyone like, thinks of me as like, em, like one of the best at sports, so you like, want to keep that. And everyone like, competes against me and stuff like that, so I try to keep up, like, highest I can.
Right. But you'd want them to think that you could do that without trying hard, would you?

Yeah. Yeah.
Why would, why's that?
Dunno. Just so they think I'm better than I am.
OK. So it would be, it would make you look better, would it, if you were that good without any effort?
Yeah.
Is that the way you look at it?
Yeah.

Students, particularly boys, also spoke about being effortlessly popular (see also Chapter 1). Boys who were regarded as *trying* to be popular were presented as 'inauthentic wannabes'. For example, Alistair suggested that the boys in his school 'see past' the inauthentic behaviours of boys in his class who act 'bad' to attract attention. Similarly, Alan spoke of boys being laughed at for *trying* to be popular.

Alistair (Ashgrove)
People won't like you if you talk properly; they'd rather you talk like slang. And they'd like you if you were, not like, they see people if they're bad in class then they're just doing it to attract attention and they see past that, but if you're bad in class and it's funny they'll sort of take a liking to you for that. But sometimes they just think you're attracting attention so you can be known and seen.

Alan (Ashgrove)
So would your group be quite a popular group then?
Yes it's quite popular but they don't try and be popular.
They're just popular without trying?
Yes.
So do some people try to be popular?
Yes.
What sorts of things do they do?
They just try and do what the really popular people do but it doesn't work half the time.
Why is that?
Because if they're trying, like everybody just laughs at them for trying to be popular.
So how do you get to be popular without trying, what sorts of things do you have to do?
If you've got like a good group of friends then you're just popular, I don't know really.

The distinct impression presented by these and other pupils is that some boys (and girls) are 'naturally' 'bad', funny, cool and so on; they do not have to try to be, they just are. Those who try hard to be 'bad', funny and cool are ridiculed for trying to be something that 'they are not'. The message is clear: the best achievements are those that are effortless, because then they are authentic.

Yet most pupils recognize that achievements cannot really be effortless. For example, Martin's comments earlier about the ways in which he tries to present himself as an effortless achiever at sport suggest a recognition that achievements cannot be without effort, but that the effort must be hidden, it must be largely invisible. Of course, behind the scenes girls and boys usually have to work very hard to appear as effortless achievers, but the pretence of effortlessness is maintained. In other words, ironically, they must try to be effortless. Power *et al.* (2003) argue that effortless achievement is displayed more easily by children from higher social class backgrounds than those from lower ones; this is explored in the next chapter.

Conclusion

This chapter outlined how pupils can explain their 'poor' performances (which are subjectively defined and relative) in ways that deflect attention away from lack of ability and focus instead upon other, less problematic reasons. There is a range of ways in which students can do this, some of which involve creating active impediments to performance (behavioural self-handicapping) and others which involve attributions (self-reported self-handicapping). These strategies (especially self-reported self-handicapping) can appeal to a broad range of students – high and low achievers – because they: (a) provide excuses for academic 'failure' that allow individuals to blame factors other than a lack of ability; (b) augment academic success by making it appear effortless; (c) enhance social status because students appear not to engage in 'uncool' academic work.

In the next chapter, I discuss how pupils attempt to balance social and academic demands, and which pupils are most likely to be successful at this balancing act.

7 Balancing acts: Who can balance the books and a social life, and how?

Can laddish lads be high academic achievers?
Yes, I tend to think I was one myself. A bit of a boy at school but when I needed to I was clever enough to make sure I was doing the work and getting on with it ... The individuals are intelligent enough to know when to do it and when not to do it; they're also intelligent enough to know how much work they need to do to get by.

(Mr Garner, Firtrees)

Chapter 5 explored the current tensions for many school pupils as a result of two competing, dominant education discourses: the 'uncool to work' pupil discourse and the 'credentials' discourse. As discussed in Chapter 5, most pupils attempt to negotiate these conflicting discourses (see also Frosh *et al.* 2002). They do this by attempting to balance the school's academic and their peers' social demands, by attempting to pursue both social and academic goals. Not surprisingly, some are more adept balancers than others, or in goal theory terms, some are more able than others to pursue and attain goals in both of these spheres (Dweck 1996). In this chapter, I discuss *strategies* that pupils employ for attempting to balance academic and social demands, and how and why certain *resources* facilitate this balancing.

Jon Swain (2004: 168) argues that the terms 'resource' and 'strategy' are sometimes conflated and the boundaries between them become hazy and indistinct. He distinguishes between the two, suggesting that 'resource' is the capital or stock that people draw upon and 'strategy' is the process that they use to apply it. In other words, he suggests that resources are about the 'what' and strategies are about the 'how'. I adopt this distinction here. The chapter starts by exploring the strategies that pupils adopted to attempt to balance the frequently conflicting demands of academic work and appearing cool and popular. I suggest that time is central to how well pupils balanced these demands. Finally, I consider how certain resources enable or facilitate pupils' use of balancing strategies. Within this section I consider the importance of time in mediating the relationship between resources (the 'what') and strategies (the 'how') and reflect on the use of resources to offset the effects of some types of 'uncool' behaviour.

Strategies

During the interviews pupils divulged a range of strategies for attempting to balance the often-conflicting demands of academic work and popularity. Strategies for 'getting away with' undertaking academic work without being cast as 'uncool' operated at two levels: 'direct' and 'indirect'. Direct strategies were those that pupils employed deliberately to *hide* their work and effort, for example, by looking like they were not listening in class when they actually were. Indirect strategies were those that enabled students to *off-set* the negative implications of school work, to negotiate more time and/or space for academic work without becoming unpopular. For example, being good at football earned boys 'popularity points' that enabled them to 'get away with' some academic work (as highlighted in Chapter 5). I start by discussing direct strategies that pupils use at home and in class. I then move on to consider indirect strategies.

Public versus private working – working mainly at home and hiding it (direct strategies)

> The least able of the three lads who were most laddish wouldn't do anything after school; that was not acceptable: 'I don't do that' ... and yet I've a real soft spot for him ... he would respond to one-to-one with no-one around and he would come back and he would secretly give me his work. But in the classroom he was a bloody nuisance, you know, and that poor guy was torn between wanting to be a lad, you know, and knowing that he could do ... the academic stuff. And the laddishness will, you know, he'll not get the grade he could get.
>
> (Mr Lee, Beechwood)

Numerous pupils reported messing around at school but then catching up when they were at home, away from the surveillance of their peers. Previous researchers have suggested that girls have no need to hide work and effort because, unlike boys, it's not a problem for girls to work hard in school (Osler and Vincent 2003; Power *et al.* 2003; Francis and Skelton 2005). For example, Power *et al.* (2003: 68) argue that 'although some of our young women also recall the stigma of being identified as a "swot", they do not appear to have engaged in "secret" work in the same way as their male counterparts'; although later they do go on to suggest that 'irrespective of the kind of school attended, academic success was not commensurate with social success' (p. 69). However, many of the girls in my research – in single-sex and co-educational schools, high achievers and low achievers – reported hiding work and effort; of the interviewees, a roughly equal proportion of girls and boys talked about hiding work and effort (37 per cent and 36 per cent respectively).[1]

> Diane (Firtrees)
> *Is it cool to work hard at school?*
> Cool? Mn, not really, you get called a spiff and all these words.
> *So does that put you off working, or?*
> Yeah, 'cos you don't want to be called [insulted] all the rest of your life. But if you just work at home, like, then your mates won't know that you're working at home.

As I've argued throughout this book, the motives underpinning these behaviours and strategies are frequently not singular. Diane's comments above suggest that she is primarily, although not necessarily exclusively, concerned about hiding her work so as not to be called a 'spiff' by her peers (social status concerns). However, as I've argued, hiding work and effort can serve a dual purpose, and a second motive of not wanting to appear academically unable (fear of academic failure) is articulated by Zuber (Oakfield):

> I'll just say 'oh I were watching TV' or summat. But I don't, I'll do some revision really.
> *Right. So why do you do that?*
> Don't know. Just in case like, I get poor marks or summat. Then they'll think oh he didn't revise anyway, so that's why.
> *OK. And do you do that a lot?*
> Not a lot, but sometimes if I'm like, expecting to do badly at some-thing.

Although home activities are usually less visible to peers than school activities, surveillance did extend to the home as well. When students did not want to go out with their friends because they had homework to do, many of them presented alternative explanations for their unavailability that masked the actual reason:

> Jenny (Firtrees)
> *So how do you manage the balance, how do you balance it* [school work and socializing]*?*
> … When I get home I say 'right, I'm going to do my work and then I'm going to go out'. And if they [friends] come round beforehand

and they say 'oh Jenny are you coming out?' I say 'no I'm getting
a shower' and I've just got to carry on doing my work.
So would you tell them you were working or would you ...?
No 'cause it would make me sound, well to my mates they'd think
I was weird, they'd think I was ill or something.

While Jenny's strategy was fairly common, it was not without its problems.
Once back in school questions about, and comparisons of, homework can
reveal who has, and who has not, undertaken the work set. As discussed in
Chapter 6, pupils are well versed in presentations of themselves that downplay their work and effort even if there is concrete evidence of them having
worked. So, for example, students would frequently claim to have spent less
time on work than they actually had spent on it. This could sometimes
involve rather elaborate excuses:

Zoe (Elmwood)
I don't pretend that I don't work hard, but I do pretend that maybe
I haven't worked as hard as I actually have.
Right. Can you give me an example?
Erm, projects and things. Erm, everyone else has just done a few
pages and I've, I tend to do quite a lot, and I just tend to say things
like 'Oh I've used a big font on the computer so that's why it looks
like it's so many pages, and I haven't actually tried hard', and 'I've
been at library and just read a load of books and copied it out of
books', and I didn't but it's just summat you say 'cos people are like
'why did you try so hard?' So you just tend to cover it up as best
you can.

Homework that was largely invisible was easier for students to manage;
revision for tests fell into this category. Again there are two principal
reasons why denying or underplaying revision for tests is regarded as beneficial by many students. First, it enables pupils to act in ways currently consistent with popular forms of masculinity and femininity in their schools:
to be 'laddish'. Second, it provides an excuse for failure or augments
success. Many students seemed to operate strategically in relation to school
work. For example, most popular students in high sets would undertake
enough work to enable them to maintain their high set position, but do
little enough work to enable them to maintain their high social status position. These students were able to revise for important tests in a relatively
invisible way that enabled them to balance their academic and social
priorities.

Clara (Hollydale)
I think they [popular girls] do revise during the day and do work

but they don't do their homework 'cause that shows it, whereas if you revise no one will see that. So they are quite clever.
So they'll work as long as people don't know?
Yes 'cause like homework shows you've worked to do it but in tests, tests is like you either know it or you don't at the time. And maybe people just think you know it but if you say like you're revising and stuff, like just [for] a little test, people go 'oh you swot'.

Chloe (Hollydale)
So the girls that disrupt the class, I mean do they work hard, I mean how come they're in a high set if they're disruptive?
Well, often they work hard in tests and things but it's the class work and the homework that they don't work hard on; it's just the tests that they do well in.

Strategies for working in class (direct strategies)

Darren (Ashgrove)
I've got a friend … he's good at subjects but he doesn't look like he tries at all, but then again he's bad, like messing around all the time and he gets away with it. Whereas people who are well behaved get like criticized for being clever and doing well.
So you can be clever if you're a bit bad as well in class?
Yes.
And you say your friend makes out he does it without working?
Yes, but he most probably does [work] but that's the image he's trying to give.
… How does he give the impression he doesn't work then?
I don't know really, he just doesn't look like he's paying attention and things like that. But then when you look at his book and things he's got great marks and he's just like really clever.

Darren talked about his friend with a mixed sense of admiration and envy. To be popular, bad and really clever was clearly, as far as Darren was concerned, an excellent position to be in. Both girls and boys talked about strategies they employed for attempting to balance messing around in class and working. Graham (Elmwood), for example, was explicit that he needed to hide his attempts to work in class, and he would do this by interspersing messing around and working.

So do you ever hide the fact that you work?
Probably, yeah.
What do you do?

Just like, if I'm messing around, I'll keep messing around but I'll talk like [for] two seconds, and I'll write a bit down at a time.

Craig, who was a high achiever at Beechwood, had taken time to learn that balancing work and messing around was necessary to avoid being called a swot (see also Renold's account of Stuart's story, 2005a). Having learned what he had to do, he now attempts to listen without showing he listens:

Do people get picked on if they work too hard?
Yeah, I think so.
Like they get called swots and that?
Yes.
But you don't?
I did when I was in Year 7.
So what changed?
I don't know, I just started talking to more people and then like finding out how they worked and that lot. And I just made myself work like that.
So what do you mean 'work like that'?
I don't know, like they say, you know 'listen but don't keep staring at the teachers' or something like that, and then I just wouldn't do it [stare at the teachers] and I still got what marks I needed but I just like did what they did.
So would they actually talk about it then, did you say they talked about it to you or did you just pick up on it?
Well most of the time I'd just pick up on it. But then people that I know most like, they'll just tell me.
So it's quite a deliberate strategy then is it of paying attention but not showing it?
Yeah.
What else, what other sorts of things?
Like talking while teacher's talking and that. Then you can still hear it and you write everything down but teacher won't think you were. And writing while they're talking (the teachers) but you're listening really but they don't think that.

'Fooling' the teacher in this way meant that Craig sometimes got told off, and this generally earned him extra 'cool points' among his peers. However, some of the teachers are wise to these strategies and claim to be able to tell which boys are really listening:

You get the ones who give the impression they're not really listening: 'I'm not going to listen to you. I'm not going to take any notice.' But you know full well come the exams they've taken in every word you've said. But they don't want to appear in front of their peers that they're really there. [But] they're really listening, they want to do well.

(Ms Brian, Beechwood)

Sometimes pupils would adopt varied strategies in different lessons depending on who was in the class with them. For example, Alistair (Ashgrove) said that: 'Yes, it's quite hard [managing working hard and being popular] ... I'm pretty good at geography but none of the popular lads are really in my set ... so I can really knuckle down.' Similarly, Sarah (Firtrees) suggested that she had to adopt very specific strategies for maths because she sat next to a popular girl in that class. We enter the interview below at the point where she's talking about her marks in maths.

I don't do that bad, I get like the average and sometimes one above. So I do do well it's just I try not to.
You try not to do well?
Yes, try not to concentrate and things.
So tell me a bit more about why you try not to concentrate.
I don't know because like in my maths class I'm sat next to someone whose like, hangs around and like smokes and things. So I just like try and show off and things like that, so I try to impress her ... 'cause like in primary school with this girl I got bullied and everything and I was a real swot type thing, so I don't want her to see me that way now, 'cause like we sit next to each other.
...
So it sounds like you manage quite carefully not showing that you work in maths but actually doing work.
Yes.
So how do you manage that?
It's like at the beginning of a lesson I wouldn't do anything and then I'd like rush it all at the end because I'm quite a fast writer. And so I end up getting it done but yet at the beginning I play around for a bit and then actually get down to it but like still talking in between and everything.
So actually at the end of the day you do get it done?
Yes ... or like things that I don't do in class I finish off as homework and things like that.
Yes because presumably you're clever and able to do that but presumably some people do that that just can't then pull it off?

Yes like they do do that and they try to get it done but they're not like fast enough or they don't know the answers straight away and things like that.

Sarah, who was awarded level 6 in her maths SATs, was able to articulate fluently and clearly the different, and sometimes complex, strategies that she adopts in maths to hide her work and effort. Her related fears of social 'failure' and of being bullied motivated these strategies. Sarah was particularly concerned not to be regarded as a swot because she was bullied at primary school for being 'a real swot'. So although Sarah is now in Year 9 of secondary school – and so almost three years on from leaving primary schooling – the memories of being bullied are still clearly painful and influential. What is striking from the accounts of Sarah and numerous other girls in this research is that girls as well as boys have to adopt careful strategies if they are to combine successfully the social and academic demands of schooling.

After school socializing (indirect strategies)

One way in which boys and girls could negotiate some space to work in school was by ensuring that they were sufficiently sociable outside of lessons and outside of school; this is what I referred to in the introduction as an indirect strategy for 'getting away with' undertaking academic work. For example, Jane (Firtrees) explained how girls can work hard and still be popular by making time for friends, and Anthony (Firtrees) talked about why he doesn't get called a spiff even though he does well in school:

> Jane
> *Could a girl who worked hard and did really well be popular?*
> Yes.
> *How would she manage that?*
> 'Cause you do your work and you try hard but you still have time for your friends. You don't just ignore your friends and [you] hang about with them as well as revising. Like you do your revising three days a week and go out with your friends the other three, or leave your work all the week and then do it at weekends.

> Anthony
> I think it's because like, 'cos I hang round with everyone and like, I play football and stuff. People who don't, they like, go to library and stuff like that, and just keep working.
> *So if you just work hard, then you're likely to get called names, but if you work hard and do other things?*

Yeah, like if you work hard but like, you hang around with everyone and play football and stuff like that, then I don't think people see you as a spiff, or as somebody that works hard and stuff like that.

Martin (Elmwood) shared Anthony's views, and articulated the difficulties of fitting work and other activities into the time available in a day.

And can someone at school who works hard be a lad?
Yeah. But, it depends like, if you like devote all your life to like, your working and stuff like that, then you're not [a lad]. But like, you can be good in class but like, not like, talk about work everything you do.
… So how do you manage, 'cos it sounds like you've got loads of things you do outside school? How do you manage to fit it all in?
Well, when I go home I do most of my homework then, really *quick*, and then I go out. And then at night when I come back in … sometimes I go in early so I can do it *quick* for [the] next day.
Right. So is it quite difficult, balancing?
Yeah. 'Cos it's like, I never have time to sit down, really. You go out and then go home, and you're doing your work and that's how you finish, and you're tired and you just go to bed.
So does it feel quite pressurized then, trying to manage things?
Yeah, like, fitting in all your homework and stuff like that, and revising. And then you've got, I've got like, I've got [football] training twice a week and then I do boxing twice a week, and I've only got one day free when I don't do anything. So like, I have to rush, rush everything really, to fit it all in. (my emphasis)

Time was quite a big issue for most students, and it arose in various contexts in almost all of the interviews. For example, in the extract from Sarah's interview in the last section she suggested that pupils who do not work 'fast enough' could not always finish their work in the time available. Martin in the last quote suggested that he is so busy with a combination of school work (which he does 'really quick'), sport and socializing that he never has 'time to sit down'. Time is central to the lives of school pupils, and to the ways in which they manage (or not) the demands of school and friendships. So time is the issue to which I now turn.

Time

It throws some staff sometimes because they might have this little group of almost angelic little boys in Year 7 and 8 and when they get to Year 10 they're thinking what's happened to them? And all that's happened to them is ... they've come under more pressure as they've got older, more opportunities have been opened up to them and they've got to get themselves involved in different things and they have less and less time to be angelic as it were.

(Mr Wells, Oakfield)

That's the other thing for me about our lads, is that they've got quite full lives outside [school].

(Ms Byatt, Firtrees)

Time available and used for school work was an important factor determining how well students could manage to juggle academic and social demands (see also Osler and Vincent 2003; Power *et al.* 2003). Time is central to our lives, yet is often an invisible and taken-for-granted aspect of the social world. Yet lessons about time are an important part of the school's 'hidden curriculum'. Drawing largely on the work of Barbara Adam (1995), Christina Hughes (2002b: 135) argues that:

Schooling is a key site where time discipline is instilled ... The organisation of schooling is fixed according to age and calendar. The days are divided into periods and lesson activities are also planned to linear time. The length of examinations is set to specific hours and minutes. Teaching time of lessons is set aside from play time and home time. Children learn that if they have not finished their work they are taking too long or if they finish early they have not done enough. Accurately gauging the appropriate level of input in relation to the time available is a key skill.

The school system is premised on the assumption that pupils invest a lot of time and effort outside of school on their school work in order to be academically successful (see also Frosh *et al.* 2002). Ridge (2005) argues that current demands to improve academic standards have resulted in more rigidly structured school environments and curricula, and concomitantly, pupils' social time and activities have become even more tightly controlled. However, my interviewees made it very clear that they had to invest a lot of time socializing with their friends (inside and/or outside of school) in order to be popular. So, the ways in which time is used, presented and negotiated by students is central to their academic lives *and* the activities that enable them to acquire 'popular' status. For example, among the boys, the tension between the need to spend time on academic work and the need to spend time doing 'lad' things, to prove themselves to be 'lads', was frequently explicit in the interviews.

To keep up the standards of being cool, you've got to work hard [at being cool] you know. You've got to have good social abilities, and in the end when you've got settled in with the crowd, then your schoolwork just starts to suffer because you're spending more time with the crowd and less on your schoolwork.

(Ben, School A)

If they're [boys] going to be cool then they hang out for longer, and they'll hang out till nine o'clock and they'll wait until it gets dark and they'll go home. But when they go home they'll just go straight to bed and they won't have done their homework, and if they haven't done their homework then their grades suffer and they get a detention or something like that. So if you are a lad your school work is suffering a lot 'cause you're always 'I haven't bothered to do my work, I was out all last night'.

(Terry, School A)

If you're a lad then you're always hanging out and everything, and you don't have much time to do, well you do have time to do your homework but you just go out so you just leave your homework to the last minute and you rush it. So that can harm your education.

(Fahed, School B)

Both boys and girls talked about going out with friends after school and suggested that spending time with friends was very important. Perhaps not surprisingly, those pupils who made little time for their friends tended to be excluded from friendship groups. However, the ways in which students organized and spent their time outside of school was shaped by gender, ethnicity, religion and class.

For most boys, social life outside of school was dominated by sport and/or hanging around with mates:

James (Elmwood)
I ain't started revising yet [for the SATs tests] ... I ain't really had time, 'cos I go cadets, (RAF cadets) and I do shooting and Ju Jitsu. So I have lots of extra-curricular activities to do.

Mick (Ashgrove)
So what sorts of things do you do outside school?
I fish, play cricket, go to watch football, socialize.

Sport was rarely central to girls' after-school activities, but it was important to them to socialize and see friends. Sweeting and West (2003) argue that young females (15 years old) are now just as likely as young males to be found in the 'traditional male' areas of the street or other public places, and this increased public visibility has no doubt contributed to some girls being labelled as 'ladettes' by the media and general public. In my research girls reported using public spaces during their leisure time; many described their social lives as involving hanging out with friends in parks or on the streets, going to the cinema, going shopping or going to friends' houses (see also Chapter 1 about girls and drinking; and Brown 2005).

Alice (Hollydale)
What about outside of school, do you go out with your friends outside of school?
Yes.
What sorts of things do you do?
We just hang around and everything.
What's hanging around?
It's like wander round and just sit on a bench and just talk and mess about and everything.

Melanie (Firtrees)
So you go out with friends from school?
Yeah.
What sort of things do you do?
I don't know. Walk around, go to the shops. It's quite boring, so we just go in one of our houses, or just walk around.

A small number of girls also talked about having to look after family or do household chores that took time away from studying, whereas no boys suggested that their time was taken up in this way (see also O'Brien 2003).

Shareen (Oakfield)
I look after the house mainly. My mum's like, she's not that well, and em, my brothers and sister, they're right into, you know, their own world and they don't do anything apart from just mess around. So I have to look after the house and don't exactly get time to, you know, study and revise and do stuff like that.

Fran (Beechwood)
So when you go out in the evenings and that, what sorts of things do you do?
I take my cousin out to the library to go on the computers and play with the toys, take some books and take him to the park and I'll see my Grandad, stuff like that.

Neelam (Hollydale)
Had you worked hard for them [SATs]?
Not really.
Why not?
I didn't have time.
In what way, what were you doing instead?
I've got to drop my nephew off to mosque and I've got things to do at home and my cousin's wedding is coming up and so I was busy in that way. If I had more time I would have revised more but then I didn't have the time so I just did as much as I could.

Many Muslim students spent chunks of their out-of-school time attending mosque. While the length of time spent at mosque varied, the average seemed to be around two hours per evening.

Adil (Oakfield)
So what's your, what's your typical after-school evening look like?
It's just like, em, going home and then just, well it depends. Sometimes I do my work, if I'm in the mood, and then my mum will like support me and say 'oh just go do an hour's work. It will do you good'. And then, em, for about an hour I'll play out and then we'll get ready for mosque at half five. And then we'll go. But it's OK, like, the timing and stuff.
So you say you finish [mosque] about 8?
Yeah.
And then what do you do afterwards?
We get collected and sometimes, it depends, like, if we've got homework and then, my mum no way we'll go out, she'll always have to let us do our work. So then like, and if we've got no work at all, like then we might go to our cousin's house or summat.

Shuhayb (Oakfield)
I go home [from school], I get changed, I'll go to mosque, and from there I do my homework, initial my homework, and if I need anything cleaning I'll clean it but if I'm free I'll just go play out. And then come in, to my dinner, and then go to the bathroom and wash my face and clean my teeth, brush my teeth and go back to sleep.

The strategies for hiding work and effort and balancing social and academic demands discussed in this chapter depend on pupils having the wherewithal to be able to pull them off. There are a number of factors that facilitate success, particularly whether students have the necessary resources at their disposal. Time provides an important link between strategies and resources: access to certain resources enables pupils to undertake school work quickly and privately, and leaves them with more time to undertake 'popularity work'.

Resources for study and socializing

> When I think about [the 'lads' in] this specific cohort ... the two boys who came from quite well-heeled families who had computers at home and supportive parents and money were able to pull it off better than one of the others who didn't have things at home, who didn't have the internet at home. So, whereas, you know, if it was coursework in geography and he had to get on the web, now, all three kind of did, but when they went home, the pressure was on to come up with the goods. Two of them just did it at home, and the third one couldn't, so he had to come back in and then he's got to be seen to go to the library or be seen to ask the teacher. So I think, I think environment and support helps you, whoever you are, whether you are a 'lad' or not, I think, you know, whether you're 'laddish' or not, but I think it's easier if you've got support because you can *privately achieve*.
>
> (Ms Byatt, Firtrees, my emphasis)

There is a great deal of work demonstrating how and why social class is linked to school experiences and attainment (for example, Archer and Leathwood 2003; Power *et al.* 2003; Ridge 2005). In his study of 10–11-year-old boys, Swain (2004: 171) argues that the boys' 'position in the peer group is determined by the array of social, cultural, physical, intellectual and economic resources that each boy is able to draw on and accumulate'. This extends to girls and secondary school pupils too. Further, not only does access to these resources shape the pupils' position in their peer group, but crucially, it shapes how well they are able to *balance* the different demands of their lives.

We have already seen that to be popular pupils must undertake school work as invisibly as possible. Ms Byatt's quote at the start of this section provides one very concrete example of the way in which having internet access at home enabled two 'lads' to complete their homework in a relatively *private* and *invisible* way, while another, who did not have private access to such resources, was placed very differently. In the remainder of this chapter I explore the ways in which access to resources shaped the ways in which pupils were able to balance the social and academic demands of schooling. Time is a key factor mediating the relationship between these resources and strategies. Certain resources enable students to generate and manage time in ways that allow them to balance academic and social demands. For example, by having easy access to books, the internet, advice and so on, some students were able to do their homework more quickly and make (more) time for socializing with friends: to undertake academic work and be popular. Bilal (Oakfield) talked about how having a computer at home helped him to organize his school work and work more efficiently:

> I've got a computer at home so if I can't get things typed up at school, I can type it up at home; so it really makes it much easier. [I] just can email it from home to school and print it, print it out from home. If you've done some work at school, you can email it to [your] home email and then open it up and carry on from [there], and print it out.

Others spoke about using computers for their SATs revision, and quite a few of these used and valued the BBC's Bitesize internet revision sites. For example, Jordan (Oakfield) said he'd used the internet and Bitesize a lot for his revision, and that it was good and 'better than just looking [it up] out of a book'. While access to computers seemed to offer those who had them numerous advantages over those who did not, it was not only in terms of technology that resource differences were apparent. Zoe (Elmwood), for example, who got 7, 7, 6 in her KS3 SATs spoke proudly of having more resources at home than at school:

> When you're doing projects and things, at home you've got like an art box, and you've got all erm, like lollypop sticks and erm, sequins and cards and buttons and things. So when you're doing your work you can tend to do like little fancy borders. And I tend to do it on the computer because I think the more I write, the more my hand writing gets scruffier and my spelling gets a bit careless. So I think that's the facilities I've got there and I've not got at school.

There were marked differences between the accounts of students in terms of resources; while Zoe boasted of having more facilities at home than at school, finding space to study can be an issue for some students (see O'Brien 2003; Ridge 2005). For example, Helen (Beechwood), who got 3, 3 and a score below test level in her SATs, told me: 'I have like a cabin bed upstairs with't table and that underneath, and we don't have a table or owt downstairs, we just have a like, a breakfast bar.'

Resources are also inextricably linked to time. As O'Brien (2003: 265) argues, 'as the demand for more time on schoolwork done at home increases through second level [schooling], working-class girls [and boys] may not have the resources to meet this demand'. When the demands on time are viewed not only in terms of academic ones, but also in terms of social ones, access to resources becomes even more salient. In my research, access to resources that facilitated quick and effective home study practices left girls and boys with more time to socialize with friends and undertake activities that could earn them peer approval. Some social activities, with the aid of computer technology, could be undertaken in the home, and sometimes at the same time as homework. So, for example, Steph (Hollydale) who attained scores of 6, 7, 6 in her SATs, spoke about how she did her homework and socialized with friends simultaneously using the internet:

> I always make sure that I've done my work because that's one of the most important things. But I like, when I've done it, I always try and do it quickly so then I have time to 'talk' [on the internet]. Or you can 'talk' to your friends when you're doing it or something. And then it's like, if I'm on the internet at home doing my research I can 'talk' to my friends at the same time, so I can get both things done at the same time.

It was clear from Steph's comments that she has long periods of uninterrupted internet access at home. What was also very clear was that those girls who did not have internet access would be excluded from the regular socializing that occurred on-line between Steph and her friends. While on-line social networks did not replace face-to-face ones (Steph went out with her friends on Fridays, Saturdays and Sundays), they meant that she could balance social and academic demands with relatively little effort. Contrast that with girls (and boys) who do not have access to on-line social lives, and who have to physically meet up to socialize, the time demands are markedly different. So are the opportunities for combining work and social time; Steph could work while socializing and hide her work and effort, it is much harder to do homework in the park without being noticed. Gender may be influential here. As noted earlier, for most boys, playing sport seemed to be a central part of being a popular and sociable 'lad'; this is not something that they could do on-line. However, McNamee's (1998) research suggests that when boys are at home they tend to control domestic space, and police their sisters' access to computers.

Time for homework and socializing is even more restricted for those pupils who undertake paid work outside school. While some of the pupils who undertake paid work are motivated by their desires for consumer goods, for others it provides a vital resource to sustain themselves in their school and social lives (Ridge 2005). For example, Ridge's (2005: 26) interviews with low-income girls revealed that for some of them who were engaged in paid work there was an acute awareness of the tensions between the demands of school work and paid work. However, she argues that 'the income earned played such a significant role in their lives that overall this appeared to outweigh concerns about schoolwork'.

Overall, while many students talked about pressures of time and the difficulties of fitting in the demands of school and of being 'cool' and popular, some had the resources to make this balancing act easier. So far I have discussed the ways in which access to certain resources enables pupils to undertake school work relatively quickly and privately, and this provides them with more time for the requisite 'cool work' (direct strategies). Resources also help in a second way: certain resources help to off-set the negative implications of school work. Pupils were more likely to 'get away with' working if they were 'cool' in other ways (indirect strategies), and to an extent, 'cool' could be purchased. It was easier to be cool and popular if girls and boys wore the 'right sorts' of clothes and had the 'right sorts' of fashion accessories (see Chapter 1). Although there were some differences between the schools about what was most fashionable, the 'right sorts' of clothes and accessories were almost always very expensive (see also Swain 2002).

Aisha (Oakfield)
So what are the cool things to wear?
Cool things to wear? Em, like right now for girls it's pointy shoes, and cropped jeans ... And for boys like, for boys it can be anything 'cos like they could wear sleeveless vests and three quarters and they should have good trainers, you know, like, those really expensive ones with suspensions and everything. So you know, like, that's what's really cool. I mean, the more expensive you look, the more cool you look.

Ruth (Elmwood)
So who defines what's cool? I mean how do you decide what's cool and what's not cool?
Mm, it's probably clothes or something. Or the way you look. Like, you have, there's some lads in our year, they'd be called proper scruffy, that won't wear decent clothes or nothing. And then there's the lads that would wear proper decent makes and that. I think it's more makes than anything.
Right.
They have to wear make [branded] clothes or you look like a scruff or summat.
So the scruffy ones aren't cool?
No. I think they're sectioned into three you know; there's swots, cool and scrubbers, as they call them.

Alice (Hollydale)
We like to wear nice clothes and everything. Some people just look

like tramps and everything but most of my friends and everything
have nice clothes because we don't really want to be seen walking
around with somebody who looks a tramp. But most people, it's
not because of the clothes that they wear that we're not friends
with them, it's just we don't really get on with them if you know
what I mean.

Ruth's and Alice's comments both convey downward social comparisons in social class terms. They talk about 'scruffs', 'scrubbers' or 'tramps'
and both reveal the negative values attached to such labels. Alice's
comment that: 'it's not because of the clothes that they wear that we're not
friends with them, it's just we don't really get on with them', conveys that
it's not only clothes that make them Other but also their ways of being.
'Swots' too were placed as Other; while they were not 'scrubbers', neither
were they 'cool' because they did not wear 'fashionable' versions of school
uniform, and crucially, they wore their uniform in an 'uncool' way, which
usually meant they wore it in accordance with school rules. For example, at
Beechwood students who wore their ties according to school rules were
called 'swotknots' as their knots were 'too small' and they wore their ties
'like teachers do' (Kieran). Undoubtedly, wearing the 'right sorts' of clothes
in the 'right sorts of ways' and having appropriate accessories (for example,
the latest mobile phones) enabled students to jump a few rungs up the 'cool
ladder' as it contributed to a 'cool' image. Swain's (2002: 66) work in junior
schools has demonstrated how clothes act as 'a powerful signifier of the
pupils' worth as people, and were an essential ingredient of social acceptability (or rejection) within their specific peer group culture'.
    In addition to the ways students dressed and adorned their bodies to
portray an air of coolness, the body itself was central to the performance.
Here again, some are given a head start. Skeggs (2004) argues that certain
characteristics are inscribed on bodies. For example, she argues that black
working-classness is inscribed on the male body as cool.[2] So some boys are
more likely than others to have coolness inscribed on their bodies. In my
research it seemed that for boys, being tall, athletic and good-looking are
definite advantages in the 'cool stakes'.

> You know, interestingly, they all (our 'laddies') are tall. I don't know
> if that's a physical trait of 'laddishness', but all our 'laddies' are tall,
> and they're all quite attractive in conventional terms. They've got,
> sort of features that the girls did find attractive and that the boys
> aspired to … They stand out, they physically stand out.
>
> (Ms Byatt, Firtrees)

> We've had quite a few fairly high achieving boys who you would
> consider to be 'lads', but they have always been lads who have
> been very good at sport and always been quite good looking lads.
> If you're a good looking lad and you can pull the ladies then you're
> probably more able to cope with being a bit academic on the side.
>
> (Ms Cornish, Elmwood)

It was reported time and time again during the interviews with pupils
and teachers that boys could 'get away with' working academically if they
were heterosexually attractive, stylish, sporty and sociable (see Chapter 5).
Importantly, as discussed earlier, they had to be all of these things effortlessly which, as Power *et al.* (2003) remark, is more difficult for boys from
less advantaged backgrounds. Boys who were apparently effortlessly heterosexually attractive, stylish, sporty and sociable were granted more time and
space to undertake academic work without facing the range of negative
consequences that boys who did not display these features encountered (see
also Power *et al.* 2003; Renold 2005a). The same sorts of 'rules' also applied
to girls, although not surprisingly the ways in which girls manifest heterosexual attractiveness are very different to the ways in which the boys do.
Also, as signalled earlier, being sporty was not important for girls. So for
girls to earn more time and space for academic endeavours without it being
at the expense of their popularity, they had to be heterosexually attractive
and sociable. Furthermore, while many boys invested a lot of time in sport,
many girls invested a lot of time in their appearance. This is conveyed by
Ms Walters (Hollydale).

> I quietly laugh at my Year 9 because they have a little contingent
> that we refer to as 'the barbies', which is a lovely expression.
> *It's one that the girls used as well.*
> Did they? Well we [teachers] refer to them as that and it's no reflec-
> tion of their ability because some of them are the most able girls.
> And they're very nice natured girls and also very pretty girls and
> they've got everything going for them. But they do spend a
> tremendously long time grooming themselves and it's that sort of,
> you know, everything has to be just so and it's as though you can't
> start the day until everything is in order and in place.

According to Ms Walters, this group of popular Year 9 girls 'had it all' –
they were intelligent, charming and good-looking: 'they've got it all.
They're talented, they've got the looks, they've got the personality and I
look at one or two of these charming young women and I think well, you're
a hard act to follow love.' According to the teachers and students at
Hollydale, these girls balanced academic and social demands very well:
'they're quite clever but even though they're still always going out. They're

really clever' (Iram). Appearance was central to the image of this group, an image that very clearly reflected traditional models of white, heterosexual femininity. Like the teacher quoted above, some pupils described them as having 'everything':

> They always like, they've always got the lip-gloss and the pink shoes and they're quite rich. They always get designer clothes and [are] the one's with everything. Like, most of them have got long blonde hair and blue eyes and [are] like tall and they're all slim and they all get all the lads from [the local boys' school] and everything.
>
> (Faya)

Without a doubt, the social class position of these girls underpins and is central to their image of 'got it all'. It is their class position that facilitates their balancing of social and academic lives. The admiration of their teacher about their ability to balance academic and social demands in an apparently effortless way, and their lifestyles in general, was clear from her interview.

> They're quite cool because they've got it all. They can do it but they're not the ones that are constantly, you know, the teacher's pet ... They can be told off for inappropriate comments in the same way as somebody sitting on the front row deliberately chatting or somebody who isn't interested. That's what makes them cool, is that they're not really the swotty type. They can do it, they've got the ability, they're interested, they're well motivated, they're clever girls but they don't appear to be overly zealous when it comes to their work. Everything is done, they just quietly get on with it. They're the ones that finish their science in the double lesson, they're the one's whose books are always on the shelf on a Monday morning because they've done their homework. But they can balance it.
>
> (Ms Walters, Hollydale)

But strip away their expensive designer clothes and their charm, remould their tall, slim bodies, long blonde hair and blue eyes, and they would have a much harder time maintaining their popularity without being regarded as swotty. Their bodies and their expensive feminine accoutrements are key to enabling them to create the time and space to undertake academic endeavours without rebuke.

Conclusion

In this chapter I have discussed some of the strategies that pupils employed to balance their social demands with the academic demands of school. I have argued that some pupils are better resourced than others to be able to balance these demands successfully and that time is central to the equation. Those pupils with the resources at home to be able to undertake homework quickly and effectively are most likely to be able to manage successfully their academic demands while at the same time having the time and space to be popular. These resources also mean that it is easier for boys and girls to disguise and hide their work and effort. Further, some pupils are advantaged in terms of their physical resources (their bodies); boys who are athletic, strong, tall and good-looking, and girls who are tall and conventionally femininely attractive, earn points on the 'cool ladder' that can be used to offset points lost for undertaking school work. Unsurprisingly, by virtue of their range of resources, middle-class students are more likely than their working-class counterparts to be able to balance the demands of being popular and academically successful.

8 'If I knew how to tackle "laddishness" I'd bottle it, sell it, and make a fortune': Implications for teachers, schools and policy-makers

> Imagine how we would go about designing an educational program if our purpose were to make students hate to learn. We would not involve them [students] in establishing the purpose of their class. We would require them to perform some impossible tasks – for example, to be perfect in everything they do. Third, when we discovered that the students were failing to master the impossible tasks, we would ridicule them and report their mistakes, failures and shortcomings to their friends and relatives.
>
> (Krumboltz, cited in Covington 1998: 104)

This chapter brings together some of the key theories and empirical findings discussed in this book and explores the implications for practice. The book has endeavoured to answer the question of what motivates 'laddishness' among schoolgirls and schoolboys. I have argued that the motives are not single, but multiple, shifting, and operate at various levels of consciousness. There were two sets of motives that emerged particularly strongly in the research, one academic and the other social. In summary, I argued that many aspects of 'laddishness' can be understood in terms of students' avoidance motives, prompted by fears about academic and/or social failure. Given this, the question that many teachers are left with is, what can they do to tackle 'laddishness'? Before I attempt to answer that question, there are two key points to stress.

First, although 'laddishness' is frequently presented as problematic, not all aspects of 'laddish' behaviours are a cause for concern. For example, the increased confidence and assertiveness that is associated with 'laddish' girls is a cause for celebration rather than regret. Furthermore, the importance attached by many boys to playing sport can be regarded as positive at a time when the government is concerned about young people having unhealthy, sedentary lifestyles (for example, Winterton 2004). In addition, a number of academically 'successful' boys in my research spoke of sport as a useful form of stress relief to counteract the strains of school and testing; they presented what ostensibly seemed to be quite a sensible work:life balance. So there are aspects of 'laddish' behaviours that we should perhaps celebrate. However, there are also attitudes and behaviours which are labelled as 'laddish' that do create problems for girls and boys in schools – both 'laddish' girls and boys, and also their peers – and that it would be beneficial to tackle.

Second, it is important to stress at the outset that there are no easy answers to the question about how to tackle problematic aspects of 'laddishness', and there are certainly no quick-fix 'solutions' (see also Mills 2001; Francis and Skelton 2005; Younger and Warrington 2005). Martin Mills (2005) made a similar point in a presentation on the boys debate in Australia, when he offered the pithy and memorable reminder that: 'For every complex problem there is always a simple solution. And it is always wrong!'

Most educational research identifies and conveys the complexities of educational problems and issues. The problem with this, as Ailwood (cited in Warrington and Younger 2005: 10) points out, is that: 'as theory has become more focused and more complex, it has also become rather more difficult to translate into policy terms'. It is, nevertheless, very important to attempt to tease out from educational research the implications for policy and practice. So the challenge for me is to unravel the implications of my research for policy and practice without losing the complexity inherent in the data.

So what are the implications of my research for teachers and policy-makers who want to tackle some of the more problematic aspects of 'laddishness'? In this book I have mapped out and attempted to explain key motives underpinning 'laddish' behaviours. I argued that they are motivated by a combination of academic and social concerns. Drawing on goal theory, self-worth theory and empirical data, I argued and demonstrated that academic performance and standards discourses encourage self-worth protection strategies among some students. Students adopt these defensive strategies because, when faced with pressures to attain results in a climate in which so much value is attached to academic ability (measured by academic 'success'), many pupils fear failing academically and being regarded as academically deficient. These defensive strategies include, among others, procrastination, intentional withdrawal of effort, rejection of academic work, and disruptive behaviours; all of which provide excuses for academic 'failure' that deflect attention away from a lack of ability. So they do not help students to avoid academic failure – in the long term, they may actually make failure more likely – but they protect students against the most damaging implications of academic failure, that is, that they lack ability. It is no coincidence that these behaviours are also ones that are labelled 'laddish' in schools. Many 'laddish' behaviours and attitudes – central to which is the notion that it is 'uncool to work' – can act to protect an individual's self-worth from the implications of academic failure. In the short term, these defensive strategies can feel like 'friends' because of their academic self-protective advantages (Martin and Marsh 2003); but in the long term, they are almost always 'maladaptive' in terms of educational experiences and results.

'Laddish' behaviours can also be motivated by social goals because they are generally regarded as 'cool' and earn pupils 'popularity points' among peers. Social relationships constitute a crucial component of school life, and their importance to students must not be underestimated. The consequences of social failure – frequent marginalization and/or bullying – can be very damaging for pupils. As such, fears of social failure motivate many pupils to try to 'fit in' because they are scared of becoming unpopular. So in addition to serving academic self-worth protection purposes, 'laddish' behaviours can also serve to protect against social failure. In other words, some students may behave 'laddishly' in an attempt to be popular, or to avoid being unpopular. Overall, the combined protective benefits that 'laddish' behaviours can offer against social failure, and against the implications of academic failure, can make them very attractive to students. But the long-term costs in terms of educational experiences and results can be high.

In this chapter I concentrate on ways in which policy-makers and teachers can attempt to reduce the sorts of 'laddish' behaviours that are frequently prompted by students attempting to defend themselves from the detrimental consequences of academic and social failure. The current emphasis on competition, performance, standards and testing is at the heart of promoting academic defensive behaviours among students; this emphasis also has implications for the ways in which students attempt to gain popularity. As such, I start by discussing some of the problems generated for teachers and schools by this current emphasis, particularly those created by high-stakes testing. I then go on to consider possible ways forward.

High-stakes testing, fears of failure and 'laddishness'

Competitive performance climates are likely to encourage the types of defensive academic behaviours that have been labelled 'laddish'. As Chapter 4 demonstrated, the academic performance discourse is a dominant one in schools; many pupils feel under considerable pressure to perform well academically, and the SATs seem to add substantially to this pressure. The pressures that many children experience to perform well in the SATs are a cause for concern among many parents, teachers and researchers, and opposition has been voiced from numerous groups about the negative effects that this testing regime has upon children (see, for example, *Guardian* 2003; Mansell 2005). Ms Holtby (Hollydale), for example, told me:

[Increased testing has] had an impact from junior school onwards ... several of my colleagues have got children at junior schools who are just doing their SATs and they are saying that their children are showing signs of anxiety. Even though they're trying to say 'it doesn't matter, just do your best, forget them, just get rid of them and think how good life will be on Friday' [the children say] 'oh no it won't because I'll have to worry until August' ... I am absolutely dead against the testing that there is. That's my personal opinion.

While the focus here is on the consequences of testing, performance-oriented climates for 'laddishness', it is worth mentioning and noting that such climates have implications for learning more broadly. For example, the psychological effects of exams, and in particular of feeling a failure, can be long-lived and extend way beyond the immediate time of the testing period and of school (Walkerdine *et al.* 2001). While the longevity of these feelings was not the focus of this research, there is evidence from other research that they have implications for the way people feel about 'life-long learning'. Diane Reay (2001b: 339) explored the long-term effects of educational 'failure'. Interviews with working-class, mature students on an access course revealed that their in-school experiences had stayed with them and were still influential:

The mature students' largely negative, sometimes fragmented educational histories reveal no easy union of the academic with personal satisfaction and achievement. Any attempt at transformation [in terms of social class] runs all the risks of the academic failure and shame many experienced in their early schooling. As Janice says 'I don't ever want that sick feeling in my stomach again'.

The decisions that Reay's interviewees were making about where to undertake higher education were influenced by memories of schooling. For example, Janice, who Reay (2001b: 339) cites again below, was keen to avoid academic competition.

The shadow of earlier academic failure hung over the students' decision making. As Janice asserts 'I don't want to compete with anybody. I don't want to be in any of this competitiveness'. This makes the transition to higher education particularly problematic when, for working-class students like Janice, the field of higher education is constituted as a forum in which 'community is dissolved in the acid bath of competition'. (Beck 1992: 94)

High-stakes testing and pressures to perform academically increase the risk of fears of failure among pupils and the subsequent defensive strategies often prompted by these. In addition, such testing regimes also impact upon pupils' behaviours and their engagement with, and enjoyment of, learning in a broader sense (see, for example, Remedios *et al.* 2005). Regular, high-stakes testing frequently means that: (a) teachers teach a narrow range of topics (those that will be tested), in streamlined ways, because of time constraints; (b) students focus on the subjects that will be tested; (c) there is little time or space for teachers to work with students on non-testable issues. All of these have implications for 'laddishness', so I'll take a look at each of these points separately.

Teachers teach a narrow range of topics (those that will be tested), in streamlined ways, because of time constraints

High-stakes testing encourages teachers to teach the skills and knowledges that will be tested (Reay and Wiliam 1999; Midgley *et al.* 2001; Hursh 2005). As Midgley *et al.* (2001: 83) argue in relation to the USA, testing and accountability changes teaching: 'rather than promoting thinking, under-standing, and creativity, they [teachers] feel pressured to teach facts and test-taking strategies'. Some interviewees in my research echoed this view. For example, Damian (Ashgrove) reported that: 'since I started the third year [Year 9] we started for our SATs and we went all the way through for our SATs, and now [after the SATs] we're doing work for the end of year tests'. That teachers concentrate on teaching topics that are to be tested in SATs is understandable; a lot hinges on SATs results for the individual pupils, the teachers and the schools. Unfortunately, teaching to a very pre-scribed curriculum that is heavily circumscribed by what will be tested can leave students uninterested and disengaged. This results, in part, from students having little scope for pursuing their own interests (Reay and Wiliam 1999), and is problematic in motivational terms because as Covington (1999: 132) argues: 'people enjoy and appreciate learning more about what already interests them than about topics that hold little inter-est'. This view is now considered 'common sense' and was voiced by a lot of my interviewees.

> Faya (Hollydale)
> I work hard in the lessons I like working hard in. If there's some-thing interesting to do that will keep my mind occupied, that I enjoy, I'll work hard and I'll get a good grade. But if there's some-thing that really bores me then I'll sit there and put my head on the desk and say 'I'm bored', or talk.

Dana (Beechwood)
If I like what I'm doing, then I'll do it.

If students find the curriculum boring, it provides little incentive for them to counter the 'uncool to work' discourses associated with 'laddishness'. While providing subject matter that interests pupils will not in itself be sufficient to challenge 'uncool to work' attitudes, it is likely to be a necessary first step. Research by Covington (1999) has confirmed the importance of subject-matter interest (see also Krapp 2003). He argues that success in conjunction with interest is a particularly powerful and positive combination in terms of learning and subject-matter appreciation. However, interest was important in conditions of failure as well as success. He argues:

> In short, people enjoy and appreciate learning more about what already interests them than about topics that hold little interest. What is intriguing about this bit of otherwise common-sense wisdom is that these results applied to failure as well as to success experiences. Indeed, what most merits our attention here is the degree to which pursuing one's interests offsets failure experiences when it comes to valuing learning. The power of this dynamic is illustrated in our data by the fact that appreciation for what one is learning was far greater in a failing but task-interested cause than it was when the same student succeeded, gradewise, but for subject-matter content that held little or no interest. (pp. 132–3)

Andrew Martin (2003) also stressed the importance of interest. In research that focused on how to enhance the motivation and educational outcomes of boys in Australia, Martin asked boys what they would change about school if they had the chance. The dominant responses revolved around greater choice and greater sense of control, with greater subject choice, choices of materials and methods within subjects being particularly desirable.[1]

However, while interest clearly is important, there are three notes of caution to raise here. First, individual interests have to be regarded as just that – as individual. Unfortunately, all too often interests are assumed, and these assumptions are based on gender stereotypes. For example, schools have adopted a number of strategies to attempt to raise the performances of boys in English. One method that seems increasingly fashionable, both in England and elsewhere, involves the introduction of single-sex classes into co-educational schools for certain curriculum subjects (Kenway and Willis 1998; Sukhnandan *et al.* 2000; Jackson 2002b; Martino and Meyenn 2002; Mulholland *et al.* 2004; Van de Gaer *et al.* 2004; Martino *et al.* 2005). Syal and Trump (1996), for example, reported on a school in England that introduced single-sex classes for English lessons. This scheme involved teaching

English to girls and boys in separate classes, but also it involved tailoring the texts studied in classes to provide appropriate 'masculine' and 'feminine' reading materials to meet the (assumed) interests of the boys and girls, respectively. For example, while the boys studied 'macho' texts such as war poems, *Lord of the Flies* and *Macbeth*, the girls studied *Jane Eyre*, *Romeo and Juliet* and *The Lady of Shallot*. This reading scheme falls back on and reinforces stereotypical assumptions about girls' and boys' interests, that is, girls enjoy reading about romance while boys prefer to read about war and death. One wonders how many of the girls would have preferred to have substituted *Macbeth* for *Romeo and Juliet*, and how many of the boys would rather have read *Jane Eyre* than *Lord of the Flies*.

Second, and related to the first point, encouraging students to build on their interests does not mean that teachers should not encourage them to adopt new interests or diversify their studies. As we have seen, many boys are reluctant to engage with materials or activities regarded as 'feminine' for fear of being Othered, harassed and bullied. Yet this does not mean that teachers should be complicit in allowing boys to ignore and/or downgrade activities and topics stereotyped as 'feminine'. But stereotypes need to be challenged carefully, and as Mills (2001) points out, teachers need to understand the social organization of masculinity (and femininity) within the gender regime of the school. Programmes to challenge stereotypes take time and careful planning, which, unfortunately, are precisely what teachers lack in the current high-stakes testing climate (discussed more fully later in this chapter).

Third, while in some circumstances failure experiences may be offset if the subject matter is considered interesting (Covington 1999), it is important not to forget that in performance climates a lack of interest – boredom – can sometimes be invoked as an excuse for students not engaging with work that they find difficult (Muldoon 2005). In other words, claiming that work is boring and so unworthy of attention can be a self-worth protection strategy. Students have less to lose by claiming that they are not doing work because it is boring, than because they are not able to do it, or are anxious that they might do it wrong. Carol Dweck's work confirms this. Dweck's (2000: 8) studies revealed that students (in this case fifth and sixth grade): 'had been quite pleased with themselves, the task, and the situation during the successful trials, but they began to express a variety of negative feelings once they began to have trouble with the task. Many claimed they were now bored, even though they had been happily involved only moments before.'

Students focus on the academic subjects that will be tested

In climates that prioritize results, and where performance is emphasized over enjoyment of learning and interest, students are more likely to concentrate on those academic topics and subjects that 'matter'. They employ their efforts strategically. Ms Christie (Hollydale) was certain that the increased testing was contributing to students neglecting modern foreign languages: 'I see the effect in my subject and it's just about destroyed it. One of the things that it does is that it makes children prioritise certain subjects.' This was reinforced by the students themselves, not specifically in relation to languages, but in terms of prioritising academic subjects that they would be taking exams in at GCSE.[2]

> Stu (Ashgrove)
> I work quite hard it depends which lesson I'm in.
> *Tell me a bit more?*
> Well some lessons this year you can't really be bothered [with] because you know that you're dropping them [at the end of Year 9] so you just sort of give up towards the end of the year and don't really bother. And then others you concentrate more in.

Definitions of which academic subjects 'matter' are also influenced by gender (Spender 1989; Paechter 1998, 2000). So, for example, 'wannabe' hegemonic boys are likely to emphasize the importance of 'masculine' subjects such as maths and science and denounce the importance of 'feminine' subjects such as French. So which academic subjects students prioritize are likely to be influenced by a number of different factors, but whether they are tested and also their gender associations are key to this process.

Rudduck and Urquhart (2003: 181) suggest also that school years are given lesser or greater strategic significance depending on whether they include high-stakes tests: 'In a climate dominated by the pursuit of grades, schools are in danger, but not of their own making, of defining and presenting learning as a series of "quick fixes" – intensive bursts of revision for the next test – and students, not surprisingly, see years without tests or exams as unimportant, as "on the back burner" years, as "rest years".'

Although the varying importance of different school years was not something that I asked about explicitly in the interviews, a few pupils raised it. For example, Faya (Hollydale) told me:

> I used to be like dead swotty in Year 7. Then in Year 8 it's like a doss year because there's no tests or anything. But Year 9 we've got SATs so it's been like why I've got to work a bit more. Year 8 is when I started messing about and now I can't get out of the habit, just messing about thinking I'll get away with it.
> *And that's because there weren't any tests in that year?*
> Yes, Year 7 you tend to be really good and do all the homework and tests and everything and I used to get good marks, I used to be really good in Year 7. And then Year 8 there's nothing, no big

pressure or tests or anything, so I started messing about. And in Year 9 I just carried on messing about and that's probably why people start getting bad marks in the SATs and stuff, because they can't get out the habit of messing about from Year 8.

While pro-testing policy-makers might interpret Faya's comments as a sign that we need to add tests into Year 8, my analysis would lead to the opposite conclusion. Strategic approaches concerned mainly with exam success are far more likely to promote performance approaches (concerned with *demonstrating* competence) than learning ones (concerned with *developing* competence). Moreover, those performance-goal-oriented students who are not 'successful' in exams are more likely than students who adopt learning goals to disengage from schooling and to adopt defensive, 'laddish' protection strategies.

There is little time or space for teachers to work with students on non-testable issues

A common complaint voiced by teachers is that they have barely enough time to cover topics on which pupils will be tested, and so being able to cover extra-curricular issues is regarded as a luxury that practical constraints seldom allow. This can be a source of dissatisfaction for teachers, parents and pupils. For example, in Osler and Vincent's (2003) research, students and parents in a school that served a diverse, multicultural population regarded the curriculum as narrow and largely monocultural. In my research, Ms Holtby (Hollydale), among others, expressed regret that she did not have enough time to engage with issues that are not tested:

> *And presumably you as teachers feel that pressure [of the testing] as well?*
> Oh yeah, definitely ... Obviously, you have a goal and that's for kids to answer those [test] questions. And sometimes you'll see maybe like, poor social interactions in class or in the corridor and you think, you know, we could spend a bit of time and sort of go through this. But in essence, I have an agenda and I have a timeline and I've got to get this done and that's more important.

Unfortunately, because teachers feel that they have insufficient time to deal with non-tested topics, issues relating to social justice tend to be sidelined. We have seen that 'popularity' is important for boys and girls, and that popularity is gendered. Furthermore, we have seen that overt hard work is inconsistent with popular versions of femininity and masculinity. It might be fruitful to implement programmes in schools that encourage students to explore and question these dominant associations, with a view to challenging them. For example, Martin Mills (2001: 81; also 2000) provides useful discussions of the ways in which 'boyswork' programmes in schools can help to 'intervene in those gendering processes that normalise the links between masculinity and violence'. Pro-feminist, boyswork programmes more generally have attracted some criticism for making 'boys and men teachers feel bad about themselves!' (Francis and Skelton 2005: 138). However, it is possible to devise programmes that do not result in boys or girls feeling anger or guilt, and which encourage students to work critically and constructively on issues of social justice. To be effective, these need to be long-term programmes, not individual sessions. They need to be designed carefully, not thrown together by teachers who do not have time allocated to such developments because they are not tested. They need to take place in a climate within which they are valued by pupils, not seen as worthless because they are not tested. They need to pervade the whole school (Francis and Skelton 2005; Younger and Warrington 2005), not be contained only within certain classes. They need the time, space and recognition that most secondary school teachers would regard as completely impossible in the current education system. Ironically, some teachers argued that the emphasis on testing and competitive individualism means that there is even more of a need to encourage the development of 'life skills', and to remind students of values other than those that encourage a race for credentials.

> Because of the way society does focus them so much on … their SATs, GCSEs, AS levels, A levels, university … it's almost like you've got to sprint on this race and you just don't even look round to see who else is there anymore. And I think that's what's really changed … the pressure's on *you*, not on you to look at others. And I think if you pressure them to look at others … I think they feel that they'll be missing out themselves in the process. I think some of them see life as a race, but you know, I know there's a lot of pressure on them … you know it's exams every year now for probably ten, well between eight to ten years, you know, for the bright ability kids, and you think well, you know, that is tough … I think that the education system is skewed towards results and value added, you know, people have forgotten the values, the life skills as well, that are also important. I think that's kind of the problem with it, really.
>
> (Ms Holtby, Hollydale)

The almost exclusive focus on academic credentials and performance means that 'education' in contemporary schools can be very narrow.

Possible ways forward

In thinking about ways forward, it is important to be explicit about where we are trying to go. I made clear at the outset that not all aspects of 'laddishness' are problematic (although of course, perceptions of what is problematic are always highly subjective). At the core of teachers' concerns seems to be the 'uncool to work' aspects of 'laddishness'. This dominant discourse means that girls and boys are likely to disrupt learning, avoid work (or at least hide it), avoid challenge and so on, in order to look cool among their peers and to be popular. So the key aim – and it's a big one – is to make learning cool. Importantly, it is learning that needs to be cool, not demonstrating competence. This means that we need to encourage students and teachers to value effort, strategy, and the process of learning, rather than to emphasize and reward 'right' answers. Such a shift would involve, as Dweck (2000: 121) argues, tackling the perception that effortless achievement is the 'pinnacle of accomplishment'. This will not be an easy task, because as Michelle Cohen (1998) demonstrates, the glorification of effortless academic achievement has a long history.

Learning is unlikely to be regarded as 'cool' while there are so many reasons to fear academic failure. The educational climate needs to shift from a performance climate in which pupils fear academic failure and its implications, to one in which pupils feel safe to experiment with learning. I am not suggesting that all assessment is 'bad'; assessment has numerous benefits (Pollard 2005). Neither am I suggesting that children should not experience 'failure'. In the right context, 'failure' (although it may need to be reconceptualized) can have positive consequences. As Covington (1998: 215) argues: 'failure is interesting partly for the fact that successful thinkers actually make more mistakes than those who give up easily and thereby preserve their unblemished record of mediocrity, and also for the fact that mistakes can usually be set right by trying again'. Students who are learning-goal-oriented are far more likely than students who are performance-goal-oriented to see 'failure' in positive terms: as a learning opportunity, a challenge to be navigated. But to encourage this view of 'failure' among all students would involve significant educational change, both at the level of policy and classroom practice.

Policy-level strategies

A competitive, performance climate in education is at the root of many of the problems discussed in this book. While this is discussed here mainly in relation to academic concerns, it also has important implications for pupils' social lives: hierarchies of femininities and masculinities are premised on competition to be 'the best', the most 'popular', on 'jockeying for position' (Edley and Wetherell 1997). So, arguably, if we want to reduce defensive 'laddish' behaviours, we need to reduce competition and shift the climate in schools from a performance-oriented one to a learning-oriented one (ideally, both academically and socially). Clearly, this is much easier said than done, and I am not offering a solution; but certainly in academic terms, reducing the amount of high-stakes testing in schools would be a substantial step in the right direction.

Many teachers, teaching unions, parents and educational researchers have for some time been calling for SATs tests to be abolished in England.[3] But despite this lobbying, in the short to medium term it seems unlikely that SATs will be abolished in England.[3] Given that, are there steps that can be taken to reduce the negative impacts of this testing regime, including 'laddish' behaviours? Midgley *et al.* (2001) argue that in a climate in which there is an escalation on the emphasis on standards, testing and accountability, there needs to be a distinction made between standards rooted in learning goals and those rooted in performance goals. They argue that standards that reflect learning goals are both necessary and important, but that performance goals are likely to drive out learning goals in large-scale testing programmes. Midgley *et al.* (2001: 83) provide the following example.

> The National Council of Teachers of Mathematics (NCTM) articulated specific standards a decade ago that were based on the principle that it was more important for students to understand how they arrived at an answer than the answer itself. These standards were adopted in part or in whole by 49 states [in the USA]. The problem arises when there is a need to assess whether a student has achieved these standards. Good classroom teachers, if they have the opportunity to spend a reasonable block of time with their students, can do this. But when this is a massive testing program ... there is a movement away from mastery [learning] standards to standards based on facts and 'right answers' that can be assessed with multiple-choice questions ... What is happening to understanding? Performance goals may indeed be driving out mastery goals.

In a nutshell, if there is to be high-stakes testing, the tests should be designed to foster learning goals by rewarding understanding, rather than encourage performance goals by rewarding memory and 'right answers'.

Classroom-level changes

A key difficulty for teachers and schools wanting to improve the learning contexts for their students is that, to a large extent, many of the problems are externally imposed and there is little that teachers can do to counter them. In other words, many teachers regard the system as problematic, and feel frustrated and powerless within it. It is crucial that we recognize that many current problems are generated by the way the education system is organized and operates, and avoid approaches that 'blame the individual'. In Chapter 3 I critiqued 'blame the individual' approaches – which are sometimes implied by motivation researchers and theorists – and I argued that most motivation theorists need to engage more fully and critically with the broader educational framework and discourses that shape individual actions. I have attempted to do this throughout the book, and in my recommendations in the previous section. However, while such macro-level engagement is essential, it does little, in the short term, to help the individual classroom teacher or school who may be looking for recommendations for practice. So, without suggesting that teachers are to blame for the faults of the system, it is legitimate to ask whether there are things that teachers can do on a day-to-day basis to make the best of a far-from-perfect system. Can teachers work at the classroom level to discourage a performance-goal culture and build a learning-goal culture? I suggest that the answer to this question is a tentative yes. Tentative in the sense that while it is not possible to provide a formula for building a learning-goal classroom structure (a classroom that makes learning goals salient), it is possible to say which factors are likely to encourage one. Furthermore, it is possible to state with even more certainty which factors promote performance-goal classroom climates, which in turn encourage 'laddishness', and so should be avoided.

Encouraging safe, cooperative learning environments

Andrew Martin (2003: 28) highlights the importance of cooperative learning environments, arguing that 'it is important to reduce students' fear of failure by developing a class and school climate of cooperation, allowing students to make and learn from mistakes, and showing students that their worth as a person is independent of their academic achievement'. Yet, as we have seen, many classroom practices promote competitive climates where there are 'winners' and 'losers'; publicly announcing test results is one of those practices. Publicly announcing test results to encourage relative ability social comparisons was common in the schools in my research (although it was more common in some than others). This practice was disliked by most pupils and was seen to add to the pressure of the test. It created anxiety and, in some cases, contributed to defensive posturing. Although at Ashgrove teachers gave the boys the opportunity to receive their scores in private, as we saw in Chapter 4, this particular option was not a 'real' option for boys who wanted to present an image of cool, laid-back, 'laddish' masculinity. Overall, publicly announcing results fosters a classroom performance structure – it reinforces the importance of relative performance levels. An easy step for teachers to take in order to move away from a performance classroom climate is to avoid public relative ability social comparisons, and to discourage them among pupils.

I realize that students find other ways to undertake relative ability social comparisons of grades after tests. We saw in Chapters 4 and 6 that some pupils actively seek out the results of some classmates, and that this prompts some students to deliberately hide their results from peers and, if necessary, lie about poor marks. So moving away from a system whereby teachers publicly announce results will not stop grade comparisons, but it would mean that teachers are not encouraging or endorsing them in the same way that they are with a public results system.

Anderman *et al.* (2002) point out that while relative ability social comparisons can be problematic, some informational comparisons can be useful. So, for example, teachers might highlight the features of a particularly good piece of work, or point to a strategy that was particularly effective in approaching a problem. These strategies are not about highlighting differences in grades between students, nor about fostering competition. Rather, they are about sharing good practice and ideas. They are about helping to generate the sort of cooperation between students that can foster new approaches and strategies for learning and understanding. Fostering student cooperation rather than competition is crucial for reducing fears of failure; students need to feel that they are in an environment that is safe enough for them to explore their understandings. They need the time and (safe) space to discuss their learning, to do what Younger and Warrington (2005) refer to as 'talking themselves into understanding'. In such environments setbacks are not discouraged, but are presented as valuable opportunities to learn and develop (Midgley *et al.* 2001). A number of other researchers have highlighted the need for teachers to create 'safe' classroom environments in which students cooperate rather than compete. For example, Lucey *et al.* (2003: 55) warn against teachers providing space for confident students to compete and attempt to demonstrate their ability:

> We would suggest that teachers need to be wary of letting whole class sessions become a public arena for confident children, predominantly boys, to demonstrate their autonomy and creativity, and in which less confident children, mainly girls, dread being exposed ... pauses for group discussion may take the spotlight off individual performance; allowing less confident children to report the conclusions of their group, rather than their own answers.

Younger *et al.* (1999: 339) also endorse cooperative teaching and learning environments in their discussion of how to raise boys' attainment levels, and point out that the standards discourse militates against them.

Possibly the greatest challenge in raising boys' achievement levels is to support teachers, and to raise awareness of trainee teachers, in devising ways of working more effectively with boys, encouraging the implementation of teaching strategies which foster more discussion and collaboration in the classroom, and which support cooperative and interactive teaching and learning. It is ironic that the prevailing educational discourse of the early 1990s, with its emphasis upon league tables and competition, appears to have restricted the development and implementation of these strategies!

While reducing academic competition in class is not guaranteed to reduce competition between pupils in social contexts outside of the classroom, it is likely to have some effect. Schools that encourage cooperation rather than competition inside and outside the classroom are likely to reduce academic and social fears of failure, and so discourage academic performance goals and social status goals (competitions for social prestige within the larger peer group).

Unfortunately, at the moment there is more evidence that schools are increasing competition than reducing it.[4] As Younger and Warrington (2005: 67) point out: 'it has become conventional wisdom that boys respond to and benefit from competition rather than collaboration, and that pedagogies which emphasise competitive activities will engage and motivate boys more readily'. Based on this conventional wisdom that boys like and benefit from competition, some schools have deliberately increased competition in the classroom in an attempt to raise boys' attainment levels (see, for example, Swan 1998).[5] However, given that the pressures of competition are at the root of defensive behaviours, this strategy is likely to exacerbate the adoption of defensive strategies among boys and girls in these classes. Covington and Manheim Teel (1996: 6) argue that there is a need to reduce competition in schools if defensive behaviours are to be reduced. Indeed, they argue that learning is the first casualty in highly competitive school environments and that 'when fear is the stimulus, there are few winners in the learning game. And even the winners may pay a heavy price.'

Praising effort not intelligence
Praising children for their achievements is widely perceived to be beneficial; the benefits of it are largely unquestioned and generally regarded as 'common sense'. However, Dweck (2000) argues that praising achievement is problematic, and her case, and the evidence she presents to support it, are persuasive. Her research over many years, in a series of different studies with a diverse range of students, has shown that praise for achievements is related to a range of negative, albeit unintended, consequences. Overall, Dweck argues that praise for intelligence for a job well done has a host of

drawbacks. First, she demonstrated that this type of praise can make children sacrifice learning by shying away from challenging tasks that could jeopardize this positive judgement of their intelligence. Instead, they gravitate towards easier tasks that reaffirm the view that they are clever. Second, she found that intelligence praise makes students so oriented towards performance goals that they will lie about failure. We saw that this was relatively common among interviewees in my research. Third, it also makes students vulnerable to failure so that after they encountered a setback their persistence and their enjoyment dwindled, their performance suffered and their faith in their ability plummeted. Fourth, it cultivates the view that intelligence is fixed rather than incremental, which means that students are more likely to give up, rather than try harder, when they encounter failure.

By contrast, Dweck argues that effort praise promotes a host of desirable outcomes. First, effort praise leads to learning goals. Second, it promotes the view that challenge promotes learning; challenge is not something that indicts their ability. In other words, it is more likely to encourage persistence in the face of a setback. Third, effort praise encourages the view that intelligence is malleable and developed through effort, rather than fixed.

Dweck's theory and research is interesting, and from a motivation point of view makes a lot of sense. She is not suggesting that pupils are not praised for their success, but that they are praised for the effort that went into it, and the strategies the students adopted, rather than for being 'clever'. In so doing, she argues that we can begin to chip away at the notion that effortless achievement – which is at the core of 'laddishness' – is the ideal. For example, she raises the question of what teachers should do when there is no effort to praise: when a student has done something quickly, easily and perfectly. This, she argues, is a time when we are sorely tempted to give intelligence praise. But she suggests that instead the teacher should apologize for wasting their time with something that was not challenging enough for them to learn anything from. Dweck (2000: 121) argues that 'We should not make easy successes the pinnacle of accomplishment and we should not be teaching our children that low-effort products are what they should be most proud of. We should direct them to more profitable activities where their time will be better invested.' What is crucial to bear in mind about Dweck's suggestion is that it must be applied consistently, in social as well as academic domains. It is essential that teachers do not fall into the trap of praising some children for ability and others for effort, or those praised for effort will quickly assume that they are being praised for effort because they lack ability.

While from an academic motive point of view Dweck's suggestions have much to recommend them, when we bring social motives into the equation the situation gets more complex. We have seen, for example, that many pupils hide their work and effort because it is not regarded as cool to work hard, and that effortless achievement is positioned as an ideal. As a result of the dominance of the uncool to work discourse, students in Younger and Warrington's (2005) research suggested that although students welcome praise from teachers for their work, it should not be too overt. Presumably praise from teachers that is too obvious makes them look swotty. Furthermore, praise for effort is even more problematic for students who do not want to appear swotty than praise for performance (good performance is desirable if it is effortless). So how can we reconcile this with Dweck's suggestions about praise?

If we accept the argument that I have put forward in this book, then hiding work and effort is motivated by both fears of academic and social failure. If we can attempt to shift the academic climate from one in which academic ability and performance concerns dominate to one in which learning goals are fostered and cooperation is enhanced, fears of academic failure are likely to be reduced. Indeed, Dweck's suggestion about praising effort and strategy rather than intelligence is aimed at de-emphasizing performance and encouraging learning. Adopting Dweck's strategy of praising effort is not, on its own, going to be sufficient for changing the classroom climate. However, in combination with other strategies, it could be one step towards creating a cooperative and 'safe' environment in which pupils feel able to undertake challenges without the risk of being labelled as stupid.

This does not tackle directly the social motives underpinning some pupils' desires to hide their work and effort. However, the impact of reducing pupils' fears of failure may mean that classroom environments generally feel safer spaces for pupils to explore these social motives and the ways in which they are problematic. Other writers (such as Juvonen 1996) have suggested that decreasing competition and creating cooperative class-room environments in which pupils work together towards common goals[6] may well be enough to start to shift 'uncool to work' attitudes. Furthermore, if we can begin to tackle the notion that effortless achieve-ment is an ideal, we will be beginning to tackle a belief that is at the very heart of 'laddishness'.

Conclusion

In this chapter I drew out a number of implications for policy-makers and schoolteachers from the key theories and findings presented in this book. While there are no straightforward ways of eradicating some of the prob-lematic aspects of 'laddish' behaviours, I have discussed various ways in which they might be reduced. I focused in particular on the 'uncool to work' aspect of 'laddishness'. I argued that this is fostered by performance climates in which fears of failure are common. If schools want to encourage 'cool to learn' attitudes, they need to reduce defensive strategies and promote positive reasons for learning. I discussed: reducing high-stakes testing; using tests that encourage learning rather than performance goals; creating 'safe' cooperative learning environments; and praising effort not intelligence.

Conclusion

If it was really cool to work hard in school and you got status from working hard, would you work hard?
Yes I would, I would if it was [cool]. But because at the moment it's not, I just don't [work hard]. I don't try and I don't intend to.

(Sandy, Hollydale)

Sandy's unambiguous and resolute declaration conveys the power of the 'uncool to work' discourse; a discourse that lies at the heart of 'laddishness'. Within this discourse 'cool' is associated with an overt rejection of academic work, messing around in class, and prioritizing social over academic pursuits. Throughout this book, I have explored the attitudes and behaviours that are frequently labelled as 'laddish' in contemporary secondary school contexts, focusing in particular on the 'uncool to work' aspect that is voiced so determinedly by Sandy. I have endeavoured to understand what motivates 'laddishness', and suggested that the motives are not single, but multiple, shifting, and operating at various levels of consciousness. Importantly, these motives are underpinned by both academic and social concerns.

Drawing on goal theory, self-worth theory and empirical data, I argued and demonstrated that in some cases 'laddish' behaviours are motivated by fears of academic failure. Fears of academic failure are relatively common in contemporary secondary schooling, and are fuelled by dominant and powerful standards and credentials discourses. These discourses, which operate in conjunction with broader neoliberal discourses, emphasize the value and importance of academic 'success' and attaining academic credentials. Academic credentials are positioned as key to building a 'successful' life. Pupils in my research were acutely aware of the importance of academic credentials for their futures. Without exception, interviewees were able to recount well-rehearsed links between good exam results and successful careers. They were equally able to recount warnings and horror stories about the consequences of academic failure, namely 'dead-end' jobs and no prospect of wealth or happiness. Messages about the consequences of academic failure were both omnipotent and ubiquitous.

The high value attached to academic ability combined with the current, regular, high-stakes ability testing programmes in schools is a potent recipe for fostering fears of academic failure. These fears may then prompt a range of defensive strategies that act to protect a student's self-worth by providing 'explanations' for academic 'failure' that deflect attention away from a lack of academic ability onto other, less damaging reasons. These defensive behaviours include, among others, an overt rejection of academic work, messing around in class, and prioritizing social over academic pursuits – the same set of behaviours that are labelled as 'laddish'. These strategies hold substantial appeal for students who fear looking 'stupid' as a result of (actual or potential) 'poor' test results; they can also appeal to students who want to bolster their achievements by presenting them as effortless. However, in the long term, defensive strategies may lead to problems both for a student's academic attainment and experiences of schooling. Overall, there is a strong case for arguing that 'laddish' behaviours are motivated in part by fears of academic failure; but that is clearly not the end of the story.

'Laddish' behaviours can also be motivated by social goals because 'laddish' ways of performing masculinity or femininity are generally regarded as 'cool' and earn pupils 'popularity points' among peers. In other words, some students may behave 'laddishly' in an attempt to be popular, or to avoid being unpopular. Social relationships constitute a crucial component of school life, and the consequences of social failure – frequent marginalization and/or bullying – can be extremely distressing for students. Fears of social failure motivate many pupils to try to 'fit in' because they are afraid of the consequences of becoming unpopular. 'Fitting in' generally involves conforming to models of hegemonic masculinity or normative femininity for boys and girls, respectively. In recent accounts, boys' 'laddish' behaviours – especially the 'uncool to work' facet – have most commonly been explained by reference to theories about hegemonic masculinity. According to this theory, academic work is perceived as 'feminine' and therefore incompatible with hegemonic masculinity. However, I have argued that this theory does not enable us to explain the ways in which some boys' relationships with overt academic work vary according to whether they do well on, or 'fail', an achievement-related activity. For example, it does not explain why some boys hide their work and effort in relation to academic tasks only when they 'fail', and do not do this in relation to tasks on which they are 'successful'. Neither does it explain why many girls regard academic work as uncool. By considering pupils' social and academic goals *in combination*, however, we are able to interpret and understand a broader range of 'laddish' behaviours.

The narratives of the vast majority of interviewees in this research brought into sharp relief the importance of both social and academic goals in their daily school lives. Students who are seen to 'have it all' in school are those who can balance academic and social demands: those who are socially and academically 'successful'. What's more, they must manage to be socially and academically 'successful' with little apparent effort. This is a very difficult act to manage, but is undoubtedly facilitated by the types of resources that are more readily accessed by middle-class students.

While students' accounts highlight the importance of social relationships for their school experiences, the importance of these is generally marginalized in standards discourses which emphasize testing, targets and results. The 'success' of schooling is judged almost exclusively in terms of exam results; consequently, there is a danger that we are increasingly losing sight of 'non-academic', non-testable aspects of school life. This is particularly the case for boys, for whom concerns about 'laddishness' are inextricably linked to fears about 'underachievement'. For girls, the picture is slightly different. Girls are presented in popular discourse as 'successful' – despite lots of evidence to the contrary – so concerns about 'laddishness' among girls relate less to the consequences of 'ladette' behaviours for their academic achievements, and more to the ways in which they transgress normative femininity. Gender double standards are ubiquitous. There is an argument for celebrating some aspects of 'ladette' behaviours, for example assertiveness and confidence, but being wary of the ways in which other aspects might impact negatively on girls' experiences and attainment in school.

The task I set at the start of this book was to explore 'laddish' behaviours among girls and boys with a view to attempting to understand what motivates them, particularly the 'uncool to work' aspect. I have argued that academic and social status motives are central to 'lad' and 'ladette' behaviours. Ironically, it may be in part the measures that were introduced to raise standards – the increased testing, monitoring, competition, emphasis on performance – that actually encourage defensive, 'laddish' attitudes among boys and girls.

Notes

Introduction

1   I employ the term 'discourse' to refer to 'groups of statements which structure the way a thing is thought, and the way we act on the basis of that thinking. In other words, discourse is a particular knowledge about the world which shapes how the world is understood and how things are done in it' (Rose 2001: 136).

2   I recognize that the term 'underachievement' is problematic in a whole host of ways, not least because it raises questions about who, or what, pupils are defined as 'underachieving' in relation to, and how and why these points of comparison are established. Furthermore, definitions of 'underachievement' vary considerably. See West and Pennell (2003) for a discussion of this. Despite these issues, it would still be grossly misleading and problematic to suggest that all 'laddish' boys are 'underachievers', or that all 'underachievers' are 'laddish'.

3   In a very small number of cases, pupils that I had selected were unavailable, so others were substituted based on availability.

Chapter 1

1   In this book I make a distinction between social and academic goals or motives. While I recognize that this distinction is artificial in some senses – in that learning is inevitably social – at many levels the distinction is both useful and valid.

2   In response to the statement 'playing sport is important to me', where pupils responded on a 5-point scale where 1 was 'not at all true' and 5 was 'very true', the mean and median scores for boys at Oakfield were 3.28 and 3 compared to: Elmwood 3.49 and 4; Firtrees 3.68 and 4; Beechwood 3.43 and 3.5; Ashgrove 3.52 and 4.

3   Although 'ladettes' were portrayed as similar to 'lads' in terms of some behaviours, they are not 'tomboys'. There are important differences between 'ladettes' and 'tomboys' (see Jackson 2006 for a full discussion of these). In summary, unlike 'tomboys', 'ladettes' are (hetero)sexualized and they 'hang around' with boys in very different ways to 'tomboys'. While 'tomboys' are typically 'honorary lads' and so insufficiently feminine to be sexually attractive to them (Frosh *et al.* 2002; Paechter and Clark 2005; Renold 2005b), 'ladettes' are generally sexually attractive to boys. Feminine appearance and fashion are generally important to 'ladettes'.

4   See Jackson and Tinkler (forthcoming) for a comparison and analysis of press representations of post-school-age 'ladettes' and 'Modern Girls' of the 1920s.

5   The 'expected' or 'target' level for KS3 SATs is 5. The maximum levels are 7 for English and science and 8 for maths.

6   The girls who identified as 'ladettes' had not necessarily heard the term prior to the interview. However, they identified with the pattern of behaviours that we talked about as being typical 'ladette' behaviours according to media definitions (see Appendix 3).

7   Much recent writing suggests that while it is uncool for boys to work hard, it is acceptable for girls (Osler and Vincent 2003; Power *et al.* 2003; Francis and Skelton 2005).

8   Although Francis and Skelton (2005) argue that the 'boys will be boys' discourse is in decline, there was lots of evidence of it among teachers and pupils in this research.

9   Of course, not all girls are 'successful' in school examinations. For example, in 2003, 43.3 per cent of girls overall failed to attain five or more A*–C grades at GCSE or GNVQ. There are marked differences between girls' results when ethnicity and social class are taken into account. For example, while in 2003, 70.3 per cent of Indian girls attained five or more A*–C grades at GCSE or GNVQ, only 40.3 per cent of black Caribbean girls did (Francis and Skelton 2005: 163).

Chapter 2

1   In using the term 'performance-approach-oriented student' I am suggesting neither that goals are a feature of the individual nor that they are stable. Rather, I regard goals as fluid and dynamic. As Dweck (1996: 190) argues, 'an event like failure, conflict, or rejection can elicit new goals (or change the relative values of existing goals)'.

2   Academic efficacy, also termed self-efficacy, refers to an individual's beliefs about their capacity to succeed on specific tasks, for example a set of algebraic problems.

3   Self-handicapping involves an individual creating obstacles to success-ful performance on tasks that s/he considers important. For example, purposely getting drunk the night before an exam, or deliberately not studying for an exam, would constitute self-handicapping (Urdan and Midgley 2001: 116). Self-handicapping is discussed more fully in Chapter 6.

4   Researchers are now beginning to explore the ways in which perform-ance-approach goals can combine with learning goals to promote optimum learning, as there is evidence that students can and do pursue multiple goals (Harackiewicz *et al.* 2002). It seems likely that the emphasis in achievement goal theory on multiple goals will continue (Freeman 2004), as will the recent but increasing interest in social goals (Ryan *et al.* 2004). However, research in both of these areas is still in its infancy (Pintrich 2003).

5   The values attached to different areas tend to be gendered and classed, with 'masculine' and 'academic' areas being attributed more worth than 'feminine' and 'manual' ones (Spender 1989; Paechter 1998, 2000).

6   While Covington talks about Western societies in general, it is worth bearing in mind that there will be variations between countries in the value attached to academic attainment. The work of Marilyn Osborn and Patricia Broadfoot, for example, highlights some interesting differ-ences between England and France in terms of classroom pedagogy (see Broadfoot and Osborn 1993; Osborn and Broadfoot 1993; Osborn *et al.* 1997). Elliot *et al.* (2005) highlight important differences in teaching styles and pupil motivation in Sunderland (England), Kentucky (USA) and St Petersburg (Russia).

7   While Covington stresses the importance of academic attainment for students' self-worth, he tends to neglect the importance of social rela-tions; this is discussed in Chapter 3.

8   While self-worth and social worth are conceptually different (self-worth relates principally to an individual's self-perceptions and social worth relates principally to the individual's perceptions of what other people think of them), in practice it is often difficult to separate them. As such, some authors argue that self-worth and social worth are inseparable and operate mutually in self-protective behaviour (Thompson 1999: 23). In this book I use the term 'self-worth' to incorporate self-worth and social worth.

Chapter 3

[1]   In some subject areas boys are less likely, or unlikely, to need to hide work and effort. For example, working hard in physical education (P.E.) is acceptable, although even here 'effortless achievement' is particularly desirable (see Chapter 6).

[2]   Frequently, a combination of social and academic motives are at work. Whether social or academic motives are foregrounded in any particular case is likely to depend on the individual and the context.

Chapter 4

[1]   Although there have been attempts to indicate how much progress students make within a school by including information about 'value-added', methods for calculating value-added are the subject of much controversy and critique (e.g. Gorard 2005). Furthermore, it is exam results rather than the 'value-added' data that tend to be prioritized.

[2]   While being able to cope has traditionally been associated with masculinity, it is increasingly associated with both female and male 'successful' neoliberal subjects.

Chapter 5

[1]   *Post hoc* analyses for the Kruskal-Wallis test are commonly Mann-Whitney tests. Unfortunately, conducting lots of Mann-Whitney tests will inflate the Type I error rate. The Bonferroni correction is applied to counter the build up of Type I errors. The Bonferroni correction means that instead of using .05 as the critical value for significance, the critical value is .05 divided by the number of tests conducted. If too many tests are conducted, the critical value becomes prohibitively small (Field 2005). As such, after studying the descriptive statistics, I conducted six tests that I thought would be most useful in determining where differences between schools were located. In this case the application of the Bonferroni correction meant that all effects are reported at a .008 level of significance.

Chapter 6

1 As mentioned earlier, this is always subjective. For example, some students may consider a 'poor' performance to be one in which they did not attain one of the top five scores in their set.
2 As outlined in Chapter 1, while self-worth and social worth are conceptually different, in practice it is often difficult to separate them. In this book I use the term 'self-worth' to incorporate self-worth and social worth as they operate mutually in self-protective behaviour.

Chapter 7

1 These figures are likely to be an underestimate of how many pupils hide work and effort', as some pupils may not admit to themselves that they do this.
2 She also argues that cool, black working-classness is also equated with criminality.

Chapter 8

1 In the UK there is currently a lot of discussion about 'vocational education', particularly since the publication of what is commonly referred to as the 'Tomlinson Report' (2004) on 14–19 curriculum and qualifications reform. The Tomlinson Report recommended that there should be more scope for young people to follow their interests by introducing a greater choice of relevant vocational programmes and activities. Such programmes were flagged as being particularly important for those young people who currently 'disengage' from school learning. It would be interesting to explore the implications of vocational education for 'laddish' behaviours, but it is beyond the scope of this project.
2 In this section I refer specifically to academic subjects; physical education (P.E.), which is frequently referred to as a non-academic subject, is an exception. As we saw in previous chapters, sporting prowess is central to popularity for boys and so, although not formally tested, P.E. is nevertheless given high priority by most boys who are or want to be popular. This illustrates the complex ways in which social and academic concerns interrelate.
3 SATs are no longer compulsory in Wales.
4 Some professional development programmes for teachers attempt to counter this trend by employing models that encourage students to work in collaborative learning communities, and create 'safe' classroom environments; for example, the Critical Skills Programme (Marshall

2005). An evaluation of the Critical Skills Programme in Jersey revealed that 68 per cent of children who had experienced critical skills approaches reported (via questionnaires) that they 'liked a lot' working in a team (Wragg *et al.* 2004).

5   This approach has the problems I noted earlier in that it relies on stereotypes about boys and treats boys as a homogeneous group.

6   Linda Marshall (2005), a Critical Skills Programme (CSP) manager, makes the point that there are benefits to be gained from students negotiating their own goals and criteria for success with their teachers and peers, so that they are clear about what they have to do. The CSP programme also endorses forms of peer assessment, suggesting that it helps students to recognize the strengths and weaknesses of their own work, and also helps them learn how to provide and receive feedback.

Appendix 1: Pupil questionnaire

Girls and boys had separate questionnaires; there were only a few differences between the girls' and boys' versions and these are noted below. Pupils responded to the statements on a 5-point scale which was labelled as follows: 1 – not at all true; 2 – a little true; 3 – somewhat true; 4 – mostly true; 5 – very true.

1 Being popular and having lots of mates at school is important to me.
2 I work harder at school work than I admit to my friends.
3 Doing well at school is important in order to get a good job in later life.
4 It's important to me that other students in my school think I'm cool.
5 Sport is more important to me than school work.
6 It's cool to be seen to work hard at school.
7 One of my goals is to look like I don't work hard at school.
8 I'd rather mess around in class than work hard.
9 It's important to me that I don't look geeky in school.
10 Being seen to be cool at school is important to me.
11 One of my goals is to avoid looking like I have trouble being cool.
12 There is a lot of pressure in school to get good grades.
13 It's important to me that my mates don't think I'm less cool than others at school.
14 If necessary, I would stay in to do my homework rather than go out with my mates.
15 One of my goals is to look cool in comparison to other pupils in my school.
16 I like to be 'the best' at activities that are important to me.
17 One of my goals is to show others that I'm cool.
18 It is important to me to be 'one of the lads'. [boys]
18 It's cool for girls to behave 'laddishly' at school. [girls]
19 Playing sport is important to me.
20 One of my goals is to keep others from thinking I'm not cool.

21 Being good at school work is important to me.
22 It's important to me that I look cool compared to others in my class.
23 It's important to me that I spend time outside of school going out with my mates.
24 Having the 'right sorts' of clothes and shoes is important to me.
25 Being attractive to girls is important to me. [boys]
25 Being attractive to boys is important to me. [girls]
26 If I knew that I could get a good grade in a test if I worked hard, then I would work hard.
27 I wish it was cool to work hard at school.
28 I consider myself to be 'one of the lads'. [This question was not included on the girls' questionnaire]

Appendix 2:
Brief profiles of the interviewees quoted in the book

KS3 levels: A = absent; N = no test level awarded; B = below test level.

Social class: this should be treated as a rough indicator and was assigned according to the students' declarations of the occupation(s) of their parent(s)/guardian(s). Working class = wc; middle class = mc; upper working class or lower middle class = uwc/lmc; question marks indicate cases when it was especially difficult to judge.

Ethnicity: reported by the students on the questionnaires from a list of: Indian, Pakistani, Chinese, Asian other, black Caribbean, black African, black other, mixed race, white UK/Irish, white-other.

Elmwood

Pupil	KS3 SATs levels	Social class	Ethnicity
Stacey	6, 7, 6	wc	white UK/Irish
Ruth	5, 6, 4	wc?	white UK/Irish
Penny	6, 6, 6	uwc/lmc	white UK/Irish
Zoe	7, 7, 6	uwc/lmc	white UK/Irish
Gail	6, 8, 7	mc	white UK/Irish
Lyn	7, 7, 6	mc	white UK/Irish
Chinella	7, 7, 7	mc	black other
Rosie	5, 5, 5	uwc/lmc	white UK/Irish
Louise	6, 7, 7	mc	white other
James	7, 8, 7	mc	white UK/Irish
Rob	A, 3, 2	unknown	white UK/Irish
Tahir	5, 6, 5	wc	Pakistani
Lewis	5, 6, 6	mc	white UK/Irish

cont.

Pupil	KS3 SATs levels	Social class	Ethnicity
Richard	4, 5, 3	wc	white UK/Irish
Tom	6, 7, 6	Unknown	white UK/Irish
Graham	4, 6, 5	wc	white UK/Irish
Jack	N, 3, 4	unknown	white UK/Irish
Martin	6, 6, 6	wc	white UK/Irish

Hollydale Girls'

Pupil	KS3 SATs levels	Social class	Ethnicity
Steph	6, 7, 6	mc	white UK/Irish
Paula	6, 6, 6	mc	white UK/Irish
Sandy	4, 4, 3	mc	white UK/Irish
Faya	unknown	wc	white UK/Irish
Chloe	5, 6, 5	wc	Indian
Amy	5, 6, 5	mc	white UK/Irish
Julie	5, 6, 5	mc	white UK/Irish
Clara	6, 7, 6	mc	white UK/Irish
Neelam	5, 5, 5	wc?	Indian
Hazel	5, 6, 6	mc	white UK/Irish
Lisa	5, 6, 6	uwc/lmc	white UK/Irish
Lesley	5, 7, 6	mc	white UK/Irish
Hannah	5, 6, 6	uwc/lmc	black other
Samantha	6, 6, 6	mc	white UK/Irish
Alice	5, 7, 5	mc	white UK/Irish
Iram	6, 6, 5	mc?	Pakistani
Alysia	4, 4, 4	wc	white UK/Irish

Firtrees

Pupil	KS3 SATs levels	Social class	Ethnicity
Julia	5, 7, 6	wc	white UK/Irish
Jade	4, 4, 4	wc	white UK/Irish
Sarah	6, 6, 6	mc	white UK/Irish
Clare	5, 4, 4	unknown	white UK/Irish
Diane	5, 5, 5	unknown	white UK/Irish
Hannah	6, 6, 6	mc	white UK/Irish

cont.

Pupil	KS3 SATs levels	Social class	Ethnicity
Jenny	6, 6, 6	unknown	white UK/Irish
Sally	5, 6, 5	mc	white UK/Irish
Jane	5, 5, 5	wc	white UK/Irish
Melanie	6, 6, 6	mc	white UK/Irish
Paul	6, 6, 6	mc	white UK/Irish
Anthony	5, 7, 5	uwc/lmc	white UK/Irish
Ian	4, 5, 4	unknown	white UK/Irish
Keith	5, 4, 4	wc	white UK/Irish

Beechwood

Pupil	KS3 SATs levels	Social class	Ethnicity
Jan	5, 5, 4	uwc/lmc?	white UK/Irish
Fran	4, A, 5	wc	white UK/Irish
Wendy	5, 5, 5	wc	white UK/Irish
Dana	5, 4, 5	wc	white UK/Irish
Tamina	5, 5, 5	wc	Indian
Amina	N, 4, 4	wc	Pakistani
Becky	5, 5, 5	uwc/lmc?	white UK/Irish
Judy	5, 4, 4	wc	white UK/Irish
Helen	3, 3, B	wc	white UK/Irish
Wayne	3, 3, 5	mc?	white UK/Irish
Mark	4, 3, 4	unknown	white UK/Irish
Danny	3, 3, A	unknown	white other
Craig	6, 5, 6	uwc/lmc	white UK/Irish
Kieran	5, 6, 4	mc?	white UK/Irish

Oakfield

Pupil	KS3 SATs levels	Social class	Ethnicity
Nassima	6, 6, 5	mc	Pakistani
Aisha	6, 6, 6	wc?	Pakistani
Shareen	5, 5, 5	unknown	Pakistani
Salma	N, 2, 3	unknown	Pakistani

cont.

Pupil	KS3 SATs levels	Social class	Ethnicity
Rehana	5, 5, 4	unknown	Pakistani
Sameena	4, 3, 3	unknown	Pakistani
Imran	N, 3, 3	wc?	Pakistani
Sikander	5, 6, 4	mc?	Pakistani
Jawad	5, 7, 6	wc	Pakistani
Zuber	5, 6, 6	mc	Indian
Jordan	6, 7, 7	mc	white UK/Irish
Masoom	5, 6, 6	mc	Bangladeshi
Adil	4, 6, 5	unknown	Pakistani
Shuhayb	4, 3, 3	unknown	Pakistani
Bilal	5, 6, 5	wc?	Pakistani

Ashgrove Boys'

Pupil	KS3 SATs levels	Social class	Ethnicity
Dean	5, 7, 6	mc	white UK/Irish
Damian	3, 5, 4	unknown	white UK/Irish
Stu	6, 7, 6	unknown	unknown
Liam	6, 8, 6	mc?	white UK/Irish
Mick	4, 6, 6	mc	white UK/Irish
Pete	5, 7, 6	mc	white UK/Irish
Alistair	6, 6, 5	mc	white UK/Irish
Talha	5, 6, 6	unknown	Indian
Julian	5, 5, 5	mc	white UK/Irish
Darren	6, 7, 6	mc?	white UK/Irish
Simon	5, 6, 6	mc	white UK/Irish
Jim	5, 7, 6	mc?	white UK/Irish
Doug	5, 7, 5	mc?	white UK/Irish
Nigel	4, 6, 5	mc	white UK/Irish
Zahir	6, 6, 7	mc	Indian
Andrew	7, 7, 7	mc	white UK/Irish
Alan	5, 6, 5	mc?	white UK/Irish
Lawrence	5, 7, 6	wc?	white UK/Irish

Appendix 3:
Pupil interview schedule

This is a guide to the types of questions asked in the interviews. Questions were amended slightly according the school and the time of year. For example, questions about 'laddish' boys were not asked at the girls' school; questions about the SATs were amended depending on whether they were asked before or after the exams. Most questions were followed up by additional probing questions; the discussions were, to a large extent, interviewee led.

School work

1 Do you work hard at school?
2 Do you do well at school?
    How do you know how well you do/how do you judge your performance?
3 I believe that you've got SATs tests coming up soon.
    Are you working hard for them?
    Are you nervous about them?
4 Can you tell me about the last time that you felt that you had failed an exam or a piece of work or the last time that you felt very disappointed by a mark? How did this make you feel? Why?
    What caused you to get this mark that you were disappointed with?
5 Do you get nervous or worried about tests or work?
    How do you feel if you work hard at something and get a poor mark? Why?
6 Would you feel better if you worked hard at something but got a low mark or if you didn't work hard at something but got a low mark?
7 What do you tell your friends if you get a low(er) mark? How do you explain it?
8 Would you ever pretend that you'd not worked hard at something when really you had?

9   Do you ever put obstacles in the way of your work so that you have an excuse if you don't do as well as you hoped?
10 Do you ever not do school work because you worry that you won't be able to do it? Do others? Evidence/examples?
11 Would you ever pretend that you had worked hard at something when really you hadn't?
12 How do you feel when you get a good mark?
      What do you tell your friends?
13 Is there pressure on you to get good marks?
      From whom?
      Is there any pressure *not* to work hard?
      From whom?
      Do you hide the fact that you work?

Laddishness

14 Do pupils talk in school about being 'one of the lads'?
      What does it mean to be a lad?
      What does a lad do?
      What does a lad not do?
15 Can someone who works hard at school be a 'lad'?
16 Is it seen as cool to work hard?
      Who defines what is cool?
      What are the consequences of being cool or not cool?
17 Some people argue that boys' attempts to be 'one of the lads' make their school work suffer. Do you agree?

Ladettes

18 Do pupils talk in school about 'ladettes'?
      What does it mean to be a ladette?
      Are there any 'ladettes' in your year?
      What does a ladette do?
      What does a ladette not do?
      Do you consider yourself to be a ladette?
19 Can someone who works hard at school be a ladette?
      How would she manage working hard and being cool?
20 Is it seen as cool to work hard?
      Who defines what is cool?
      What are the consequences of being cool or not cool?
21 Some people argue that girls' attempts to be a ladette make their school work suffer.
      Do you agree?
      Why?

As far as possible I wanted to explore pupils' own perceptions of what 'ladettes' might be like before discussing how they are represented in the media. The vast majority of pupils had never heard the term 'ladette'; the small minority that had interpreted it broadly to mean 'tomboy' (see Jackson 2006). Where pupils interpreted 'ladette' to mean 'tomboy', I usually explored this with them and then went on to discuss 'ladettes' as portrayed in the media. The girls who identified as 'ladettes' had not necessarily heard the term prior to the interview. However, they identified with the pattern of behaviours that we talked about as being typical 'ladette' behaviours according to media definitions.

Appendix 4:
Teacher interview schedule

This is an outline of the key interview topics that were provided to teachers in advance of the interview. As with the pupil interview schedule, it was tailored to some degree to the school – particularly the single-sex schools. Questions were followed up by additional probing questions; the discussions were, to a large extent, interviewee led.

What do you understand 'laddishness' to mean?

- What is a 'lad'?
- What does a lad do? What are 'laddish' behaviours?
- Is 'laddish' behaviour problematic? Is it always?
- Can 'lads' be high academic achievers? How? Who?
- Why is 'laddish' behaviour attractive to some boys?

Is 'laddishness' (among boys) an issue at your school?

- How?
- Why?
- Which groups?

Is 'laddishness' an issue among girls?

- How?
- Why?
- Which groups?

How is 'laddishness' dealt with at your school?

- Individual teacher level
- School level

How could schools/teachers tackle 'laddish' attitudes?

References

Aapola, S., Gonick, M. and Harris, A. (2005) *Young Femininity: Girlhood, Power and Social Change.* Basingstoke: Palgrave Macmillan.

Adam, B. (1995) *Timewatch: The Social Analysis of Time.* Cambridge: Polity Press.

Anderman, L.H. and Freeman, T.M. (2004) Students' sense of belonging in school, in P.R. Pintrich and M.L. Maehr (eds) *Motivating Students, Improving Schools: The Legacy of Carol Midgley.* London: Elsevier.

Anderman, L.H. and Midgley, C. (2002) Methods for studying goals, goal structures, and patterns of adaptive learning, in C. Midgley (ed.) *Goals, Goal Structures, and Patterns of Adaptive Learning.* London: Lawrence Erlbaum Associates.

Anderman, L.H., Patrick, H., Hruda, L.Z. and Linnenbrink, E.A. (2002) Observing classroom goal structures to clarify and expand goal theory, in C. Midgley (ed.) *Goals, Goal Structures, and Patterns of Adaptive Learning.* London: Lawrence Erlbaum Associates.

Archer, L. (2003) *Race, Masculinity and Schooling: Muslim Boys and Education.* Maidenhead: Open University Press.

Archer, L. and Leathwood, C. (eds) (2003) Diverse working class femininities and education, special edition of *Gender and Education,* 15(3).

Archer, L., Halsall, A., Hollingworth, S. and Mendick, H. (2005) 'Dropping out and drifting away': an investigation of factors affecting inner-city pupils' identities, aspirations and post-16 routes. Executive Summary Report. London: Institute for Policy Studies in Education, London Metropolitan University.

Arnot, M., David, M. and Weiner, G. (1999) *Closing the Gender Gap: Postwar Education and Social Change.* Cambridge: Polity Press.

Arnot, M. and Miles, P. (2005) A reconstruction of the gender agenda: The contradictory gender dimensions in New Labour's educational and economic policy, *Oxford Review of Education,* 21(1): 173–89.

Arnot, M. and Weiner, G. (eds) (1987) *Gender and the Politics of Schooling.* London: Hutchinson in association with Open University Press.

Beck, U. (1992) *The Risk Society.* London: Sage.

Broadfoot, P. and Osborn, M., with Gilly, M. and Bucher, A. (1993) *Perceptions of Teaching: Primary School Teachers in England and France.* London: Cassell.

Brown, J. (2005) 'Violent girls': same or different from 'other' girls?, in G. Lloyd (ed.) *Problem Girls: Understanding and Supporting Troubled and Troublesome Girls and Young Women.* London: RoutledgeFalmer.

Brown, P. (1997) Cultural capital and social exclusion: some observations on recent trends in education, employment, and the labour market, in A.H. Halsey, H. Lauder, P. Brown and A. Stuart Wells (eds) *Education, Economy, Culture and Society.* Oxford: Oxford University Press.

Brown, P., Halsey, A.H., Lauder, H. and Stuart Wells, A. (1997) The transformation of education and society: an introduction, in A.H. Halsey, H. Lauder, P. Brown and A. Stuart Wells (eds) *Education, Economy, Culture and Society.* Oxford: Oxford University Press.

Butler, J. (2004) *Undoing Gender.* London: Routledge.

Carrigan, T., Connell, R. and Lee, J. (1985) Toward a new sociology of masculinity, *Theory and Society*, 14: 551–604.

Clare, J. (2003) Respect for teacher 'is key to boys doing well': Ofsted study finds bad teaching can promote a laddish culture, *Daily Telegraph*, 11 July.

Clark, L. (2004) The ladettes aged 15, *Daily Mail*, 26 January. www.dailymail. co.uk/pages/live/articles/health/womenfamily.html?in_article_id=2066 76&in_page_id=1799 (accessed 26 August 2004).

Cohen, M. (1998) 'A habit of healthy idleness': boys' underachievement in historical perspective, in D. Epstein, J. Elwood, V. Hey and J. Maw (eds) *Failing Boys? Issues in Gender and Achievement.* Buckingham: Open University Press.

Connell, R.W. (1995) *Masculinities.* Cambridge: Polity Press.

Connell, R.W. (2005) *Masculinities* (2nd edn). Cambridge: Polity Press.

Connolly, P. (2004) *Boys and Schooling in the Early Years.* London: RoutledgeFalmer.

Covington, M.V. (1992) *Making the Grade: A Self-Worth Perspective on Motivation and School Reform.* Cambridge: Cambridge University Press.

Covington, M.V. (1998) *The Will to Learn: A Guide for Motivating Young People.* Cambridge: Cambridge University Press.

Covington, M.V. (1999) Caring about learning: the nature and nurturing of subject-matter appreciation, *Educational Psychologist*, 34(2): 127–36.

Covington, M.V. (2000) Goal theory, motivation, and school achievement: an integrative review, *Annual Review of Psychology*, 51: 171–200.

Covington, M.V. (2002) Patterns of adaptive learning study: where do we go from here?, in C. Midgley (ed.) *Goals, Goal Structures, and Patterns of Adaptive Learning.* London: Lawrence Erlbaum Associates.

Covington, M.V. and Beery, R.G. (1976) *Self-Worth and School Learning.* New

York: Holt, Rinehart & Winston.

Covington, M.V. and Manheim Teel, K. (1996) *Overcoming Student Failure: Changing Motives and Incentives for Learning*. Washington DC: American Psychological Association.

Cox, C.B. and Giuliano, T.A. (1999) Constructing obstacles vs. making excuses: examining perceivers' reactions to behavioural and self-reported self-handicapping, *Journal of Social Behavior and Personality*, 14(3): 419–32.

David, M.E. (2004) A feminist critique of public policy discourses about educational effectiveness, in S. Ali, S. Benjamin and M.L. Mauthner (eds) *The Politics of Gender and Education: Critical Perspectives*. Basingstoke: Palgrave Macmillan.

Davies, J. (2005) The roar of gender in the classroom: Twenty years on from 'Schools for the boys?'. Paper presented at the Fifth International Gender and Education Conference, University of Cardiff, 29–31 March.

Day, K., Gough, B. and McFadden, M. (2004) 'Warning! Alcohol can seriously damage your feminine health'. A discourse analysis of recent British newspaper coverage of women and drinking, *Feminist Media Studies*, 4(2): 165–83.

Deem, R. (ed.) (1984) *Co-education Reconsidered*. Milton Keynes: Open University Press.

Delamont, S. (1984) *Sex Roles and the School*. London: Methuen.

Delamont, S. (1999) Gender and the discourse of derision, *Research Papers in Education*, 14: 3–21.

Department for Education and Employment (DfEE) (2000) Boys must improve at same rate as girls – Blunkett, www.dfee.gov.uk/pns/DisplayPN.cgi?pn_id=2000_0368

Dweck, C.S. (1996) Social motivation: goals and social-cognitive processes. A comment, in J. Juvonen and K.R. Wentzel (eds) *Social Motivation: Understanding Children's School Adjustment*. Cambridge: Cambridge University Press.

Dweck, C.S. (2000) *Self-Theories: Their Role in Motivation, Personality and Development*. Hove: Taylor and Francis.

Edley, N. and Wetherill, M. (1997) Jockeying for position: the construction of masculine identities, *Discourse and Society*, 8: 203–17.

Elliot, A.J. and Harackiewicz, J.M. (1996) Approach and avoidance goals and intrinsic motivation: a mediational analysis, *Journal of Personality and Social Psychology*, 70: 461–75.

Elliot, J.G., Hufton, N.R., Willis, W. and Illushin, L. (2005) *Motivation, Engagement and Educational Performance: International Perspectives on the Contexts for Learning*. Basingstoke: Palgrave.

Epstein, D. (1997) Boyz' own stories: masculinities and sexualities in schools, *Gender and Education*, 9: 105–15.

Epstein, D. (1998) Real boys don't work: 'underachievement', masculinity, and the harassment of 'sissies', in D. Epstein, J. Elwood, V. Hey and J. Maw (eds) *Failing Boys? Issues in Gender and Achievement*. Buckingham: Open University Press.

Epstein, D. and Johnson, R. (1998) *Schooling Sexualities*. Buckingham: Open University Press.

Epstein, D., Elwood, J., Hey, V. and Maw, J. (eds) (1998) *Failing Boys? Issues in Gender and Achievement*. Buckingham: Open University Press.

Erdley, C.A. (1996) Motivational approaches to aggression within the context of peer relationships, in J. Juvonen and K.R. Wentzel (eds) *Social Motivation: Understanding Children's School Adjustment*. Cambridge: Cambridge University Press.

Evans, J., Rich, E. and Holroyd, R. (2004) Disordered eating and disordered schooling: what schools do to middle class girls, *British Journal of Sociology of Education*, 25(2): 123–42.

Field, A. (2005) *Discovering Statistics using SPSS*, 2nd edn. London: Sage.

Fielding, M. (1999) Target setting, policy pathology and student perspectives: learning to labour in new times, *Cambridge Journal of Education*, 29(2): 277–87.

Francis, B. (1999) Lads, lasses and (new) Labour 14–16-year-old students' responses to the 'laddish behaviour and boys' underachievement' debate, *British Journal of Sociology of Education*, 20(3): 355–71.

Francis, B. (2000) *Boys, Girls and Achievement: Addressing the Classroom Issues*. London: RoutledgeFalmer.

Francis, B. (2005) Not/Knowing their place: girls' classroom behaviour, in G. Lloyd (ed.) *Problem Girls: Understanding and Supporting Troubled and Troublesome Girls and Young Women*. London: RoutledgeFalmer.

Francis, B. and Archer, L. (2005a) Negotiating the dichotomy of Boffin and Triad: British-Chinese pupils' constructions of 'laddism', *Sociological Review*, 53(3): 495–521.

Francis, B. and Archer, L. (2005b) British-Chinese pupils' and parents' constructions of the value of education, *British Educational Research Journal*, 31(1): 89–107.

Francis, B. and Skelton, C. (2005) *Reassessing Gender and Achievement: Questioning Contemporary Key Debates*. London: Routledge.

Freeman, K.E. (2004) The significance of motivational culture in schools serving African American adolescents: a goal theory approach, in P.R. Pintrich and M.L. Maehr (eds) *Motivating Students, Improving Schools: The Legacy of Carol Midgley*. London: Elsevier.

Frosh, S., Phoenix, A. and Pattman, R. (2002) *Young Masculinities: Understanding Boys in Contemporary Society*. Basingstoke: Palgrave.

Furlong, A. and Cartmel, F. (1997) *Young People and Social Change: Individualisation and Risk in Late Modernity*. Buckingham: Open University Press.

Galloway, D., Rogers, C., Armstrong, D., Leo, E., with Jackson, C. (1998) *Motivating the Difficult to Teach*. London: Longman.

Gilbert, R. and Gilbert, P. (1998) *Masculinity Goes to School*. London: Routledge.

Gleeson, D. and Husbands, C. (eds) (2001) *The Performing School: Managing, Teaching and Learning in a Performance Culture*. London: RoutledgeFalmer.

Gorard, S. (2005) Value-added is of little value. Paper presented at the British Educational Research Association Conference, University of Glamorgan, 14–17 September.

Griffin, C. (2000) Discourse of crisis and loss: analysing the 'boys' under-achievement' debate, *Journal of Youth Studies*, 3(2): 167–88.

Guardian (no named reporter) (2003) Exams taking their toll on children, *Education Guardian*, 25 April, http://education.guardian.co.uk/schools/story/0,5500,943430,00.html (accessed September 2005).

Harackiewicz, J.M., Barron, K.E., Pintrich, P.R., Elliot, A.J. and Thrash, T.M. (2002) Revision of achievement goal theory: necessary and illuminating, *Journal of Educational Psychology*, 94(3): 638–45.

Hardy, F. (2005) Ladettes to ladies, *Daily Mail*, 15 January.

Harris, A. (2004) *Future Girl: Young Women in the Twenty-First Century*. London: Routledge.

Haywood, C. and Mac an Ghaill, M. (2003) *Men and Masculinities*. Buckingham: Open University Press.

Henry, J. (2003) 'Ladette' culture blamed for rise in young girls being locked up, *Daily Telegraph*, 7 September. www.telegraph.co.uk/news/main.jhtml?xml=/news/2003/09/07/nladet07.xml (accessed 26 August 2004).

Heron, L. (2002) Tackling the laddish culture among pupils, *Leicester Mercury*, 22 August.

Hey, V. (1997) *The Company She Keeps: An Ethnography of Girls' Friendships*. Buckingham: Open University Press.

Holland, S. (2004) *Alternative Femininities: Body, Age and Identity*. Oxford: Berg.

Hughes, C. (2002a) *Women's Contemporary Lives: Within and Beyond the Mirror*. London: Routledge.

Hughes, C. (2002b) *Key Concepts in Feminist Theory and Research*. London: Sage.

Hursh, D. (2005) The growth of high-stakes testing in the USA: accountability, markets and the decline in educational equality, *British Educational Research Journal*, 31(5): 605–22.

Jackson, C. (1999) 'Underachieving' boys? Some points for consideration, *Curriculum*, 20(2): 80–5.

Jackson, C. (2002a) 'Laddishness' as a self-worth protection strategy, *Gender and Education*, 14(1): 37–51.

Jackson, C. (2002b) Can single-sex classes in co-educational schools enhance the learning experiences of girls and/or boys? An exploration of pupils' perceptions, *British Educational Research Journal*, 28(1): 37–48.

Jackson, C. (2003) Motives for 'laddishness' at school: fear of failure and fear of the 'feminine', *British Educational Research Journal*, 29(4): 583–98.

Jackson, C. (2006, forthcoming) 'Wild' girls? An exploration of 'ladette' cultures in secondary schools, *Gender and Education*.

Jackson, C. and Tinkler, P. (forthcoming) 'Ladettes' and 'Modern Girls': 'troublesome' young femininities, *Sociological Review*.

James, W. (1890) *Principles of Psychology*. Chicago: Encyclopedia Britannica.

Juvonen, J. (1996) Self-presentation tactics promoting teacher and peer approval: the function of excuses and other clever explanations, in J. Juvonen and K.R. Wentzel (eds) *Social Motivation: Understanding Children's School Adjustment*. Cambridge: Cambridge University Press.

Juvonen, J. and Wentzel, K.R. (eds) (1996) *Social Motivation: Understanding Children's School Adjustment*. Cambridge: Cambridge University Press.

Kaplan, A. (2004) Achievement goals and intergroup relations, in P.R. Pintrich and M.L. Maehr (eds) *Motivating Students, Improving Schools: The Legacy of Carol Midgley*. London: Elsevier.

Kaplan, A., Gheen, M. and Midgley, C. (2002b) Classroom goal structure and student disruptive behaviour, *British Journal of Educational Psychology*, 72(2): 191–211.

Kaplan, A., Middleton, M.J., Urdan, T. and Midgley, C. (2002a) Achievement goals and goal structures, in: C. Midgley (ed.) *Goals, Goal Structures, and Patterns of Adaptive Learning*. London: Lawrence Erlbaum Associates.

Kehily, M.J. (2001) Issues of gender and sexuality in schools, in B. Francis and C. Skelton (eds) *Investigating Gender: Contemporary Perspectives in Education*. Buckingham: Open University Press.

Kenway, J. and Fitzclarence, L. (1997) Masculinity, violence and schooling: challenging 'poisonous pedagogies', *Gender and Education*: 117–33.

Kenway, J. and Willis, S., with Blackmore, J. and Rennie, L. (1998) *Answering Back: Girls, Boys and Feminism in Schools*. London: Routledge.

Kenway, J., Willis, S. and Nevard, J. (1990) The subtle politics of self-esteem programs for girls, in J. Kenway and S. Willis (eds) *Hearts and Minds: Self-Esteem and the Schooling of Girls*. London: The Falmer Press.

Krapp, A. (2003) Interest and human development: an educational-psychological perspective, in L. Smith, C. Rogers and P. Tomlinson (eds) *British Journal of Educational Psychology Monograph Series II, Part 2* (Development and motivation: joint perspectives): 57–84.

Kupersmidt, J.B., Buchele, K.S., Voegler, M.E. and Sedikides, C. (1996) Social self-discrepancy: a theory relating peer relations problems and school maladjustment, in J. Juvonen and K.R. Wentzel (eds) *Social Motivation:*

Understanding Children's School Adjustment. Cambridge: Cambridge University Press.

Lees, S. (1986) *Losing Out.* London: Hutchinson.

Lees, S. (1993) *Sugar and Spice: Sexuality and Adolescent Girls.* London: Penguin.

Linnenbrink, E.A. (2004) Person and context: theoretical and practical concerns in achievement goal theory, in P.R. Pintrich and M.L. Maehr (eds) *Motivating Students, Improving Schools: The Legacy of Carol Midgley.* London: Elsevier.

Lloyd, G. (ed.) (2005) *Problem Girls: Understanding and Supporting Troubled and Troublesome Girls and Young Women.* London: RoutledgeFalmer.

Lucey, H., Brown, M., Denvir, H., Askew, M. and Rhodes, V. (2003) Girls and boys in the primary maths classroom, in C. Skelton and B. Francis (eds) *Boys and Girls in the Primary Classroom.* Maidenhead: Open University Press.

Mac an Ghaill, M. (1994) *The Making of Men: Masculinities, Sexualities and Schooling.* Buckingham: Open University Press.

Maehr, M. and Arbor, A. (2002) Foreword, in C. Midgley (ed.) *Goals, Goal Structures, and Patterns of Adaptive Learning.* London: Lawrence Erlbaum Associates.

Mahoney, P. (1985) *Schools for the Boys? Co-education Reassessed.* London: Hutchinson.

Mansell, W. (2005) Call to scrap key stage tests, *The Times Educational Supplement*, 1 April.

Marsh, P., Rosser, E. and Harre, R. (1978) *The Rules of Disorder.* London: Routledge.

Marshall, L. (2005) Personal communication. For information about the Critical Skills Programme, see: www.criticalskills.co.uk

Martin, A.J. (2003) Enhancing the educational outcomes of boys, *Youth Studies Australia*, 22(4): 27–36.

Martin, A.J. and Marsh, H.W. (2003) Fear of failure: Friend or foe? *Australian Psychologist*, 38(1): 31–8.

Martin, A., Marsh, H.W. and Debus, R.L. (2003) Self-handicapping and defensive pessimism, and goal orientation: a qualitative study of university students, *Journal of Educational Psychology*, 95(3): 617–28.

Martin, A., Marsh, H.W., Williamson, A. and Debus, R.L. (2003) Self-handicapping and defensive pessimism: a model of self-protection from a longitudinal perspective, *Contemporary Educational Psychology*, 28: 1–36.

Martino, W. (1999) 'Cool boys', 'party animals', 'squids' and 'poofters': interrogating the dynamics and politics of adolescent masculinities in school, *British Journal of Sociology of Education*, 20(2): 239–63.

Martino, W. and Meyenn, B. (eds) (2001) *What about the Boys? Issues of Masculinity in Schools.* Buckingham: Open University Press.

Martino, M. and Meyenn, B. (2002) 'War, guns and cool, tough things': interrogating single-sex classes as a strategy for engaging boys in English, *Cambridge Journal of Education*, 32(3): 303–24.

Martino, M. and Pallotta-Chiarolli, M. (2003) *So What's a Boy? Addressing Issues of Masculinity and Schooling*. Maidenhead: Open University Press.

Martino, W., Mills, M. and Lingard, B. (2005) Interrogating single-sex classes as a strategy for addressing boys' educational and social needs, *Oxford Review of Education*, 31(2): 237–54.

McLellan, R. (2002) Socio-cultural approaches to raising boys' achievement at secondary school. Paper presented at the British Educational Research Association Conference, University of Exeter, September.

McLaughlin, C. (2005) Exploring the psychosocial landscape of 'problem' girls: embodiment, relationship and agency, in G. Lloyd (ed.) *Problem Girls: Understanding and Supporting Troubled and Troublesome Girls and Young Women*. London: RoutledgeFalmer.

McNamee, S. (1998) Youth, gender and video games: power and control in the home, in T. Skelton and G. Valentine (eds) *Cool Places: Geographies of Youth Cultures*. London: Routledge.

Meikle, J. (2004) Health ads urged for young drinkers, *Guardian*, 15 December.

Middleton, M.J. and Midgley, C. (1997) Avoiding the demonstration of lack of ability: an underexplored aspect of goal theory, *Journal of Educational Psychology*, 89(4): 710–18.

Midgley, C., Kaplan, A. and Middleton, M. (2001) Performance-approach goals: good for what, for whom, under what circumstances, and at what cost? *Journal of Educational Psychology*, 93(1): 77–86.

Mills, M. (2000) Issues in implementing boys' programme in schools: male teachers and empowerment, *Gender and Education*, 12(2): 221–38.

Mills, M. (2001) *Challenging Violence in Schools: An Issue of Masculinities*. Buckingham: Open University Press.

Mills, M. (2005) Australian directions in the boys' debate: getting it right or going to the Right? Presentation at a Gender and Education Association north-west regional seminar, Lancaster University, 1 June.

Muldoon, J. (2005) *The Significance of Teachers and Relational Change During Children's Psychological Transition to Secondary School*. Unpublished PhD thesis, Lancaster University.

Mulholland, J., Hansen, P. and Kaminski, E. (2004) Do single-gender classrooms in coeducational settings address boys' underachievement? An Australian study, *Educational Studies*, 30(1): 19–32.

O'Brien, M. (2003) Girls and transition to second-level schooling in Ireland: 'moving on' and 'moving out', *Gender and Education*, 15(3): 249–67.

Office for Standards in Education (OFSTED) (2005) Managing challenging behaviour, HMI 2363. London: OFSTED.

Osborn, M. and Broadfoot, P. (1993) Becoming and being a teacher: the influence of the national context, *European Journal of Education*, 28: 105–16.

Osborn, M., Broadfoot, P., Planel, C. and Pollard, A. (1997) Social class, educational opportunity and equal entitlement: dilemmas of schooling in England and France, *Comparative Education*, 33: 375–93.

Osler, A. and Vincent, K. (2003) *Girls and Exclusion: Rethinking the Agenda*. London: RoutledgeFalmer.

Paechter, C. (1998) *Educating the Other: Gender, Power and Schooling*. London: The Falmer Press.

Paechter, C. (2000) *Changing School Subjects: Power, Gender and the Curriculum*. Buckingham: Open University Press.

Paechter, C. and Clark, S. (2005) Who are tomboys and how do we recognize them? Paper presented at the British Educational Research Association Annual Conference, University of Glamorgan, 14–17 September.

Parry, O. (1997) 'Schooling is fooling': Why do Jamaican boys underachieve in school?, *Gender and Education*, 9: 223–31.

Patrick, H., Anderman, L.H. and Ryan, A.M. (2002) Social motivation and the classroom social environment, in C. Midgley (ed.) *Goals, Goal Structures, and Patterns of Adaptive Learning*. London: Lawrence Erlbaum Associates.

Phoenix, A. (2004) Neoliberalism and masculinity: racialization and the contradictions of schooling for 11- to 14-year-olds, *Youth and Society*, 36(2): 227–46.

Pintrich, P.R. (2003) A motivational science perspective on the role of student motivation in learning and teaching contexts, *Journal of Educational Psychology*, 95(4): 667–86.

Pollard, A., with Collins, J., Maddock, M., Simco, N., Swaffield, S., Warin, J. and Warwick, P. (2005) *Reflecting Teaching*, 2nd edn. London: Continuum.

Power, S., Edwards, T., Whitty, G. and Wigfall, V. (2003) *Education and the Middle Class*. Buckingham: Open University Press.

Reay, D. (2001a) 'Spice girls', 'Nice girls', 'Girlies', and 'Tomboys': gender discourses, girls' cultures and femininities in the primary school, *Gender and Education*, 13(2): 153–66.

Reay, D. (2001b) Finding or losing yourself?: working-class relationships to education, *Journal of Education Policy*, 16(4): 333–46.

Reay, D. and Wiliam, D. (1999) 'I'll be a nothing': structure, agency and the construction of identity through assessment, *British Educational Research Journal*, 25(3): 343–54.

Redman, P. (2005) Who cares about the psycho-social? Masculinities, schooling and the unconscious, *Gender and Education*, 17(5): 531–8.

Remedios, R., Ritchie, K. and Lieberman, D.A. (2005) I used to like it but now I don't: the effect of the transfer test in Northern Ireland on pupils' intrinsic motivation, *British Journal of Educational Psychology*, 75(3): 435–52.

Renold, E. (2001) 'Square-girls', femininity and the negotiation of academic success in the primary school, *British Educational Research Journal*, 27: 577–88.

Renold, E. (2005a) *Girls, Boys and Junior Sexualities: Exploring Children's Gender and Sexual Relations in the Primary School*. London: RoutledgeFalmer.

Renold, E. (2005b) Queering 'girlie' culture, negotiating heterogendered childhoods: tomboys, top-girls and moshers. Paper presented at the British Educational Research Association Annual Conference, University of Glamorgan, 14–17 September.

Renold, E. and Allan, A. (2004) Bright and beautiful: high-achieving girls and the negotiation of young 'girlie' femininities. Paper presented at the British Educational Research Association Annual Conference, UMIST, Manchester, 16–18 September.

Ridge, T. (2005) Feeling under pressure: low-income girls negotiating school life, in G. Lloyd (ed.) *Problem Girls: Understanding and Supporting Troubled and Troublesome Girls and Young Women*. London: RoutledgeFalmer.

Rose, G. (2001) *Visual Methodologies*. London: Sage.

Rudduck, J. and Urquhart, I. (2003) Some neglected issues of transfer: identity, status and gender from the pupils' perspective, in C. Skelton and B. Francis (eds) *Boys and Girls in the Primary Classroom*. Maidenhead: Open University Press.

Ryan, A.M., Kiefer, S.M. and Hopkins, N.B. (2004) Young adolescents' social motivation: an achievement goal perspective, in P.R. Pintrich and M.L. Maehr (eds) *Motivating Students, Improving Schools: The Legacy of Carol Midgley*. London: Elsevier.

Sherriff, N.S. (2005) *Peer Group Cultures and Social Identity: An Integrated Approach to Understanding Masculinities*. Unpublished PhD thesis, Lancaster University.

Simons, H.D., Van Rheenen, D. and Covington, M.V. (1999) Academic motivation and the student athlete, *Journal of College Student Development*, 40(2): 151–62.

Skaalvik, S. (1993) Ego-involvement and self-protection among slow learners: four case studies, *Scandinavian Journal of Educational Research*, 37: 305–15.

Skeggs, B. (2004) *Class, Self, Culture*. London: Routledge.

Skelton, C. (2001a) *Schooling the Boys: Masculinities and Primary Education*. Buckingham: Open University Press.

Skelton, C. (2001b) 'Typical boys?' Theorising masculinity in educational settings, in B. Francis and C. Skelton (eds) *Investigating Gender:*

Contemporary Perspectives in Education. Buckingham: Open University Press.

Spender, D. (1989) *Invisible Women: The Schooling Scandal.* London: The Women's Press.

Spender, D. and Sarah, E. (eds) (1980) *Learning to Lose: Sexism and Education.* London: The Women's Press.

Sukhnandan, L., Lee, B. and Kelleher, S. (2000) *An Investigation into Gender Differences in Achievement. Phase 2: School and Classroom Strategies.* Slough: NFER.

Swain, J. (2002) The right stuff: fashioning an identity through clothing in a junior school, *Gender and Education*, 14(1): 53–69.

Swain, J. (2004) The resources and strategies that 10–11-year-old boys use to construct masculinities in the school setting, *British Educational Research Journal*, 30(1): 167–85.

Swain, J. (2005) Sharing the same world: boys' relations with girls during their last year of primary school, *Gender and Education*, 17(1): 75–91.

Swan, B. (1998) Teaching boys and girls in separate classes at Shenfield High School, Brentwood, in K. Bleach (ed.) *Raising Boys' Achievement in Schools.* Stoke on Trent: Trentham Books.

Sweeting, H. and West, P. (2003) Young people's leisure and risk-taking behaviours: changes in gender patterning in the west of Scotland during the 1990s, *Journal of Youth Studies*, 6(4): 391–412.

Syal, R. and Trump, S. (1996) Single-sex classes raise boys' grades, *Sunday Times*, 25 August.

Thompson, T. (1999) *Underachieving to Protect Self-Worth.* Aldershot: Ashgate Publishing Ltd.

Tomlinson, M. (2004) *14–19 Curriculum and Qualifications Reform: Final Report of the Working Group on 14–19 reform.* Annesley: DFES Publications.

Urdan, T. (2004a) Can achievement goal theory guide school reform?, in P.R. Pintrich and M.L. Maehr (eds) *Motivating Students, Improving Schools: The Legacy of Carol Midgley.* London: Elsevier.

Urdan, T. (2004b) Predictors of academic self-handicapping and achievement: examining achievement goals, classroom goal structures, and culture, *Journal of Educational Psychology*, 96(2): 251–64.

Urdan, T. and Midgley, C. (2001) Academic self-handicapping: what we know, what more there is to learn, *Educational Psychology Review*, 13(2): 115–38.

Urdan, T., Ryan, A.M., Anderman, E.M. and Gheen, M.H. (2002) Goals, goal structures, and avoidance behaviours, in C. Midgley (ed.) *Goals, Goal Structures, and Patterns of Adaptive Learning.* London: Lawrence Erlbaum Associates.

Van de Gaer, E., Pustjens, H., Van Damme, J. and De Munter, A. (2004) Effects of single-sex versus co-educational classes and schools on gender differences in progress in language and mathematics achievement, *British Journal of Sociology of Education*, 25(3): 307–22.

Walkerdine, V., Lucey, H. and Melody, J. (2001) *Growing Up Girl: Psychosocial Explorations of Gender and Class*. Basingstoke: Palgrave.

Warrington, M. and Younger, M. (1999) Perspectives on the gender gap in English secondary schools, *Research Papers in Education*, 14(1): 51–77.

Warrington, M. and Younger, M. (2000) The other side of the gender gap, *Gender and Education*, 12(4): 493–508.

Warrington, M. and Younger, M. (2005) Working on the inside: discourses, dilemmas and decisions. Paper presented at the Fifth International Gender and Education Conference, University of Cardiff, 29–31 March.

Warrington, M., Younger, M. and Williams, J. (2000) Student attitudes, image and the gender gap, *British Educational Research Journal*, 26: 393–407.

Warrington, M., Younger, M. and McLellan, R. (2003) 'Under-achieving boys' in English primary schools? *The Curriculum Journal*, 14(2): 139–56.

Weiner, G. (ed.) (1985) *Just a Bunch of Girls*. Milton Keynes: Open University Press.

Wentzel, K.R. and Wigfield, A. (1998) Academic and social motivational influences on students' academic performance, *Educational Psychology Review*, 10(2): 155–75.

West, A. and Pennell, H. (2003) *Underachievement in Schools*. London: RoutledgeFalmer.

Whitelaw, S., Milosevic, L. and Daniels, S. (2000) Gender, behaviour and achievement: a preliminary study of pupil perceptions and attitudes, *Gender and Education*, 12(1): 87–113.

Willis, P. (1977) *Learning to Labour: How Working Class Kids Get Working Class Jobs*. Farborough: Saxon House.

Winterton, R. (2004) Speech to Tackling Obesity in Young People Conference. www.dh.gov.uk/NewsHome/Speeches/SpeechesList/SpeechesArticle/fs/en?CONTENT_ID=4074909&chk=haNP5E (accessed October 2005).

Wolters, C.A. (2004) Advancing achievement goal theory: using goal structures and goal orientations to predict students' motivation, cognition, and achievement, *Journal of Educational Psychology*, 96(2): 236–50.

Wragg, E.C., Wragg, C.M. and Chamberlin, R.P. (2004) *Jersey Critical Skills Programme: An Evaluation*. www.gov.je/statesreports/reports/JerseyCriticalSkillsFinalReport%2018.1.05.doc

Younger, M. and Warrington, M. (1996) Differential achievement of girls and boys at GCSE: some observations from the perspective of one school, *British Journal of Sociology of Education*, 17: 299–313.

Younger, M. and Warrington, M. (2005) *Raising Boys' Achievement in Secondary Schools*. Maidenhead: Open University Press.

Younger, M., Warrington, M. and McLellan, R. (2002) The 'problem' of 'under-achieving boys': some responses from English secondary schools, *School Leadership and Management*, 22(4): 389–405.

Younger, M., Warrington, M. and Williams, J. (1999) The gender gap and classroom interactions: reality and rhetoric? *British Journal of Sociology of Education*, 20(3): 325–41.

Index

Aapola, S. 45–6, 47
Academic efficacy 26, 35
Achievement goal theory 25–9,
    35, 36–40, 44–6, 101, 123,
    140
Alcohol xviii, 1, 11, 12, 15–18, 20,
    74, 80, 86,
Anderman, L.H. xiv, 135
Appearance – see body and
    fashion
Arnot, M. 30
Augment success xxi, 33, 84, 85,
    93, 95, 100, 104
Avoidance goals – see
    performance-avoid goals

Balancing academic work and
    popularity 80, 81, 84,
    101–21, 142
Barbies (at Hollydale School)
    119–20
Blunkett, D. xii
Body 118–121
Boyswork programmes 131
Brown, P. 38–9, 48, 73
Bullying 2, 9, 11, 15, 41, 84, 106,
    107, 108, 124, 128, 141
Byers, S. xi

Career prospects xiii, 13, 49, 53,
    54, 59, 72, 82, 83, 84, 140
Closet achievers 32, 34, 96

Clothes – see fashion
Cohen, M. 96, 132
Competition 10, 27, 30, 38, 39,
    47–8, 50, 51, 52, 57–8, 60–2,
    71, 73, 81, 124, 125, 131–6,
    138, 142
Competitive individualism (see
    also competition) 39, 47–8,
    71, 73, 131
Computers 12, 104, 112, 114–16
Connell, R.W. 10
Cooperative learning 39, 134–6,
    139
Coping with pressure 52, 55–6,
    65, 71–2
Covington, M. 29–34, 39–40, 96,
    126, 127, 132, 136
Cox, C.B. 93
Credentials discourse 24, 48, 53,
    61–2, 73, 74, 79–83, 84, 96,
    101, 131, 140
Cricket 90–1, 111
Critical Skills Programme 147–8
Curriculum 110, 126, 127, 130,
    139

Disruptive behaviour 1, 6, 8,
    12–15, 20, 21, 22, 24, 32,
    34–5, 37, 75, 81, 82, 91–2,
    105, 106, 123, 132, 140.
Domestic responsibilities 112–13
Drinking – see alcohol

Dweck, C. 31, 88, 128, 132, 136–8, 144

Effortless achievement xx, 8, 9, 32, 34, 46, 69, 73, 85, 93, 95–100, 119–20, 132, 137, 138, 141, 146
Ego goals – see performance goals
Employment (paid) 116–17
English 63, 68, 127–8, 144
Epstein, D. xii, 40
Ethnicity xiv, xvi, xx, 2, 4, 6, 49, 55, 74, 77–9, 84, 111, 144
Excuses for failure xxi, 32–5, 56–7, 83–4, 86–95, 123,

Fashion 5–8, 17–19, 117–20
Football 6–8, 29, 102, 108–9, 111
Francis, B. 3–4, 6, 9, 23, 55, 131, 144,
Frosh, S. 10, 62, 80–1

Galloway, D. 33, 34
GCSEs xi, xv, 53, 56, 59, 66–7, 69, 129, 131, 144
Geek (see also swot and spiff) 7, 74, 84
German 90–1
Girl power xiii, 45–6
Goal theory – see achievement goal theory
Goal structures 27–8, 36, 48, 50, 134
Good girl femininity 15, 45–6
Griffin, C. 4

Hegemonic masculinity xix, 2, 9, 10–11, 23, 33, 36, 40–4, 45, 62, 129, 141
Heterosexuality 4, 10, 11, 17, 19, 119, 120, 154
Hiding work and effort (see also effortless achievement) xx, 23, 32, 34, 37, 41–43, 45, 46, 62, 73, 75, 85, 89, 92, 93, 94–100, 102–8, 113–16, 119, 120, 121, 132, 136–8, 141, 142, 146
Higher education 125
Holland, S. 5
Hughes, C. 47, 71, 110

Interest 126–8, 147
Internet 114–16

Jobs See career prospects

Kaplan, A. xiv, 26, 27, 28, 39–40

Ladette to Lady 11
League tables of school performance 48, 136
Learning goals 25–6, 27, 28, 48–9, 130, 133–4, 137, 138
Lees, S. 13
Lie about results 85–86
Life-long learning 125
Loveable rogue 21

Mac an Ghaill, M. 96
Martin, A. 80, 87–8, 127, 134
Mastery goals – see learning goals
Maths 27, 53, 56, 68, 80, 88, 107–98, 129, 133, 144
Midgley, C. 25, 126, 133
Mills, M. 10, 123, 128, 131
Mosque 113

Neoliberalism 38–9, 44, 47, 65, 140, 146
Normative femininity 17–23, 119–21, 141–2

OFSTED xv, xvii, 14, 48
Osler, A. 130

Performance goals 25–9, 48–9, 50, 51, 125, 130–7, 139

Performance-approach goals 25–6,
    28–9, 144
Performance-avoid goals 25–6,
    28–9, 32, 37, 60, 122
Phoenix, A. 38
Physical education (P.E.) 146, 147
Policy implications 122–39
Power, S. 100, 102–3, 119
Practice implications 122–39
Praise 136–8
Pressure to perform academically
    47–74
 Parental pressure 54–60
 Peer pressure 60–3, 85–100
 Teacher/school pressure 50–4,
    63–70
Procrastination 32–3, 86, 123
Public announcement of test
    results 27–8, 50–3, 87, 134–5

Reay, D. 21–2, 29–30, 31, 48, 59,
    125
Renold, E. 10
Research methods xv–xix, 87–91
Resources 101–21
Revision (exam) 1, 41–2, 62,
    63–70, 72, 55–6, 86, 87,
    89–91, 94–5, 97, 103, 104–5,
    108–9, 111–13, 115, 129
Ridge, T. 110, 116–17
Rudduck, J. 129
Rugby 41

SATS xvi, xviii, xx, 28, 30, 48, 49,
    53, 55–59, 63–73, 108, 111,
    113, 115–16, 124–6, 144
Anxiety – see also fear of failure
    (academic) 30, 49, 55–9,
    63–73, 124–6, 131
School differences 65–70
 Use of results 65–70
Science 61, 63, 68, 87, 120, 129,
    144,

Scrubber 117–18
Self-efficacy – see academic
    efficacy
Self-handicapping xv, xvii, 26, 32,
    86–100, 145
 Behavioural 86–93
 Self-reported 93–100
Self-worth protection xx, 29–35,
    36–40, 44–6, 84, 85–100,
    123–4, 128, 140–2
Self-worth theory 29–35, 36–40,
    44–6, 123–4, 140
Sibling rivalries 56–9
Single-sex classes 127–8
Single-sex schools xv, xvi, xviii,
    103
Skeggs, B. 4, 118
Social class xii, xvi, xx, 2, 3–4, 11,
    15, 49, 55, 58–59, 74, 77–9,
    84, 114–21, 125–6, 142, 144,
    145
Social comparisons 26–8, 31, 32,
    34, 50–3, 56–59, 61, 86, 87,
    104, 118, 134–5
Social justice 130–1
Social status motives xiv, xix,
    1–23, 24–5, 36–46, 62,
    74–84, 85–6, 91, 92, 98, 100,
    101–21, 122–4, 128, 132,
    136–8, 140–2, 147
Spiff (see also geek and swot) 75,
    83, 103, 108, 109
Sport 5–8, 29, 41, 76–7, 80,
    90–1, 98, 100, 102, 108–9,
    111, 116, 119, 122, 143,
    147
St Trinians 14
Standards discourse xiii, xx, 20,
    28, 31, 37–9, 44–5, 47–9, 53,
    85, 110, 123–124, 133, 135,
    140–2
Swain, J. 101, 114, 118
Sweeting, H. 111–12

Swot (see also geek and spiff) xi, 6, 7, 15–17, 35, 41, 74–76, 80–84, 85, 92, 97–98, 102, 105, 106, 107, 108, 117, 118, 120, 129, 138

Task goals – see learning goals
Testing (academic) (see also SATs) xx, 26, 27, 31, 37, 42, 47–73, 85–100, 104–5
Anxiety – see fear of failure (academic) 122, 124–39, 141–2
Time 102, 108, 109–21
Tinkler, P. 20
Tomboys 144, 156
Tramps (see also scrubbers) 118

Urdan, T. 24, 29, 86, 94–95
Uncool to work discourse xi–xii, xix, 1–23, 35, 36–7, 40, 43, 45, 52, 60, 62, 69, 74–84, 91, 92, 95–6, 98, 100, 101–21, 123–4, 127, 132, 138–9, 140–2
Underachievement xi–xiii, 20, 22, 23, 142, 143

Uniform (school) 118

Vocational education 147

Walkerdine, V. 44, 58–9
Warrington, M. xiii, 24, 33
Willis, P. 3–4
Withdrawing effort 32, 33–4, 123

Younger, M. 91, 135, 136, 138